The British Aircraft Industry during the First World War

In loving memory of the Engineers
Leslie Richard Manning (1944–2022)
John Leslie Manning (1979–2020)

The British Aircraft Industry during the First World War

The Dope Scandal

Tim Jenkins

BLOOMSBURY ACADEMIC
LONDON • NEW YORK • OXFORD • NEW DELHI • SYDNEY

BLOOMSBURY ACADEMIC
Bloomsbury Publishing Plc, 50 Bedford Square, London, WC1B 3DP, UK
Bloomsbury Publishing Inc, 1385 Broadway, New York, NY 10018, USA
Bloomsbury Publishing Ireland, 29 Earlsfort Terrace, Dublin 2, D02 AY28, Ireland

BLOOMSBURY, BLOOMSBURY ACADEMIC and the Diana logo
are trademarks of Bloomsbury Publishing Plc

First published in Great Britain 2024
This paperback edition published in 2025

Copyright © Tim Jenkins, 2024

Tim Jenkins has asserted his right under the Copyright,
Designs and Patents Act, 1988, to be identified as Author of this work.

Cover image © General view of dope room in aircraft factory, 1915–1918.
Science & Society Picture Library/Getty.

All rights reserved. No part of this publication may be: i) reproduced or transmitted in any form, electronic or mechanical, including photocopying, recording or by means of any information storage or retrieval system without prior permission in writing from the publishers; or ii) used or reproduced in any way for the training, development or operation of artificial intelligence (AI) technologies, including generative AI technologies. The rights holders expressly reserve this publication from the text and data mining exception as per Article 4(3) of the Digital Single Market Directive (EU) 2019/790.

Bloomsbury Publishing Plc does not have any control over, or responsibility for, any third-party websites referred to or in this book. All internet addresses given in this book were correct at the time of going to press. The author and publisher regret any inconvenience caused if addresses have changed or sites have ceased to exist, but can accept no responsibility for any such changes.

A catalogue record for this book is available from the British Library.

A catalog record for this book is available from the Library of Congress.

ISBN: HB: 978-1-3502-9707-4
       PB: 978-1-3502-9710-4
       ePDF: 978-1-3502-9708-1
       eBook: 978-1-3502-9709-8

Typeset by Integra Software Services Pvt. Ltd.

For product safety related questions contact productsafety@bloomsbury.com.

To find out more about our authors and books visit www.bloomsbury.com
and sign up for our newsletters.

Contents

List of figures — vi

Introduction: 'Britain and aerial navigation' — 1

1 'Common instruments of locomotion' — 15
2 'Aeroplanes in war' — 39
3 'Mysterious deaths of the liver' — 59
4 'Dope poisoning in aircraft factories' — 73
5 'The Air Committee fiasco' — 87
6 'British Cellulose & Colonel Grant Morden' — 117
7 'No departmental favouritism' — 137

Conclusions: 'A plane truth' — 157

Notes — 169
Bibliography — 190
Index — 204

Figures

1. Voisin Boxkite Biplane, 1909. Courtesy of Hulton Archive/Stringer/Getty Images — 3
2. S.F. Cody in the First Successful British Aeroplane at Farnborough in 1908. Courtesy of Science & Society Picture Library/Getty Images — 16
3. Royal Aircraft Factory B.E.2. Courtesy of Steve Stringer Photography/Getty Images — 33
4. Bleriot XI Monoplane, Farnborough 1915. Author's Collection — 46
5. Voisin III with Mounted Cannon, Gosport 1915. Author's Collection — 55
6. Workers at the Short Brothers Seaplane Works at Rochester, Kent. Courtesy of A.R. Coster/Stringer/Getty Images — 66
7. Female Workers Outside an Aeroplane Factory in Birmingham, 1918. Courtesy of Fotosearch/Stringer/Getty Images — 84
8. Royal Aircraft Factory Planning Department. Author's Collection — 104
9. B.E.2e, 140 Squadron, Royal Air Force, March 1918. Author's Collection — 107
10. Waring and Gillow Furniture factory, Hammersmith, London, November 1916. Courtesy of Heritage Images/Getty Images — 152

Introduction: 'Britain and aerial navigation'
The birth of an industry (1909 onwards)

The development of aviation during the First World War is a story often told through the analysis of a particular aircraft type, the experiences of gallant aviators, or a daring offensive mission. Although these approaches remain extremely entertaining, by necessity, the history of technological progress and the supply-chain challenges faced by the embryonic British aircraft industry have often been relegated to the footnotes, if indeed space is found to reference them at all. That is not to say that there are no exceptions to this observation. Hugh Driver's work on the development of the British aviation industry in the years immediately preceding the outbreak of the war is a thorough examination of the early aerial policy and technological progress.[1] And additionally, there are some fascinating works exploring company histories as well as the official histories regarding the conduct of the air war.[2] Nevertheless, there remains a gap in defining the interdependence between manufacturers and the materiel needs of the wartime state, and this research aims to begin and address this oversight.

Ultimately, modern historiography now enables us to legitimately explore the more ill-defined economic, technological and industrial occurrences that take place during total war and put them into their proper historical perspective. Invariably, and most conveniently, this can be conducted long after any initial fury at government incompetence or, in this instance, allegations of war profiteering have subsided.[3] This exploration of the interrelationship between the wartime government and the emerging aviation industry aims to unpick, for the very first time, some of these finer machinations through the analysis of one of the most intriguing episodes of the First World War, what became known to contemporary commentators as the dope scandal.

More recent examinations of the British post-1918 aircraft industry have invariably approached the subject from the perspective of analysing military effectiveness, exploring the lessons learnt from the experiences of the First World War and ensuring future designs were equipped to deal with the rigours of aerial combat.[4] However, in the case of the British military aviation experience between 1914 and 1918, the technology was simply too new to apply such a methodology. Consequently, this research attempts to redress this balance by exploring the interrelationships between government research establishments and the private contractor, the complications of procurement and supply, the ensuing international scandals, and the political manipulation of emergency wartime regulation in an attempt to conceal blunders and incompetencies from an increasingly enlightened and informed contemporary public. Only after these elements have been thoroughly analysed can the true nature of Britain's rich aviation heritage be put into a context that is fully digestible. This is even more important in the present time, whereby the frequent reports of ineptitude in holistic government contracting, which have thus far characterized the first quarter of the twenty-first century, continue to desensitize society's reaction to such occurrences and consider them as commonplace, rather than exceptional.

Between 1908 and 1912, aeroplane design developed increasingly rapidly with the French taking a commanding lead over early American and British innovations, a precedent that is represented in the aviation parlance that persists to this day through the continued use of terminology such as fuselage, empennage and aileron. The aeroplane designs of Frenchmen such as Farman, Bleriot and the aerodynamic research of Gustave Eiffel made significant contributions towards the development of sound established aviation engineering principles. In turn, these developments inspired British designers in their quest to develop safer, more stable heavier-than-air machines.

In Great Britain, for example, George Hartley Bryan defined the design rules for aeroplane stability through the analysis of flight dynamics, whilst Leonard Bairstow was responsible for developing wind tunnels at the National Physical Laboratory that facilitated in-depth scientific investigation and rapid progress. Bairstow had entered the Engineering Department at the National

Figure 1 Voisin Boxkite Biplane, 1909. Courtesy of Hulton Archive/Stringer/Getty Images.

Physical Laboratory in 1904, and in 1909 he was appointed the principal of the Aerodynamics Division. It is during this period that he carried out pioneering investigations into wind tunnel development and the practical application of stability theory using small mica aeroplane models.[5] It was the definition of scientific principles and the development of the improved practical means of testing them that enabled Geoffrey de Havilland, and later Edward Teshmaker Busk, to design the famous B.E.2c British military biplane that became the first inherently stable machine of its kind. The British it seems, then, were starting to make some progress of their own but not without considerable divergence of opinion regarding future strategic direction.

This initial progress soon appeared to be short-lived, however. A report by the Sub-Committee of the Committee of Imperial Defence on Aerial Navigation would further delay immediate increased government investment in aviation. In February 1909, in a report entitled *The British Armed Forces and the Committee of Imperial Defence on 'Aerial Navigation'*, the appointed investigating Committee concluded that fixed-wing aircraft were of little practical threat to the security of British military forces. They believed that the aeroplane possessed only slight practical offensive capabilities and speculated that aircraft would be considerably more expensive to develop and manufacture than their lighter-than-air balloon and airship alternatives which were already tried and tested. Consequently, the recommendation was that all further expenditure in aeroplane design at the Royal Aircraft Factory, the British government aviation experimental establishment, should be immediately curtailed and the associated risks of developing such new technology should be left to the private sector.[6] In fairness, even when the government attempted to make improvements to its emerging policies concerning the developing science of aerial navigation, they were invariably ridiculed in the press. For example, *The Times* aeronautical correspondent stated quite assiduously on 6 May 1909 that it was impossible to make comment on something that, in his opinion, was so ill defined that it simply did not exist, namely a 'British national institution for tackling the problems of aerial navigation'.[7]

Nevertheless, an event that both inspired and shocked the British government into more determined action in the development of national aviation policy was the successful crossing of the English Channel in an aeroplane by Louis Bleriot on 25 July 1909. This anxiety was caused by the sudden realization that Britain was no longer an island national that could be protected by the traditional means of naval expenditure. The much-feared phenomenon of aerial bombardment was now a distinct possibility in any future conflict, and this trepidation alone was enough to initiate demands for rapid exploration of how Britain might be defended against such an act of aggression. Following Bleriot's accomplishment, it was commented in *The Times* on 26 July 1909 that 'it would be folly to set limits to the power of accommodation' concerning the future potential of the aeroplane as an offensive weapon and warned the public that such technology meant that nobody was now safe within the previous comfort of the British shoreline.[8]

However, the government was petitioned to invest in the development of the aeroplane not only out of military necessity but out of a genuine, potentially more devastating concern that national pride may also be perilously at stake if the British failed to compete in forthcoming international competitions. The 'Grand Aeronautique Week', hosted by the French at *Le Champagne, Reims*, in August 1909, brought together the emerging aviation talent from around the world who competed against one another for the coveted Gordon Bennett Trophy. Throughout the course of the event, records for speed and flight duration were repeatedly broken and re-broken by intrepid aviators and the British were desperate to be part of the action.[9]

The aviation 'Grand Prix' race was the international barometer of aeronautical evolution at the time. The first ever race in 1909 had been won by the American aviation pioneer Glenn Curtiss and took place over an endurance course of some 20 kilometres.[10] Technological progress was such that by the following year, the race, held at Belmont Park, took place over a 100-kilometre course and was narrowly won by the British aviator and designer Claude Grahame-White. The third race was held on 1 July 1911 at East Church, Isle of Sheppey, by which time the distance was increased to 150 kilometres. For perspective regarding the pace of technological progression, the *Scientific American* reported that Glenn Curtiss' victory in 1909 was both splendid and well deserved but that the race of 1910 was more the result of complete fluke during which the steady flying of Grahame-White eventually prevailed. This was largely due to the fact that the French aviator, Alfred Leblanc, who was the race leader for the duration, crashed at the last moment presenting the British airman with an unlikely victory. Albeit one no less welcome from a British perspective.[11]

Notwithstanding Grahame-White's success, none of the principal manufacturers represented at Belmont were British, and machines designed and manufactured by Bleriot, Wright and Nieuport were coveted as the fastest, most manoeuvrable and most reliable aeroplanes in the field of competition. More interestingly, however, from an aerodynamic perspective, the races proved that monoplane designs were the fastest, whilst the biplane configurations were more inherently stable in flight and manoeuvrability. In 1915, the French director of Military Aeronautics announced that the *Armée de l'air* would no longer purchase monoplanes, stating limited carrying capacity, limited pilot vision from the cockpit and low speed range as the main reasoning behind the decision, and arguments regarding the individual merits of each design from a military perspective were not settled until the cessation of the Second World War.[12]

Despite continued technological development throughout the early years of the twentieth century, the science of aeronautics did not become a university subject until after the First World War, and consequently, in those years leading up to the outbreak of the conflict, governments throughout Europe struggled to justify increased national expenditure on such emerging technology without a defined military purpose. Beyond the possible use of aeroplanes and airships for military reconnaissance, many remained sceptical regarding the offensive potential of aviation. Even in Germany, doubts remained about the practicalities of offensive airpower following unsuccessful bomb-dropping trials at Gotha in August 1912, during which minimal hits were scored on predetermined targets by ordnance released from both aeroplanes and airships.[13]

Notwithstanding the disappointment experienced by the early proponents of military aviation following the results of the Gotha bombing trials, the potential threat of aerial bombardment had certainly caught the imagination of the British public. There was an emerging phenomenon of reported sightings of airships flying over the UK between 1912 and 1913, and these were widely believed to have been German Zeppelins sent to test the preparedness of Britain's aerial defences prior to their deployment in a future war. Winston Churchill, as First Lord of the Admiralty, admitted in the House of Commons that a supposed sighting over Sheerness on 14 October 1912 was most certainly not a British aircraft, and this only served to further fuel public anxiety and suspicion.[14] The fear that an enemy airship could roam at will above the military installations of the British Isles caused a frenzy, which encouraged multiple reports of airships being spotted the length and breadth of the archipelago. However, most of these reports were undoubtedly false, as accurately deduced by *The Times* Berlin correspondent, who concluded in February 1913 that the British continued to greatly overestimate the capabilities of German's lighter-than-air machines.[15] Nevertheless, there can be little doubt that such hyperbole was effectively utilized by the proponents of British airpower for the immediate expansion of Britain's military aerial capabilities.[16]

Eventually, following continued pressure in Parliament and the press, the War Office issued the first government specification for a military aeroplane on 14 December 1911 as part of a competition to be held the following year at Larkhill on Salisbury Plain. Entrants had to deliver their machines by 31 July 1912, and although thirty-eight entries were originally received, only twenty-five were delivered in time for evaluation.[17] The winning machine was the

Samuel Franklin Cody Biplane (No. 31), but despite impressive performance, its complicated design did not lend itself easily to mass-production as stipulated in the competition requirements and an alternative design had to be sought to equip Britain's fledgling air services in the interim. Entry to the Army Aeroplane Competition was restricted to private manufacturers in accordance with the recommendations previously made by the Committee of Imperial Defence on 'Aerial Navigation', and consequently the B.E.2, the inherently stable flying machine designed and manufactured at the government's own Royal Aircraft Factory, was unable to take part.

Nevertheless, it was decided to use the B.E.2 as a general runabout during the competition, and in August 1912 Geoffrey de Havilland and the commandant of the Royal Flying Corps, Major Sykes, achieved the British aeroplane height record of 10,500 feet in an early example of the type whilst the Military Aircraft Trials were underway at Larkhill.[18] Although Cody's machine being declared overall winner, it was obvious that the Farnborough design outperformed every other aeroplane in the competition and the War Office duly placed orders for the machine. However, to placate private manufacturers and encourage their development, orders were placed with Armstrong-Whitworth, Coventry Ordnance and Handley-Page to manufacture the B.E.2a under license and support the production programme already established at the Royal Aircraft Factory.[19] Despite these best efforts, the B.E.2 became synonymous in the emerging British aircraft industry with government monopoly and unfair advantage.

However, once the authorities realized that the British aircraft industry was as yet incapable of producing an aeroplane of suitable performance and ease of manufacture to suit the nation's emerging military requirements, the War Office had little choice but to put their faith in the Farnborough-designed B.E.2 machine and its derivatives. The B.E.2 was originally designed by de Havilland and Frederick Green. Green was an exceptional aeronautical engineer and the first recruit of Mervyn O'Gorman at the Royal Aircraft Factory before leaving to become the chief engineer at the Armstrong Whitworth Aircraft Company in January 1917.

This adoption of the B.E.2 was considered an interim measure, implemented to allow the private firms to fully establish themselves and perfect their manufacturing techniques and designs. Nevertheless, the

Farnborough-designed machine was to become synonymous with accusations from the private British manufacturers of government monopoly and manipulation of the industry, an accusation that persisted well into the 1920s. The reality, however, was that aeroplanes designed by government scientists were desperately required in the early years of British aviation whilst independent manufacturers perfected their own machines and construction processes. In fact, many famous British designers, such as Geoffrey de Havilland himself, started their careers in government-controlled aeronautical facilities before going on to establish their own successful companies. In essence, without the research conducted at government-funded establishments, such as the Royal Aircraft Factory and the National Physical Laboratory, Britain would have been unable to transform itself into the world's principal aviation power by 1918.

Through necessity therefore, the B.E.2c became the primary British machine used for both training and operations in the early stages of the war but it would nonetheless be wrong to assume that the British authorities were unable to recognize the potential of a privately manufactured British design or embrace its potential. This is evident in the early adoption of the AVRO 504 by both the Royal Flying Corps and Royal Naval Air Service. This aircraft, designed by Alliot Verdon Roe, saw service throughout the conflict in a variety of different roles. In fact, the AVRO 504 was already in military service at the outbreak of the First World War and holds the dubious honour of being the first British plane shot down in action on 22 August 1914.[20] More than 10,000 were manufactured in total and remained in military and civilian use well into the late 1930s, with some examples even brought out of RAF storage to be used as glider tugs during the development of British airborne forces in 1940.[21]

In August 1916, during a crisis in the British administration concerning the future conduct of the Air War, Lord Montagu of Beaulieu shared his recollections of the early development of British military aeroplanes during a debate in the House of Lords:

> I pass on to 1912, when, after trials held by the aeronautical authorities, the first B.E.2 plane was produced. It was a tractor biplane, and it really put up a very good performance and answered expectations. It was thought to be too slow, and so a more powerful engine was put into it; and necessarily, because we had not the same knowledge then as we have now, it became more

dangerous and killed several pilots. During 1912–13 various machines of the B.E.2 type were produced. In 1914, just before the war, the Royal Aircraft Factory lost Mr. De Havilland, who went over to a private firm which is now manufacturing aeroplanes on a large scale. A few days before the war broke out our first real auto stable plane was produced – the B.E.2c. Although at the beginning of the war these machines did good work, they are admittedly out of date now. At that time this was the only machine we had in quantities, and the only really well-designed machine. Therefore, I do not blame the authorities for having built them in considerable quantities.[22]

Unfortunately, such politically motivated debates detracted considerably from the incredible progress made by British scientists in government employment both at the Royal Aircraft Factory and on the Aeronautical Advisory Committee and even resulted in some leaving for employment in private industry. In his autobiography de Havilland even admitted that he relied on the aerodynamic qualities achieved in the B.E.2 as the principle for all his early aeroplane designs as a private concern, high praise indeed for an aeroplane that had received nothing but criticism in the Parliament and the British press.[23]

By July 1913, interest was beginning to be shown in the House of Commons concerning the endurance capabilities of British military machines, flying range being recognized as a key performance quality in the success of their future military application. In response to a written question posed by Lord Beresford, Colonel Seely, the Secretary of State for Air, proudly announced that the B.E.2 machine was capable of carrying enough fuel to remain in the air for approximately four hours or around 280 miles. Regarding the longest non-stop flights covered by Royal Flying Corps personnel to date, Seely stated:

> The longest flight carried out by an officer of the Military Wing, without landing, is 249 miles, which took four and a half hours. Another officer, unaccompanied by a passenger, flew about 516 miles in one day. His actual flying time was six and a quarter hour, and he landed twice for fuel.[24]

The pace of progress was indeed remarkable, particularly when compared to Bleriot's achievement some four years previously during which he covered a distance of approximately 31 miles between Calais and Dover.[25] The flight that became such a catalyst for British aeronautical development was already a technologically distant memory.

However, progress was not simply limited to technological developments such as endurance statistics, and the wider military capabilities of British airpower also began to come into ascendance. By July 1913, the number of certified pilots in the Royal Flying Corps had increased from around 20 the previous year to 191, and of these 82 had already qualified for their military flying certificate.[26] Yet the problem would not prove to be one of recruitment in the early stages of the war, but the challenge of supplying quantities of adequate machines and the supply of the materiel resources necessary for their construction.

The complications of materiel supply, in particular, the ability of armaments manufacturers and their sub-contractors to deliver orders of new designs in unprecedented volumes, became a growing business in which corruption and profiteering invariably became prevalent. However, when sub-contracts were finally placed by Farnborough for the manufacture of the B.E.2 under license, the results were often far from satisfactory, as in the case of an order for five machines with Handley-Page.[27]

Necessity created business opportunity and for those of a less scrupulous nature the temptation for personal gain became all too great. The Canadian prime minister, Sir Robert Laird Borden, delivered a speech before the Canadian Club at Winnipeg on 29 December 1914, during which he stated:

> Already our factories are turning out not only clothing and equipment of all kinds, but munitions of war on a great scale and of character that we did not dream of producing four months ago. Our inexhaustible resources in the forests, the fisheries, the coal and minerals of Canada are tremendous assets in this war. All this must tell in the long run, as Germany will yet know. In a word, we have the resources, while Germany has the preparation.[28]

Canada's materiel contribution during the First World War was indeed great, but some of its citizens saw the opportunity to take advantage of an almost fatal omission in the British strategic approach to the logistics of aeroplane manufacture, the adequate supply of aircraft dope. Or to be more precise, the cellulose acetate required for its production.

Aeroplane dope at first appeared to be a mundane accessory in the development of British aviation, but its significance to Britain's ability to manufacture aeroplanes in increasing quantities soon became apparent and threatened the entire production programme. Dope was brushed onto the fabric covering on the wings and fuselage of aeroplanes to ensure the cloth was taut, thus increasing both the aerodynamic qualities of the machine and the strength of the overall structure. Although the *British Cellulose Committee Enquiry Report* of 1919 acknowledged the oversight in strategic planning, it failed to attribute sufficient gravitas to the potential consequences:

> At the outbreak of the war the use of Cellulose Acetate and certain necessary solvents in the manufacture of 'dope' for aeronautical purposes was not widely known, and indeed the aeroplane programme itself was then on a small scale. After the outbreak of war, however, its value was more fully realised, and with the increasing growth in the aeronautical programme the question of supply became important.[29]

Nevertheless, this simple miscalculation not only risked pilot casualties during the ensuing air war through the continued deployment of technologically redundant machines but also resulted in fatalities in the aeroplane factories on the Home Front, a recurring situation throughout the course of the ensuing conflict which 'fused the formerly dichotomous images' of 'home' and 'front' depicting these places as both strikingly similar and equally as dangerous.[30]

The dope shortage resulted in the prolonged use of products which contained a poisonous chemical called tetrachlorethane. This was used as a solvent to dilute the dope and made it easier to apply by brush to the aircraft fabric. The problem was that dopes containing tetrachlorethane were highly toxic and, if used in spaces without sufficient ventilation, could prove fatal to those employed in its application. Once deaths from tetrachlorethane poisoning became widely reported from 1914 onwards, the government became increasingly embroiled in what later became known as the 'dope scandal'.

It has often been argued that Britain's capability to manufacture aircraft was limited principally by the supply of engines. Although the issue did indeed cause a temporary bottleneck in production, particularly when competition arose between the Royal Flying Corps and the Army concerning priority over the delivery of engines with the arrival of the tank in increasing numbers from early 1917, the primary problems remained the supply of raw materiels and sufficient factory space for manufacture.[31] Consequently, the government had little choice but to invest in a controversial factory at Spondon, Derby, constructed expressly for the purpose of producing cellulose acetate even though some of the private sector promoters of the new facility were known to be of dubious character.

Much of the investment programme in extra manufacturing facilities remains attributed to David Lloyd George, who recognized, whilst Minister of Munitions, that the violence and unprecedented destructiveness of the conflict would be irreversibly transformative. The demands of materiel supply not only contributed to the principles of modern management and logistics but were also the precursors of the arguments concerning the merits and associated negatives of nationalized and privatized industry, the very models that characterized British politics in the latter half of the twentieth century.[32]

The growing output of British armaments manufacture began modestly with four National Cartridge Factories responsible for producing rifle ammunition. However, carefully controlled aircraft manufacture followed closely behind and was initially centred at both the Royal Aircraft Factory in Farnborough and Shepard's Bush in London. By 1918, however, the Ministry of Munitions directly supervised 250 factories and the output of approximately 20,000 'controlled' establishments which represented 'a new industrial infrastructure where outputs counted more than costs'.[33] Nevertheless, despite the obvious success, towards the end of the conflict there were arguments that supply should be proportionate to military dividend and the capital invested.[34] It was this principle that ultimately threatened to undermine all the progress made in the development of military aviation during the years of conflict when Britain began to rebuild her economy in the immediate post-war period.

These achievements were particularly hard fought because from the inception of military aviation until the formation of the Royal Air Force, there was a complete lack of consensus regarding the most effective methods of administering and managing the emerging British aerial capability from a strategic perspective. This was largely due to the pre-war divergence of the two Royal Flying Corps wings which culminated in the formation of an independent Royal Naval Air Service and the effective divorce of the military and naval aviation arms and their strategic requirements throughout the course of the war.[35] Repeated attempts to achieve greater cooperation in terms of aeroplane design and training requirements by the Joint War Air Committee, and later Air Boards, failed primarily due to inter-service rivalries and mutual suspicions. Ultimately, these difficulties attracted political attention, which further detracted from more pressing problems such as securing an adequate supply of aircraft dope to meet the demands of the forces in military theatre.

By 1918, the situation had changed irrevocably from the inception of Royal Flying Corps in 1912, when the flying of aeroplanes was primarily intended for the purpose of reconnaissance. If pilots did experience the opportunity for aerial combat during those early stages of the war, it was through the aiming of their personal revolvers or rifles at an opponent from an equally unarmed machine. However, by the cessation of the conflict the list of front-line aircraft of specially designed types, neatly subdivided by their military purpose into groups of fighters, reconnaissance, tactical and strategic bomber, was in sharp contrast to the in-fighting experienced in the early evolution of the British aircraft industry. Similarly, the predominance of design and manufacture had swung squarely in favour of private manufacturers such as A.V. Roe, Sopwith and de Havilland, who obtained specially designed aero-engines from companies such as Rolls Royce and Sunbeam to power their own designs through the highly sophisticated machinations of an innovative and efficient engineering supply chain.[36]

Indeed, the confusing and complicated origins regarding aerial navigation policy and the British technological response appeared to be a distant memory by the time the Air Ministry and the independent Royal Air Force were established in April 1918. However, this milestone represented not only the culmination of an intensive struggle for the efficient and effective development of British aviation technology and the subsequent application of military airpower but also the creation of a component supply mechanism that was no less impressive, if not even harder fought to develop.

1

'Common instruments of locomotion'

Technical development (1909–14)

The development of new technologies invariably comprises the slow process of research and development before the product is finally perfected and introduced to the open market. For the British, the period between the first practical demonstration of powered flight by the Wright Brothers on 17 December 1903 and the outbreak of The Great War in 1914 was one of vigilant experimentation accelerated beyond all expectation following the start of hostilities. This progress intensified dramatically following the true dawn of aerial combat in 1915, when the Germans first armed their aircraft with synchronized machine guns firing through the propeller. From a foundling concern 'originally taken in by amateur gentlemen as an advocation',[1] the British aircraft manufacturing capability developed to become one of the most technologically advanced industries in the world by 1918.

To place such a manufacturing expansion into context, it is worth noting that the Royal Flying Corps (RFC) accompanied the British Expeditionary Force to France with sixty-six aeroplanes in August 1914, approximately half the number of machines then available to the French *Service Aéronautique*. However, British industry soon embraced the challenge of both design and manufacture of aircraft, and national and private enterprise ultimately collaborated to perform a remarkable achievement. One of the most perceptive contemporary commentaries on the accomplishment of the British aircraft industry was written by C.H. Claudy for the *Scientific American*:

> At the beginning of the war Great Britain's capacity for manufacturing airplanes was not greater than 100 per year. At the time the armistice was signed she was turning out planes at the rate of 800 per week! In other words,

her production possibilities were demonstrated to be in excess of 40,000 planes a year! Think of that, and remember that it is not America, with her limitless resources of men and money and factory and raw materiel but the British Isles, with their very much limited man-power, materiel resource and steel industry, which not only built the planes but engined them. And then, as do all fair-minded Americans who get the actual facts, take off your hat and bow in deep respect to a nation we of America are rather too apt to consider slow and old-fashioned in methods when it comes to factory production.[2]

When compared to the manufacturing heritage and capabilities of the United States this was high praise indeed and Claudy himself highlights the fact that at the start of hostilities there were only six aircraft factories in England. In little over four years, 126 firms and three national factories became employed in the manufacture of British aircraft by November 1918. Such exponential growth in output to meet increased military demand was inevitably a swift learning curve not only in aircraft design but also factory regulation, government procurement protocol and materiel supply. To fully comprehend the British experience, we must examine details of the regulation

Figure 2 S.F. Cody in the First Successful British Aeroplane at Farnborough in 1908. Courtesy of Science & Society Picture Library/Getty Images.

that resulted in not only the success of the industry but ultimately the safety of the workforce employed in production.

Despite this ultimate achievement, early aviation enthusiasts in Britain were initially appalled at the apathy at the War Office to the potential application of airpower. The Secretary of State for War, Lord Haldane, adopted a wait-and-see approach to development for which he was also highly criticized for allowing other nations to steal a significant lead in building their own military capabilities.[3] Haldane declined the offer to purchase the Wright Brothers' aeroplane and associated scientific information in December 1906, a move often considered a missed opportunity by aviation historians.[4] It was widely believed that the apparent lack of interest afforded to early aviation by the military authorities was due to their belief that the geography of an island nation was key to defence and the only way in which to secure the British Isles from attack was through the maintenance of a powerful Navy. This attitude remained prevalent despite reports of Count Zeppelin's successful experimentation with his navigable rigid airship in 1900 and the known advantages of using military observation balloons during the Boer War.[5] Although the airship and the aeroplane were undoubtedly in their technological infancy, they were becoming increasingly proficient at traversing the traditional military boundaries of land and sea, a capability frequently alluded to by early proponents of military aviation.[6]

Early British experiments in military aviation began in the late nineteenth century with the advent of the balloon, and following experimentation at Woolwich and Chatham, the Army Balloon Factory was established at Aldershot in 1890. By 1900, the school was under the command of Colonel Templer, who was an experienced aeronaut and no stranger to the dangers of ballooning. The *Pall Mall Gazette* described Templer as an 'actor in two of the most terrible ballooning accidents' during which both his passengers had been killed.[7] The first victim fell from the balloon basket following a collision with a gasometer and the second, Mr Powell M.P., was carried across the English Channel and never seen again.

The British secured the services of another individual who was no stranger to the dangers of early flight, Samuel Franklin Cody. An early American aviation pioneer, Cody was experimenting in the Aldershot balloon sheds with man-lifting kites powered by small petrol engines in early 1907.[8] Whilst British interest soon began to turn towards the development of aeroplanes, kite experimentation was recognized as an important research tool for determining the characteristics of manoeuvrability in flight. Accordingly, Cody continued his research, for which he was awarded a total of £5,000 grant funding in the Army Appropriation Account of 1913.[9] The Balloon Factory was relocated to Farnborough in 1911 and briefly renamed the Army Aircraft Factory before becoming the Royal Aircraft Factory (hereafter the Factory) in 1912. After the formation of the Royal Air Force in 1918 the name was once again changed to the Royal Aircraft Establishment to avoid confusion with inevitable future military acronyms.

The position of the Army Aviation Department was briefly discussed in Parliament in December 1911, where Colonel Seely, then Under-Secretary of State for War, detailed the number of aircraft held on strength.[10] These comprised a grand total of fifteen aeroplanes in War Department ownership, of which nine were of English design and six were of French manufacture. Most of these machines were new to Farnborough and had only been purchased since January 1911.[11] However, it was not just the development of aeroplanes that required dedicated attention but also the recruitment and training of the pilots required to fly these cutting-edge machines. An incentive scheme was therefore devised to recruit pilots which promised the award of £75 to every officer who obtained their aviation certificate.

The Conservative MP for Brentford, William Joynson-Hicks, raised further questions in relation to the details of the proposed aviators' certificate scheme to which Colonel Seely replied that once awarded, each candidate would be attached to the Air Battalion for a further course of instruction before being officially appointed as an Army aviator and noted that 'the original selection will be made on the recommendations of commanding and medical officers as to the suitability of the officers for aviation work'.[12] The *Penny Illustrated Paper* considered the license fee to be good value for money as it not only insured pupils against all future accidents and damages but also attracted the best talent away from the competition already posed by opportunities in civil aviation:

> It is not surprising, therefore, that with such a moderate charge a large number of pilots have passed out from Hendon school this year, especially since there are so many brilliant openings for them with the ever-increasing aeroplane companies, who are always on the lookout for careful and capable aviators for their new machines.[13]

With a commercial airman's salary ranging between £500 and £2000 a year just before the outbreak of war, the recruitment of qualified pilots for military purposes was almost as difficult as procuring suitable aircraft.

In relation to the development of new machines, the government proposed a series of competitions in which cash prizes would be awarded for the best aeroplane designs and the exchange would conclude with how these machines could be best manufactured once the winners had been ascertained. Joynson-Hicks was curious to deduce whether any winning design might be manufactured under license at the Factory and enquired regarding the possibility to produce 100 machines at Farnborough. Colonel Seely responded that the Factory was only organized for experimental work and the carrying out of general repairs and was not capable of such large-scale manufacture, but he did confirm that the potential for production of aeroplanes was under consideration. This later became a source of increasing tension and bitterness between the government and the emerging private aircraft industry.

Despite the developments in British military and civil aviation it was still widely believed in public circles that the country was much behind the rest of the world regarding technical capabilities, and it was feared that this was causing irreparable damage to national pride and the status of British industry abroad. Indeed, the Women's Aerial League had been specifically formed to address the perceived backwardness of Britain regarding the science of aviation and endeavoured to reverse the government's tendency to buy airships and aeroplanes from foreign nations – a phenomenon which they believed damaged both British commerce and national prestige.[14] However, there was also a scientific reason why the British were somewhat behind their continental neighbours in the development of aviation – namely, the weather. The British climate and insular geographical position meant that an uncertainty of wind force was always against early aviators, and it was argued that it was important to wait for technological progress to be sufficient to mitigate for the unpredictable weather experienced in the UK.[15]

However, once the government became interested in the development of aviation they were initially keen to open negotiations with private inventors for the acquisition of existing aeroplanes of foreign manufacture, and in March 1909 Lord Haldane announced in Parliament that such enquiries were already underway. It was reported in *The Times* on 11 March 1909 that arrangements had been made for Wilbur Wright to travel to England to demonstrate his flying machine before War Office experts, but in reality this was only after he had completed a tour of flying exhibitions to military representatives of other European nations.[16]

In fact, the apathy of which the British government was being accused by contemporary commentators could also be found in other countries and applied to the phenomenon of artificial flight more generally. For example, when the Wright Brothers conducted their first experiments in Springfield, Illinois, in the United States, they received very little official state-endorsed encouragement and instead experienced widespread cynicism that they would never be able to perfect heavier-than-air flight. It was in this environment of indifference that their remarkable achievement of a flight of 38,956 metres on 5 October 1905 in the Wright Flyer III bore no witnesses and no official photographs, despite Springfield itself having a population of approximately 50,000 inhabitants at the time. Some sceptics even refused to believe the flight had taken place at all, whilst those that accepted the accomplishments concluded that there was very little appetite or future in its physical application.

Wilbur Wright himself appears to have not given any serious consideration to the application of powered flight beyond sport flying and wrote the following in an article for the *Scientific American* in February 1908:

> The motor-driven flyers will become sufficiently numerous to afford great sport, not only to the amateur aviators, but also indirectly to the general public, for the flying-machine races of the future will surpass anything the world has yet seen as spectacular performances.[17]

It was not until 31 May 1909 that the true extent of the Wright's scientific achievements began to be recognized and even then, not in their native America but in France. The French aviation pioneer, Octave Chanute, promoted and publicized their flying experiments and persuaded the industrialist and politician, Lazare Weiller, to invite the brothers to France to demonstrate the capabilities of the Wright Flyer.

Unfortunately for the Wright Brothers, the general lack of interest afforded to them was largely due to the secretive attitude they had adopted since their first powered flight in 1903. Consequently, their reluctance to collaborate, or to even corroborate their own impressive aeronautical achievements, resulted in them making 'the great mistake of believing themselves considerably ahead of the French experimenters' and aeronauts of other nations, for that matter.[18] The brothers had little time for either journalists or financiers but rather considered themselves to be pure scientists and as such occasionally published their findings in the academic press such as the following abstracts from an article published on 6 April 1906:

> From the beginning the prime object was to devise a machine of practical utility, rather than a useless and extravagant toy. For this reason, extreme lightness of construction has always been resolutely rejected. On the other hand, every effort has been made to increase the scientific efficiency of the wings and screws in order that even heavily built machines may be carried with a moderate expenditure of power. The favorable results which have been obtained have been due to improvements in flying quality resulting from more scientific design and to improved methods of balancing and steering. The motor and machinery possess no extraordinary qualities. The best dividends on the labor invested have invariably come from seeking more knowledge rather than more power.[19]

Presently they attempted to offer their invention to successive governments for an unnegotiable price, but a major problem was that the 'aeroplane' as a concept was effectively an amalgamation of different inventions which were ultimately difficult to patent and distribute outright. Inevitably the Wright's technological lead was eroded by the achievements of fellow aviation pioneers who were allowed sufficient time to catch up. When the Brazilian Santos-Dumont not only set the first world record in a heavier-than-air machine on 12 November 1906 but far more importantly from a commercial perspective – being the first flight to be filmed and publicly distributed – the Wright Flyer lost significant amounts of technological and financial value.[20] Soon French inventors such as Farman, Delagrange and Bleriot were also making substantial progress in aeroplane design, and ultimately it was the progress of these French pioneers that had the greatest influence on British opinion.

Conversely, the French Senate was also facing public criticism for not recognizing the potential threat of military aviation, and in France, the key motivation for investment and development of an independent air fleet became national defence from foreign aggression. This was considered paramount particularly following German progress in the design and manufacture of dirigibles and the experiences of the Franco-Prussian war. Not only did the Germans possess more operational airships but they also manufactured and supplied many of the materiels required for their construction recognizing early that the control of materiel supply was as important as military capability. Emile Reymond, a distinguished French engineer, believed that French 'dignity as well as her security was at stake', and that France owed it to herself to ensure that every effort was made in making up the technological and industrial divide.[21] This obsession to make up for perceived lost time became a recurring theme throughout Europe, but the science of aeronautics was still in its infancy and once governments committed sufficient funds to military aviation development invariably progressed rapidly, particularly following the outbreak of war.

The British experience was undoubtedly like that of France, with the press regularly reporting that the country was dangerously behind and using the developments of other nations and their aviators as a barometer of progress. However, there can be little doubt the impact the first crossing of the English Channel, by French aviator Louis Bleriot on 25 July 1909, had upon the emerging British military defence doctrine in relation to defence against aerial threat.[22] By 1911, many exciting events were witnessed in the world of aeronautics, including long-distance cross-country flights, the advent of efficient air cargo transportation and the Paris to Madrid air race. But in Britain the national mood was of adject disappointment. It was widely believed that the government was directly responsible for putting the country at a technological disadvantage that had enabled foreign aviation pioneers to secure the most records and prizes at the expense of British designers and aviators. However, it was not just national prestige that had been deemed to suffer but also that the government had gifted continental powers an unrivalled military advantage that the British simply could not match, despite the scientific knowledge and manufacturing capabilities present in the UK.[23] Announcements in France that they were also in the process of developing a dedicated Army aviation branch did little to improve the British disposition.

However, characteristically understated progress was indeed being made in Britain as the potential of airpower became more apparent. In early 1912, the government reported that they had 'been impressed by the evidence which has been placed before them regarding the state of Aerial Navigation' when compared with that made by other military powers and had concluded that the necessity for an efficient aeronautical service was no less urgent.[24] Reports of Italian aeroplanes not only being employed in military reconnaissance duties but also dropping bombs during fighting with Ottoman forces in Tripoli meant that the importance of airpower as an addition to the military equipment of a modern armed forces could no longer be ignored. In Britain, Grahame-White argued in 1912 that French aviation was so advanced because the government were eager to encourage progress and willing to finance the constructor who had ideas.[25] This was certainly true in the design and manufacture of specialist aero-engines, such as the *Gnome et Rhône* rotary engine, whereby the French government decided to finance research and development directly. The British left development in the hands of the private sector and as a result remained significantly and were consequently dependent on the supply of French powerplants throughout the early stages of the war. Nevertheless, the British epiphany that military aviation was fast becoming an established and specialist part of modern warfare resulted in the formation of the Royal Flying Corps on 13 April 1912.

In terms of technological development, both aeroplanes and airships were designed at Farnborough until 1913, when the development of dirigibles was transferred to the Royal Navy. Although the Factory was theoretically a technical department and resource for both services, the Admiralty decided to develop their own facilities and explore the potential acquisition of aeroplanes from elsewhere, including not only private British manufacturers but designs from throughout the aviation world. An early example of Admiralty independence can be found in early 1914, when they attempted to obtain the particulars of a large Russian aeroplane, nicknamed the 'Ilya Murometz', designed by Igor Sikorsky. Although it was arranged for officers of the Naval Air Service to travel to St. Petersburg to inspect the aircraft the outbreak of war ultimately curtailed further interest and hardware solutions were sought much closer to home.[26]

Nevertheless, one of the major challenges in Britain was the relationship between private firms and government-sponsored research establishments. The advents of flying encouraged a variety of firms to enthusiastically enter into the construction of aeroplanes without fully appreciating both the financial outlay and necessary time involved for research and development. These investments were uncompromisingly required in order to perfect flying machines that would ultimately become 'a common instrument of locomotion'.[27] Those early firms also soon realized that the immediate development of aeroplanes was intrinsically linked to the demand for military orders and predefined military specifications, and that they neither possessed sufficient knowledge or financial resources to continue with independent development without the order books being full of government business. This resulted in British manufacturers reluctantly requesting official government support and a compromise being reached in which a competition would be held to identify those designs most suitable for further development. In fact, the blueprint for the development of British military aviation contained the following paragraph specifically detailing the encouragement of private enterprise as a key part of their strategy:

> Mention has already been made of the fact that importance is attached to the existence in this country of a flourishing private industry. This consideration has been given due weight to in the provisions regarding the purchase of aeroplanes, about half of which will be ordered from British firms. The arrangement under which officers and civilians desiring to enter the Royal Flying Corps as flyers will first have to obtain their Royal Aero Club certificate privately, and the rent to be paid for sheds and landing rights should render some assistance to the private aerodromes. A stimulus will thus be provided to private enterprise, which may assist the aerial industry to tide over the difficult initial period.[28]

A key part of the assistance from the public purse was the freely available dissemination of government sponsored research, but this failed to stop claims from industrialists that the sole purpose of the Royal Aircraft Factory was to obtain a government monopoly in the field of aeronautics at the expense of private enterprise. Such claims persisted and became a common theme during devise discussions concerning future policy until 1916.

It was certainly true that the facilities at Farnborough were far beyond superior to those available to private constructors, but this was exactly what the country required in order to obtain both the scientific and practical intelligence for the rapid development of military aviation. What private manufacturers initially failed to realize was that without the dissemination of the scientific research undertaken at the Factory, it was highly unlikely that they would have been able to produce suitable machines of their own design and certainly not as quickly. Some of the first technical areas in which private firms benefited from research undertaken by the engineers at Farnborough was in relation to deciding which were the best fabric coverings for aeroplane wings and fuselages. In addition, aero-engine performance data was widely also shared with manufacturers to enable improvements to be made and ensure machines were designed in the knowledge of the available thrust.

The construction of aircraft at the Factory was initially restricted to reverse engineering machines that had been purchased for the purpose of experimentation. However, some aeroplanes were designed from scratch although admittedly based on the principle of improving existing technology but nevertheless making a significant contribution towards the emerging British understanding of aeronautical science. An example of the kind of practical experimentation in which the Factory was involved was reported in the *Journal of the Royal Society of Arts* by the superintendent, Mervyn O'Gorman, in which he proudly announced that published performance information on an aeroplane as 'not a theoretical case' but based upon 'verified by trials on the design at Farnborough'.[29] The ability to physically test theories and the capabilities of existing designs thoroughly was instrumental in establishing British aerial dominance by the end of the First World War. Ultimately, the existence of centralized research facilities achieved the best possible return on investment, not only in the short term but also for the future of machines manufactured by private industry – many of which were designed by former scientists and engineers who had perfected their trade whilst employed at Farnborough.

The fifth International Aero Exhibition at Olympia in 1913 was an opportunity to demonstrate two key exhibits that were the direct products of War Office investment. The *Journal of the Royal Society of Arts* was eager to report on the technical capabilities of the Farnborough designs. First, the rather uninspiring Delta class airship, but second, and ultimately more importantly from the perspective of British aviation, the B.E.2 biplane:

> In comparison to the balloon-ships of other nations, the 'Delta' is little more than a toy. With a capacity of 165,000 cubic feet of gas, and carrying a crew of six for war purposes, the 'Delta' is to the latest type of foreign dirigibles what a torpedo boat is to a cruiser. Frankly, it's disappointing. But the B.E.2 biplane, designed and constructed at The Royal Aircraft Factory,

presents several novel and interesting features, notably its range and speed from forty-one to seventy miles an hour – which gives it at once a high speed and an ease of alighting, while it ascends 1,000 feet in two and a half minutes.[30]

The B.E.2, which stood for Bleriot Experimental, was of a 'tractor configuration' by which the engine was at the front of the machine rather than the 'pusher' type designs in which the propeller was as the back of the aeroplane. It was indeed of superior performance to any other British design before the outbreak of war but was soon outclassed in active service attracting substantial criticism in Parliament and the British press once the conflict was underway. However, in reality there were very few alternative aeroplane designs available despite the War Office Military holding an Aeroplane Competition in 1912 to encourage private sector development.

The first military aircraft competition was in fact held in France in 1911 and the national interest in aviation was such that four million francs were raised by public subscription for the purchase of military aeroplanes. Without French pioneering efforts and technological achievements, particularly in the design and manufacture of specialist aero-engines, it is unlikely that Britain would have been able to have developed her industry with such momentum. In more ways than one, the British aviation industry remained dependent on her French allies throughout the duration of the First World War.

As previously promised the War Office had issued the first specification for a military aeroplane on 14 December 1911 in preparation for the competition which was set to open the following year at Larkhill on Salisbury Plain.

The regulations for the British competition stipulated that each entry had to be delivered to the test field in a packing case on 31 July 1912 where an officer observer would note the time it took to erect the aeroplane and the relative simplicity of its assembly. In total, thirty-eight entries were initially received but the official report noted the following regarding the suitability of the twenty-five aeroplanes that were ultimately delivered to Larkhill in time for the competition:

> Four of these machines were in such an incomplete state that they were in large measure built in the sheds on the competition ground. Two machines, the Aerial Wheel monoplane and the Piggott biplane, had not made a flight

by the 24th day of the competition; the competitors who entered these machines were then instructed to withdraw them. Several other entries suffered from being either unprepared or untried.[31]

Nevertheless, following a series of stringent examinations which not only determined the aeroplanes' flight characteristics but also included glide tests, ability to landing on grass, ease of steering on the ground, ease of road transport and the field of view afforded the pilot, the judges determined that there was one clear winner. The Cody Biplane (No. 31) was awarded first place, and despite being rather unflatteringly described as a 'heavy machine, strongly and somewhat roughly constructed', it successfully achieved all the tests without difficulty.[32] Cody's prize was an additional £4,000 for his research projects which he invested in the development of his own aeroplane designs, but he was tragically killed on 7 August 1913, when his 'Cody Floatplane' broke up in mid-air during a demonstration flight over Farnborough. He was buried with full military honours in recognition of the services rendered to military aviation, but the British had lost one of its most promising and extraordinary aviation pioneers.[33]

One of the key recommendations to come from the competition judges following the competition was the importance for continued focus by British industry on independent aero-engine design. Progress had already been made in aero-engine design following the Alexander Motor Prize Competition, which offered a £1,000 prize on behalf of the Aerial League for the best aircraft engine which would be evaluated at the National Physical Laboratory, but further work was needed to produce more powerful and reliable powerplants.[34] The National Physical Laboratory had been established at Teddington in 1900 following the publication of a Parliamentary Committee report in 1898 for the 'testing and verification of instruments for physical investigation; for the construction and preservation of standards; and for the systematic determination of physical constants and numerical data, useful for scientific and industrial purposes'.[35] The institution was to become fundamental in the development of British aviation throughout the twentieth century and worked closely with specialist research establishments to overcome emerging technical and scientific challenges.

Aero-engine design for the Alexander Motor Prize Competition were to be delivered to the National Physical Laboratory for testing no later than

1 July 1910 and had to comply with a series of regulations drawn up the previous November. These stated that the submission should produce at least 35 BHP and weigh less than 245 lbs.[36] Six engines were originally entered into the competition but only three designs were delivered by the closing date from the following firms; Wolseley Tool and Motor Car Company, Limited (Birmingham), Humber, Limited (Coventry), Green's Motor Patents Syndicate: Manufactured by The Aster Engineering Company (Wembley).

Both the Wolseley and Humber entries were disqualified for failing to complete a twenty-four-hour run reliability test whilst the Green's Motor Patents Syndicate engine only produced 31.5 BHP and thus also failed to meet the regulations.[37] Despite the disappointment, improvements in British capabilities to produce adequate aero-engine designs was not the only requirement in the manufacture of reliable aeroplanes. It soon became obvious that all manufactured components, including aircraft fabrics and dopes, required more rigorous investigation and quality control, as without securing the performance of fundamental materiels, technological progress was impossible.

In the Army Estimates for 1913 to 1914 the Secretary of State for War, John Seely, specifically noted his disappointment in the slow development of British aviation:

> The supply of aeroplanes has proceeded more slowly than could have been wished. Considerable difficulties have been experienced in obtaining machines, either of British or foreign make, and from various causes there has been great delay in delivery by almost all of the makers. The experience gained, however, of the practical use of machines, by the Military Aeroplane Competition gained held in August, and by the researches of the committee which was appointed to consider the question of accidents to monoplanes, has made the selection of machines for future supply very much easier.[38]

In recognition of the work required to accelerate the development of the fledgling British aircraft industry and Royal Flying Corps, Seely more than doubled the investment for the year 1913 to 1914.

Nevertheless, despite the success of the Army aeroplane competition and the increased government expenditure there was one aircraft already available that would have more than challenged Cody's domination. Although the superior capabilities of the Royal Aircraft Factory B.E.2. were demonstrated during the Military Aeroplane Competition, it was not allowed to formally enter because Mervyn O'Gorman was one of the judges. Beyond this fact, however, this could be seen as a demonstration of a more profound reluctance within government circles to recognize the achievements of national institutions in preference to nurturing the endeavours of private enterprise.

Estimates	1913 to 1914	1912 to 1913
	£	£
Establishment of Army personnel, including Special Reserves and premium pilots' certificates	150,500	28,000
Staff of flying school	18,500	5,000
Aeroplanes, mechanical transport, stores and materiels	285,000	161,000
Buildings, including Army share of school buildings	72,000	38,000
Total	**526,000**	**232,000**
Less Admiralty contributions towards flying school	25,000	14,000
Net Provision	501,000	218,000
Increase	283,000	–

Source: J. Seely, *Memorandum of the Secretary of State Relating to the Army Estimates 1913–1914* (London, H.M.S.O., 1913).

However, the amalgam of government-funded research undertaken at Farnborough and the National Physical Laboratory was crucial in the development of British aviation and did receive occasional support in the press. On 13 November 1912, *The Times* reported that the publication of the Advisory Committee for Aeronautics Blue-Book was the principal scientific event of the year and praised the thoroughness of the scientific research and its importance to future progress. Prior to this publication there was a general belief that aeroplanes developed rather organically depending upon the preference of the individual designer and this could be evidenced in the endless forms and configurations of contemporary designs. However, the scientific principles determined by the Advisory Committee for Aeronautics set out every specific detail of construction so that in Britain at least, there was no longer any excuse for aeroplanes manufactured upon poor design principles.[39]

The report itself noted that following consultation with the War Office, systematic experiments were underway to determine the effect of variation in constructional details and conducting accurate in-flight performance measurement which were deemed 'essential for the explanation of the behaviour of a given type of machine.'[40] Ultimately, it was the dissemination of such information to the wider aviation industry that proved invaluable in future designs. These research activities were conducted at Farnborough under the control of the Director-General of Military Aeronautics at the outbreak of The Great War.

During the first two years of the conflict the Factory not only produced a substantial amount of aeroplane and aero-engine designs, but also undertook repairs and supply of aircraft general spare parts. The Factory also had a chemical laboratory and carried out research into aircraft fabric and dope. Towards the end of 1915 however, it was considered that the amount of design work undertaken at the Factory had started to prevent 'healthy competition by private firms and was the cause of jealousy on behalf of contractors'.[41] Nevertheless, the design and manufacturing of aircraft at Farnborough in the early stages of the war was necessary whilst the capacity within the fledgling independent British aviation industry was being built up to maintain supply of machines and associated spares to the Royal Flying Corps.

Perhaps more importantly, 1915 was also the year of the 'Fokker Scourge' during which armed German machines began inflicting heavy losses on British aircraft, particularly the B.E.2c for which both the Factory, and Mervyn O'Gorman in particular, faced intense and often unjust criticism. Interestingly, contemporary reports from German military aviators regarding the increasing regularity of aerial fighting often referred to their own lack of firepower in comparison with Allied machines as detailed in the following extract from March 1915:

> We attack every chance we get in spite of the fact that we have only our revolvers against the machine guns which they have mounted on their aeroplanes. We find the best defence against their machine-gun fire is to get up close to the French aeroplane and then dodge and twist in sharp dips and curves, spoiling the aim of their mounted machines gun, and giving us the advantage with our revolvers.[42]

The perceived German advantage, it would seem, was far from the absolute dominance suggested in the British press.

Ultimately however, a public enquiry into the perceived poor performance of British aeroplane designs was conducted in 1916 and although the amount of production work undertaken at Farnborough was reduced to further encourage aircraft designs by private firms, the body responsible for the administration of policy concerning the air war suggested that the Factory increased experimental activities. The Factory was restructured according to the Air Board recommendation in September 1916 and O'Gorman was replaced by Sir Henry Fowler, who was appointed Superintendent with two subordinates responsible for design and production, respectively.

A further restructure commenced in March 1917, when responsibility for the Factory was transferred to the Ministry of Munitions, although it was decided that the supply department would assume responsibility with the superintendent being managed directly by the controller of Aeronautical Supplies. In this arrangement the Factory was effectively treated like any other aviation contractor and could submit designs for the approval of the technical department, but principal experimental duties remained largely unchanged. Sir Henry Fowler was superseded as the superintendent by Sydney Smith in early 1918 and the technical department was transferred to the Department of Aircraft Production, which effectively brought the entire factory under the control of the Ministry of Munitions before being finally handed over to the Air Ministry in 1920.

Before the outbreak of the First World War there was sufficient interest within the British government in the development of aviation for military purposes that the Minister for War appointed an Advisory Committee for Aeronautics on 30 April 1909. The committee was presided over by the eminent physicist Lord Rayleigh and was principally concerned with 'the scientific study of the problems of flight, with a view to their practical solutions'.[43] Research and experimentation were the responsibility of the National Physical Laboratory, whilst construction of dirigibles and aeroplanes fell into the sphere of activity of the War Office and Admiralty. The programme of experimental work was extensive and considered general questions in aerodynamics, development of aeroplane and airship designs, experiments with propellers, engines design and meteorology.

One of the key areas under investigation by the Committee was tests on balloon and aeroplane fabrics. This primarily involved treating samples of fabric with various preparations of dope to determine improvements in the strength, durability and waterproofing of the materiel. It was reported in 1913 that the dopes in common use provided significant additional strength to aircraft fabric but this gradually diminished over time and required a process of re-application.[44] In the report for 1913 to 1914 the following observations were reported:

> In view of the expense involved in the frequent renewal of the fabric on aeroplanes in service, it is of importance to obtain the type of fabric for the purpose most fitted to withstand exposure to tearing. The weight must be as small as is consistent with the qualities desired; and the dope used should reduce the extensibility and protect the fabric from the weather. In collaboration with the naval and military authorities; it has been arranged that a more continuous series of tests shall be carried out on fabrics and dopes.[45]

Although extensive experiments upon the qualities of materiel coverings had been underway since 1911, work to determine the most efficient fabric and dope combinations intensified following a series of fatal accidents involving Royal Flying Corps monoplanes during 1912.

During September 1912 a Bristol monoplane, flown by Lieutenant Hotchkiss with Lieutenant Bettington as observer, crashed at Wolvercote near Oxford. The aircraft was seen flying over Port Meadow, Oxford, at a height of approximately 2,000 feet when it began a normal descent. At a height of around 200 feet either the fabric of the right-wing burst or the rear section of the port wing gave way and the aeroplane crashed. Although it was ultimately concluded that the fabric had been weakened following the failure of a high tensile wing cable coupling, the investigating committee recommended further experimentation into the suitability of aircraft fabric and dopes alongside exploration into a more suitable method of fixing fabric onto the ribs of wing structure.[46] Experimentation in this area was still being undertaken at the Department of Metallurgy and Metallurgical Chemistry, which included the investigation of balloon and aeroplane fabrics in their programme of investigation between 1915 and 1916. The main purpose of these experiments

Figure 3 Royal Aircraft Factory B.E.2. Courtesy of Steve Stringer Photography/Getty Images.

was to determine 'the causes and nature of deterioration in fabrics, and their mode of treatment by doping or otherwise', and this remained a fundamental problem prior to the advent of all metal aircraft.[47]

At the beginning of 1914, as the prospect of war became ever more certain, questions began to be raised in the press concerning the supply of aircraft for military purposes and whether those aeroplanes operated by the Army and Navy should be amalgamated into a single service. Despite continued press criticism, the War Office had indeed undertaken a variety of steps to assist in the establishment of a successful British aircraft industry, including purchasing examples of promising British and foreign aeroplanes for the purposes of experimentation and establishing the Advisory Committee for Aeronautics to act as an independent centre of excellence for scientific research into the principles of flight. This research and practical development would take place at the Royal Aircraft Factory, which was developed as the engineering centre responsible for disseminating scientific information to the emerging British aircraft industry, thus enabling manufacturers to produce reliable aircraft design in consistent numbers rather than individual examples. A problem did arise, however, in the decision to allow the Royal Aircraft Factory to manufacture aeroplanes of its own design at Farnborough, and although this was done with the good intention of controlling industry prices and ensuring safety through performance reliability, it ultimately caused further friction between the government and private firms who were desperate to secure contracts and satisfy shareholder demand for profits.[48]

Consequently, despite the obvious and rapid progress, continued criticism by the private firms which constituted the opinions of the emerging British industry attracted increasing attention. Effectively they accused the government of collusion and interference to manipulate the sector and their criticism was primarily aimed at the management of the Royal Aircraft Factory and their use of public funds to directly compete with private enterprise.

In reality, the Factory designs were at the time of superior performance to any other British manufactured machine. Consequently, it was decided that in order to both build up the strength of the private sector and increase industrial capacity, contracts would be awarded to private firms for the manufacture of Farnborough designs under license. These machines were principally the tried-and-tested B.E.2, and later the R.E.8. The latter machine, nicknamed the 'Harry Tate' in squadron service, was a successful two-seat reconnaissance and light bomber designed at Farnborough to succeed the B.E.2c. Over 4,000 had been successfully manufactured through the sub-contract supply chain by signing of the Armistice.

Nevertheless, private firms complained that the process stifled the development of their own designs, which would have undoubtedly been more profitable for them than delivering tenders for government designed machines, but at that time not a single prototype had been delivered either on time or to specification for evaluation. What these private firms failed to recognize was that the orders for Factory designs were crucial in the development and perfection of their own production techniques and capabilities and laid the foundations for the subsequent flourishing British aircraft industry. One of the most important lessons learnt during these early stages of development before the outbreak of war was refining the ability to manufacture component parts to standard tolerances and an accuracy which enabled interchangeability and ease of in-service replacement, which was critical in enabling firms to submit proprietary designs.

In early 1914, politicians also began to take an interest in the development of the British airpower capability, and the exchanges provide us with an interesting lens by which to measure progress. For example, in response to a question posed in Parliament on the 14 February 1914 concerning the number of men employed in Ordnance Factories, it was reported that 957 personnel were employed at the Royal Aircraft Factory, a figure which would later be scrutinized in relation to accusations of staff having little to occupy their time.[49] However, perhaps one of the most important revelations during this period was confirmation by Colonel Seely that the Factory was indeed involved in the manufacture of aircraft:

Mr Joynson-Hicks:
Asked the Secretary of State for War, whether he still adheres to his oft-expressed view that the Royal Aircraft Factory is to be used for experimental purposes only; and how many aeroplanes are now being manufactured there?

Colonel Seely:
The Royal Aircraft Factory is now making 24 aeroplanes of a special type.[50]

Questions were also raised in relation to the processes by which repairs to aeroplanes were undertaken at the Factory and why they were recorded differently to those completed at operational squadron repair shops. The financial secretary to the War Office Mr Harold Baker explained that the present practice was to enter the details of repairs directly into the logbook. In any exceptional cases whereby, the logbook was not to reach the factory at the same time as the aeroplane, a record was kept separately and entered when the logbook became available.[51] It may appear that these questions demonstrated a profound interest in practical operations, but an underlying suspicion of the activities undertaken at Farnborough and the government's strategy towards the development of British aviation by the political opposition remained prevalent.

The Factory was effectively responsible for technical investigation and the improvement in performance of aeroplane designs. During 1913–14, experiments were conducted to deduce a more suitable way of controlling the stability and manoeuvrability of aeroplanes, since the prevalent system whereby in which the wing was physically 'warped' to change direction was considered inefficient. The more effective solution involved the redesign of the wing structures to integrate an independent aileron providing the machine with greater stability and the pilot with enhanced control. These improvements were fully recorded by the Advisory Committee for Aeronautics, who reported that the modifications had been made in connection with stability and strength of construction and resulted in 'the complete re-design of certain existing types of machine, involving alterations to wings, body, tail, fin area, wires and controls'.[52] Tests of the new designs proved that it was possible, without sacrifice of controllability, 'to make the aeroplane inherently stable and capable of flying satisfactorily'.[53] Nevertheless, this did not prevent accusations that the B.E. class of aeroplanes had been temporarily withdrawn from Royal Flying Corps squadrons because the wings were unsafe rather than undergoing technical upgrades. Mr Baker, the financial secretary to the War Office, offered the following alternative explanation:

> It is contemplated that B.E. 2 aeroplanes shall in future have aileron instead of warp control. This is an improvement in design, and it must not be assumed that when an improved type of wing is adopted it is because the type displaced is unsafe. That is not so in this case.[54]

However, this simply prompted further searching questions in relation to flying accidents and the suitability and safety of Royal Aircraft Factory designs. Mr Joynson-Hicks proceeded to interrogate the financial secretary and:

> Asked whether the rudders and elevator flaps on B.E. aeroplanes in use by the Royal Flying Corps are to be changed, or have been changed recently, for stronger ones; and, if so, whether the discovery that these organs of control were too weak was due to any of the recent fatal accidents to officers of the Royal Flying Corps, or to such organs bending or showing weakness when machines were being flown by pilots employed by the Royal Aircraft Factory?

Mr H. Baker:

The steel tubing in the rudders of some B.E. aeroplanes is being replaced by tubing of increased size, not as the result of the accidents mentioned, but independently and in consequence of experience obtained by the flyers of the Royal Aircraft Factory. The rudders were not too weak, but everything observed which points to the possibility of improvements or increased safety is, of course, at once investigated.[55]

It was in this spirit of inherent suspicion and open questions relating to the professionalism and capabilities of government facilities that Britain's embryonic airpower capability was deployed during the First World War. Accusations of negligence continued, culminating in charges that Royal Flying Corps pilots were effectively being murdered for being sent into combat against superior enemy aircraft and enquiries and inevitable reorganizations would follow. One of the key findings, however, would be that it was not only pilots who were putting their lives at risk in aerial warfare but similar hazards were experienced by those involved in the manufacture of the machines they flew. Solutions were required not only on the Western Front but on the Home Front also.

2

'Aeroplanes in war'

British military aviation (1912–15)

For Britain to further develop the aeroplane into an effective military weapon it first needed to devise a method of efficient administration responsible for the management of such new and emerging technology. The scheme for the establishment and organization of the Royal Flying Corps was communicated to Parliament in a paper dated 11 April 1912, and apart from a few minor alterations in detail, the development of the Royal Flying Corps was carried out directly along the lines recommended in that scheme. The new service comprised a Central Flying School for pilot training, a Naval Wing, a Military Wing, a Strategic Reserve and the establishment of a research facility, which would become known as the Royal Aircraft Factory, for the purposes of experimentation and scientific development.[1]

The Army Aircraft Factory, which was already in existence at Farnborough in April 1912, was subsequently rebranded as the Royal Aircraft Factory when the Royal Flying Corps came into existence. The Factory was tasked primarily with conducting practical full-scale experiments to prove or otherwise what the scientists at the National Physical Laboratory, located at Bushy House, Teddington, had concluded following investigations with scale aeroplane models. The technical work carried out at the Factory was classified into a series of categories that initially included the following: design of airships, aeroplanes and propellors; physical investigations; research into fabrics, dopes and varnishes; metallurgical research; engine design and research; quality control and inspection of private firms' construction; and keeping the main aeronautical and engineering store for the Royal Flying Corps.

From the outset, the Military Wing of the Royal Flying Corps quickly decided that they simply required one good aeroplane design that was capable of being mass-produced quickly and efficiently and this resulted in the decision to hold the Military Aeroplane Trials in the summer of 1912.[2] Ironically, Samuel Cody's winning design was not at all suited to large-scale production and so it was decided to use the Royal Aircraft Factory-designed B.E.2 as the benchmark, even though this was technically outside the rules of the competition. However, the RFC Naval Wing adopted an entirely different policy altogether and decided to select machines designed and built by private firms which resulted in certain manufacturers developing close links directly with the Admiralty. Such a divergence of strategy ultimately resulted in not only confusion but also ill feeling towards the War Office on the part of British manufacturers. Much of their discontent was aimed directly at those civil servants involved in aeroplane design at Farnborough who continued, in the eyes of private industry, to be overly prescriptive in Army aeroplane requirements and determined to keep them at arms' length.

The issue of producing standardized parts was also far more complicated than had been originally perceived as the majority of components were manufactured by hand and the fledgling aero-industry was yet in a position to develop specialist tools or production practices to ensure consistency or adequate product controls. Many believed that a policy of standardizing one or two designs would smother the initiative of private design teams on which the armed forces were to become dependent when production expanded for war. However, the real impetus towards standardization was the result of increased government orders immediately before 1914 whilst the industry organized itself sufficiently to satisfy demand.[3]

To effectively coordinate these complex functions an Air Committee was established in 1912 to ensure the government's emerging aerial policy was delivered in the most efficient way possible and determine a consensus of direction among the individual services. This hierarchy enabled the Committee of Imperial Defence, and numerous other Departments of State, to refer any questions concerning the development of British military airpower directly to the Committee so that scientific experts could provide answers.[4] Although logical in peacetime, this method of governance would prove far too cumbersome under wartime conditions despite such use of advisory committees and consultative councils becoming an essential component of the machinery of public administration during the inter-war period.⁵

Initially, however, there was a far more pressing challenge that faced the Factory and that was the rapid establishment of a cordial working relationship with private aircraft manufacturers. These early pioneers resented being told where to focus their development resources and having to cooperate with government officials carrying out quality control on their products. Some of the earliest companies began manufacturing French designs, such as those of Blériot and Farman, under license but British companies soon began to emerge producing their own machines.

Some of the most famous British aircraft manufacturers emerged during this period, including Bristol, Sopwith, Handley-Page, Shorts and AVRO, but the reality was that the aeroplane was still very much in its infancy. Consequently, despite the ingenuity and dedication of British designers, many manufacturers entered wholeheartedly into aeroplane construction without appreciating the sheer quantity of research and development required before the emerging technology could become what *The Times* aeronautical correspondent had described as 'a common instrument of locomotion'.⁶ This was to become the source of the resentment and suspicion of government practices that characterized these early years of development.

By 1912, the European political situation necessitated that the immediate development of the aeroplane was directly linked to its potential adaption for military purposes. Many British aviation pioneers, such as Claude Grahame-White, conceded that reliable aeroplanes would be needed in large numbers if definitive destructive results were to be achieved against a modern enemy.⁷ However, early manufacturers simply did not possess either the finances or the required knowledge to produce suitable machines of sufficient quality in increasing quantities. Consequently, instead of embracing the establishment of the Factory as a method of accelerating their own development through the sharing of scientific data, many private constructors accused the government of trying to drive them out of business. These allegations, although largely unfounded, fuelled a suspicion and resentment that was to continue throughout the duration of the conflict and wasted a great deal of time in human resources. This inherent suspicion of government intent later had significant consequences on servicing the materiel demands of the war.

Various attempts were made by the government to raise the profile and reputation of their experimental establishment and reassure the emerging British aeronautical firms that the work undertaken at Farnborough was in the best interests of both the public and private sectors. In May 1912, the King and Queen were reportedly impressed during a visit to Farnborough during which they spent time with the Superintendent, Mervyn O'Gorman, inspecting eight military machines.[8] The positive press continued throughout the remainder of 1912 as the Secretary of State for War, Colonel Seeley, publicly reiterated in the House of Commons that the object of the Factory was not to build machines in competition with the private sector but to serve as a guide to constructors in the design and supply of British Army aeroplanes to military specifications.

Frederick Lanchester, a pioneering British aeronautical engineer and trusted member of Asquith's Advisory Committee for Aeronautics, believed that 'whatever the relative merits or demerits of private and government manufacture' new designs required sufficient standardization before any contract be undertaken. In Lanchester's informed opinion, the Factory was responsible for manufacture and experimentation of new designs until they had become an 'officially accepted type' and only then could private concerns take the reins in terms of production and innovate as necessary.[9]

It was also genuinely believed that British constructors, using the research capabilities established at Farnborough, would be able to exploit the emerging friendly markets of Australia, Canada and South Africa, whose governments had already expressed an interest in establishing their own aviation services. By September 1912, it was becoming recognized that commercial aviation was a distinct business opportunity in its own right and commercial manufacturers were starting to attract private investors eager to ensure they would be the first to see a return on any capital expended. However, there was also a realization that such investment was only as good as the firm, or the designer, responsible for the construction of a new aeroplane that could outperform its competitors in both performance and price. Although the potential was vast, many were waiting for more definitive requirements and guaranteed government orders before laying down their money.[10]

Nevertheless, the general optimism was further enhanced in November 1912 by the publication of the Advisory Committee on Aeronautics' 'Blue Book', which was an amalgamation of domestic and international scientific experiments into the development of aeronautical science. This magnum opus of aeronautical science included the work of the Factory's very own superintendent, Mervyn O'Gorman, as a recognized expert and one of the very best and brightest of British aero-engineers.[11] More importantly, however, was the fact that O'Gorman was an advocate of feely sharing information and the benefit of his considerable experience in the development of British aeronautical science. He gave numerous lectures on important developments in aeroplane design, such as the progress in stability devices, before the Aeronautical Society at the Royal United Services Institution in January 1913. However, this appeared to do little to relieve the suspicions and jealousies prevalent in the private sector.[12]

Armed with this arsenal of scientific information and access to aeronautical expertise, private firms had a wealth of knowledge at their disposal, all without having to spend excessive sums on research and development costs. The situation should have been one of perfect harmony between the public and private purse, with the government paying for research whilst the private sector delivered finished articles to predetermined specifications at safeguarded prices being mutually beneficial to client and contractor alike. Nevertheless, animosity towards the Factory continued to intensify rather than abate and all at a time when every effort should have been focused on technical investigation and building up sufficient reserves of suitable aeroplanes capable of operation in the coming conflict.

Nevertheless, by March 1913 rumours had started to circulate about the unprofessional conduct of workmen employed at the Royal Aircraft Factory which accused the workforce of institutional laziness and abusing their privileges. The Amalgamated Society of Engineers wrote to *Flight* magazine in protest against such allegations which resulted in a considered editorial response concluding that the Factory was not only a first-class national asset of international reputation but had also accomplished uncommonly good work for the money expended upon it and that this represented a sound scientific investment.[13] This was high praise indeed, particularly as the government had been continually accused of not being willing to authorize the spend of sufficient funds in the progress of British aviation which ultimately remained the root of all criticism. Private firms believed that the public finances voted for aeronautics, and the Factory in particular, would have been better spent buying British aeroplanes designed and constructed directly from the British trade rather than in the development of machines by public sector scientists and engineers.

Such arguments were effectively useless as the government had quite clearly set out its plans for future development from the outset, but the lack of forthcoming large orders effectively put private firms in a difficult financial position as they were unable to expand their capacity without the guarantee of government employment. In addition, dependence on foreign-produced components, such as aero-engines, was a genuine concern of the sector and aeronautical commentators believed that it was absolutely essential that powerplants should be designed and built in the UK if the aeroplane was to be developed to its fullest capacity as an 'instrument of war'.[14] Here there was at least a valid argument, since Factory machines such as the B.E.2 and the R.E.8 were specifically designed to take French engines, and although this was perfectly logical during peacetime, there was no guarantee that sufficient supply could be maintained during times of war.

Consequently, a stalemate developed between the aircraft trade and the government. The former, despite securing tentative contracts for the manufacture of Factory machines, complained at the lack of opportunity to produce their own designs and continued to accuse the government of using public funds to compete directly with private sector enterprise. The government on the other hand remained disappointed that the private sector had been unable to efficiently respond to demand. The press reported in January 1914 that none of the private firms had succeeded in delivering orders within contractual time frames and that the average amount of delay was four months. *The Times* even reported that it was difficult for most British industrialists to understand why the issue of government contracts should result in protests from the aircraft industry, particularly as the manufacture of government machines could not be deemed to be less profitable than for proprietary designs as there was effectively no real competition.[15] Although the press coverage appeared objective it provoked an angry response from Mr Charles Grey, aeronautical correspondent and founder of the *Aeroplane Magazine*, who blamed delays on the failure of the Royal Aircraft Factory to efficiently carry out its task of inspection regarding the quality of construction from private firms.[16]

Grey's principal quarrel centred on alternations to designs made by Royal Aircraft Factory engineers once they had been issued to manufacturers, which he believed had resulted in lengthy delays in the delivery of completed machines as the required changes took time to complete. Grey was also annoyed at the insistence by Royal Aircraft Factory officials that private firms used materiels of certain specification which he deemed more expensive and difficult to obtain than readily available alternatives.[17] Finally, consistent delay in the delivery of engines from French suppliers was also listed as a cause for the poor performance in meeting contractual deadlines. Despite the impassioned defence of the private industry, however, Grey was willing to concede that individual firms remained unprofessional and difficult to do business with, but he implored that they should be nurtured and encouraged for the sake of their ideas and 'not left desolate in a cold and unsympathetic world'.[18]

The process of government variation to original design specifications and the time required for subsequent modifications has been a continual cause of criticism throughout the history of the British aircraft industry so the fact that it was evident in its infancy is hardly surprising. But at this early stage the perfection of standardization was crucial in ensuring that all components performed within specified tolerances, and without this attention to detail, it is unlikely the industry would have been able to flourish during the forthcoming conflict. William Robson, an RFC pilot writing in 1916, certainly appreciated the Factory's attention to detail and believed that it was no exaggeration to say that aviators' lives depended on 'the good workmanship and faultless materiel' of their machines. Robson specifically argued that a higher standard of worker was required in the aeroplane industry above other branches of engineering.[19] However, in other areas of the National Munitions Factories, such as those responsible for the manufacture of explosives, pre-war standards of inspection were actually relaxed at the outbreak of conflict to increase production.[20] A decision that had devastating political consequences later in the war.

Nevertheless, in late January 1914 additional accusations started to emerge which suggested that the Factory was guilty of practicing industrial espionage during which they simply took the innovations of private firms and incorporated them into their own aeroplane designs. This was an altogether more dangerous rumour than that of institutional laziness that was circulating the previous year because it implied that any aspiration of private firms to

Figure 4 Bleriot XI Monoplane, Farnborough 1915. Author's Collection.

continue independent development was effectively hopeless. How would they ever be able to encourage capital investment in aviation from wealthy individuals if it was only going to be used to 'provide ideas to be filched' by the scientists and engineers at Farnborough with the full support of the government?[21] Once again, despite remaining unsubstantiated, these new speculations raised sufficient scepticism and conjecture to inspire certain elements within the aviation press to conduct a comparative analysis between the aircraft produced by the industry and those designed by the engineers at Farnborough to conclusively put the matter to rest once and for all.

It was certainly true that Royal Aircraft Factory had based their military aeroplane designs on the most technologically advanced examples of the day, including those constructed by Louis Bleriot, Santos-Dumont and Henri Farman. The Factory had specifically purchased these machines for the purpose of experimentation and determining the best characteristics of each individual design. With aviation in its infancy, it is hardly surprising that this should have been the case and it represented a rare example of government prudence in relation to research and design, balancing the need for rapid technological solutions with the incumbent strain on the public purse. The Aeronautical Society of Great Britain even took a principled stand against the issuing of inventors' patents and championed the principles of open cooperation and communication. The Society's Secretary, Captain Baden

Baden-Powell, effectively used his position to promote a compromise through which he 'endorsed patenting as a pragmatic means to combat secrecy amongst inventors' but only if the process ultimately assisted in the facilitation of the open exchange of ideas and latest scientific breakthroughs.[22]

The Americans also believed that the establishment of a national research facility to explore the merits of existing aeroplane designs to be quite an ingenious solution to the challenges of military aviation. In fact, the American press were even praising the British B.E.2 as a fine machine combining all 'the military qualities of speed, quick climbing powers, and the ability to stand rough usage' as late as 1916. Long after the design had been proved technologically obsolete during combat on the Western Front.[23] However, the British policy of taking the best innovations from foreign and domestic manufactured aeroplanes and incorporating them into their own designs did not go entirely smoothly. Orville Wright brought an action before the War Office in the autumn of 1914 for patent infringements which was not concluded until 1916 for the not-insubstantial settlement figure of £15,000 paid by the British government.[24] This could have been substantially more if Griffith Brewer, the Wright's UK patents agent, had not persuaded Orville to benevolently accept a far lesser sum than he had originally demanded.[25]

Claims of imitation also came from domestic manufacturers prompting *Flight* magazine to conduct their forensic analysis of numerous contemporary aeroplanes against those of Factory design. Investigations included comparisons of construction techniques employed in fuselage sections, of the materiels used for covering the bodywork, landing gear configurations, wing section designs and control surface mechanisms. The examination concluded that although similarities naturally existed between one machine and another, it was evident that the individual characteristics of the B.E. class of Factory design had been retained and had not been significantly modified 'by the introduction of fresh features copied from other machines'.[26]

If this was not evidence enough to finally dispel the myth that the Factory intended to compete directly with the British aircraft industry, an independent aeroplane manufacturer publicly praised the government establishment for its determination to encourage and assist the private constructor. More sensationally, they even argued that there was something gravely wrong within the inner working of the firms that constituted the British aviation industry and their determination to ensure the killing-off of the smaller competition. Hewlett and Blondeau was founded in 1910 and manufactured numerous aircraft types, including Farman and Avro machines, under license before becoming a subcontractor to the fledgling Royal Flying Corps. In their open letter printed in *Flight* on 31 January 1914 they argued that they had received every help and attention from the personnel at the Royal Aircraft Factory in the execution of their work and that their relationships had always been of both a professional and most favourable nature. Hewlett and Blondeau recognized that all the Factory wanted from their subcontractors was to ensure that work undertaken was done well and to the specified standards to ensure consistency and safety, and the firm believed it was 'only fair to say this, as it has been implied that all the trade constructors dislike the R.A.F. and its ways'.[27]

The support for the Factory and its meticulous methods was a revelation, as it was the first time that the private sector had formally recognized the efforts of the public sector to work with industry in the development of British aviation. Perhaps even more remarkable was that a private firm accused its own industry of an inability to form friendly relations in the pursuit of a common goal. Hewlett and Blondeau believed that some British manufacturers were purposefully building aircraft at a loss in order to put other constructors out of business and corner the market. Once this monopoly had been achieved, they could then charge whatever price they wanted for the manufacture of machines be it of their own design or those manufactured under license through sub-contract orders.

In reality, such Machiavellian commercial tactics were unlikely to succeed because new firms were emerging all the time and their smaller overheads, in comparison to those of larger more established concerns, meant that they could always manufacture machines at a lower cost. Hewlett and Blondeau believed that if the industry as a whole could have fixed a fair price of each machine built to Farnborough standards between them, then the resultant government orders would have been more than enough for existing firms to operate on a financially sound basis. Unfortunately, the emerging British aircraft industry was not immune to the age-old trick whereby larger firms attempted to undersell their smaller rivals, but Hewlett and Blondeau warned that even if this succeeded in bringing about the ruin of some of the fledgling aviation companies, larger concerns could not 'hope to keep the market to themselves long enough to get back all they have spent in reaching this end'.[28]

The letter concluded that if the industry asked a reasonable price for their efforts and accepted that universal standards were required for government contracts, then the complaints against the Factory would simply vanish. The War Office needed machines as quickly as possible to be prepared for the inevitable European conflict and would have welcomed the opportunity to award contracts if they could be certain that orders could be delivered both on time and of the quality demanded in their specification. However, the poor relationship with private manufacturers, combined with the turmoil within the industry itself, meant that Factory was working double shifts in the manufacture of B.E. machines to supply military demand rather than focusing its attention on scientific investigation. Ironically, a situation that neither the scientists at Farnborough nor the owners of private aircraft factories wanted.

The effective absolution of Royal Aircraft Factory practices and their strategic intentions in the aviation press was further assuaged by the establishment of an independent Aeroplane Inspection Branch which should have settled the matter permanently. In addition, *The Times* reported on 26 February 1914 that seventy-one of the eighty-nine aeroplanes added to the Royal Flying Corps strength since the proceeding summer had been manufactured by private firms and the correspondent expressed hope that the industry would 'settle down to the abundant work that lies before it' rather than continue to quarrel with the government.[29] Briefly, it appeared that this was indeed the case as the mutterings abated and both Factory and industry got on with the job at hand, the timely manufacture of aeroplanes for the Royal Flying Corps.

That was until a brief and anonymous editorial published in *Flight* magazine on 10 July 1914, which once again criticized the Factory for competing with the private sector by not issuing orders for B.E. designs, and received a furious response from Mervyn O'Gorman. It was obvious that the Superintendent at Farnborough had finally had enough. Inevitably however, this only served to rekindle the whole debate and alienated a previously supportive aviation press. O'Gorman's outrage was primarily concerned with the fact that the letter should have been published at all and that he had not been consulted directly to offer a counter-perspective:

In repudiating his statements, you will perhaps quote with name and date some of the many statements of responsible ministers whom you allude to; you will mention that the Director General of Military Aeronautics and his Staff who alone control the Factory's output, as well as myself as Superintendent of the Royal Aircraft Factory, have always been accessible to you, and explain how it is that no enquiry was made of any of these before you imputed bad faith to them all in an article which you close by saying that you 'suspend judgment.' In a weekly journal there can scarcely be such urgency as to excuse and still less warrant this neglect of verification.[30]

However, O'Gorman's response may well have been an over-reaction and evidence of official frustration at the continued criticism as *Flight* simply invited a response from the authorities in recognition that the allegations were lacking in evidence. The editor, Stanley Spooner, explained that the opinion of the authorities was not sought deliberately in order to ensure such rumours were not 'magnified into grave misstatements of fact' and argued that the very act of not going to the trouble of publishing an official denial was ultimately the best method of running such a false statement to earth.[31]

Unfortunately for the Superintendent, press reportage soon became the least of his worries as the activities of the Factory once again became the focus of attention in Parliament and subject to a much more destructive criticism that ultimately resulted in a comprehensive management restructure. The unwanted attention came primarily through the routine process of agreeing the Army Estimates and Expenditure for the 1914–15 financial year. The proposed expenditure for the Royal Aircraft Factory was broken down into three sub-categories which included wages, aircraft inspection, and funds for aeroplanes, stores and materiels.[32] The amount totaled £524,000, or a budget increase of £300,000 on the previous year. Although this announcement was much to the delight of the advocates for the Factory, it naturally attracted the attention of those opposed to government strategy, and the activities carried out at Farnborough in particular.

The Conservative Parliamentarian Joynson-Hicks was quick to admonish the operation of the Factory in Parliament at the first opportunity which presented itself. This happened to be on 14 March 1914 during the vote on the Army Estimates that had been published the previous month. Even though he was formally warned by the speaker that the performance of the Royal Aircraft Factory was not the topic of the debate, Joynson-Hicks successfully used the references to propose expenditure to scrutinize his Liberal colleagues, despite openly declaring that he had no desire to score political points and was driven solely in the public and national interest.

Hicks explained to the House that following independent enquiries he had discovered that there was a 'deep dissatisfaction among the officers of the Royal Flying Corps with regard to the products of the Royal Aircraft Factory' and that they had neither confidence in the machines manufactured or the standards of repairs and maintenance carried out there.[33] The prospect of government policy inhibiting the development of private enterprise was objectionable enough to Conservative politicians but the squandering of public funds in the manufacture of substandard aeroplanes was a cause in which the entire opposition could unite.

The timing of the debate could not have been worse for the reputation of the government establishment as a number of fatalities had recently occurred involving machines manufactured and maintained by the Factory, and this became the focus of growing concern. Joynson-Hicks had received a letter from the General-Manager of the Cedric Lea Company, aeronautical engineers based in Shoreham, who had taken the opportunity to inspect a Royal Aircraft Factory designed F.E.2 pusher-biplane which had claimed the lives of Mr. Kemp and his passenger Mr. Haynes at Wittering on 23 February 1914.[34] The letter stated that:

> We had just concluded some private tests of our latest flying machines when the Aircraft biplane came on to the ground, and the machine was carefully examined by our several departmental heads. The unanimous verdict was that the workmanship and finish of the machine was eminently unsatisfactory. We should have been ashamed to have completed the work, and, if we had done so, we are quite positive that it would not have been accepted by any person qualified to pass judgment on aircraft.[35]

A letter from a private manufacturer, sought from an opposition MP, may well have been perceived as simply a continuation of the old allegations against the Factory being played out on a political stage, but a statement from the secretary to the Sussex County Aero Club which claimed that 'when the F.E. 2 biplane arrived the engines and wires were covered with rust' can be considered an entirely independent witness.

Nevertheless, the allegation of sub-standard manufacturing remains slightly puzzling as many private firms had previously complained that the Factory's exacting criteria were impossibly restrictive. Conversely, Thomas Sopwith, arguably one of the most famous aviators of the day, had openly praised the meticulous requirements laid down by the Farnborough Inspectors and believed that the victory of his Sopwith Tabloid design in the 1914 Schneider Cup race was due in no small measure to the fact that his company had experience of building machines to the Army aviation authorities' specifications.[36] Something, somewhere, was obviously misaligned as it was unlikely the Factory would not operate under the same exacting conditions that it expected of private industry.

In fact, questions of workmanship and competency of repairs had previously been raised in Parliament following the death of Lieutenant Desmond Arthur on 25 May 1913 during which the serviceability of a particular aeroplane had been queried. It was that very same B.E. machine, numbered 204, that claimed the lives of Royal Flying Corps Officers Captain C. R. W. Allen and Lieutenant J. E. G. Burroughs at Netheravon on 11 March 1914. The previous day Captain Downer had been killed at Upavon flying another B.E.2 machine in which the wing collapsed.[37] It was this last tragic accident that motivated Major Brook Popham, military aviation pioneer and Downer's former commanding officer, to give evidence, in which he concluded that there were three possible causes for the accident:

> First – the design of the machine may have been wrong, and the strains miscalculated; second – the workman who did the job may, through ignorance or carelessness, have put in too weak a tube; third – the rudder-post may have been changed after reconstruction, and after it was handed over to the squadron. In any of these three cases there is evidence of criminal negligence. If it were done in my squadron, I am to blame. On the contrary, if the machine was handed over to me like this and nothing was done in my squadron, I hold the officials of the Royal Aircraft Factory responsible.[38]

Such negative comments from a senior officer in the Royal Flying Corps was the perfect ammunition for Joynson-Hicks to press home his advantage and claim that there was something fundamentally amiss with the administration at Farnborough and its inability to conduct sufficient and safe inspection of the machines in which pilots were expected to risk their lives. Johnson-Hicks implored Colonel Seely to convince the House of Commons that the country had the means necessary to develop an efficient air service whilst giving confidence to those pilots that the danger to them has been reduced to a minimum. He concluded that an enquiry was required to improve the current situation and ultimately reduce the necessity for further accusations to be levelled against either the government or 'the management of the Royal Aircraft Factory'.[39]

The Conservative MP for Wells George Sandys championed Joynson-Hick's cause later in the debate by insisting that there was an impression in the country that not everything was being done to ensure that the Royal Flying Corps had access to the best possible equipment and safety inspections. Sandys reiterated safety concerns surrounding the recent tragedies before remarking directly on the proposed £14,000 allocated in the Army Estimates for the Inspection Department in which he concluded 'nobody would begrudge a penny of it' but hoped that the duties of the inspection officers had been sufficiently considered to ensure all Factory machines were of the highest possible workmanship.[40] Ironically, Geoffrey de Havilland was appointed an inspector of aircraft within the newly established Aeronautical Inspection Directorate in December 1913, a decision that lost the government one of its most promising aeronautical engineers. Unhappy with a move away from design work, he left Farnborough to join the Aircraft Manufacturing Company, or Airco, in May 1914, where he designed the Airco D.H.2, which equipped the first dedicated British fighter Squadron in France when delivered in February 1916.

Nevertheless, Colonel Seely maintained his assertion that the Farnborough-designed B.E. biplane was the most stable and safest machine in the world. He had even enthusiastically recounted at the Wilbur Wright memorial banquet on 19 May 1914 that he had personally taken part in a demonstration in which the pilot had abandoned control at 2,000 feet and he himself had been able to easily steer the machine around.[41] In reality, the stability in flight of the B.E.2 came at the expense of manoeuvrability and this would prove the subject of significant criticism during the development of the art of aerial combat.[42]

Britain's declaration of war against Germany on 4 August 1914 resulted in the fledgling Royal Flying Corps being sent to France to carry out reconnaissance and artillery spotting duties. By the end of the year the British Expeditionary

Force's increasing request for aeroplanes resulted in the Factory-designed Bleriot Experimental machine being standardized into the B.E.2c as a multi-purpose aeroplane. The War Office also placed a 100 horse-power limit on engine power to improve flying stability and regulate technical specifications to increase production.[43] Regarding the technical development of aircraft, the numbers and type of aircraft required played a critical role in the determination of policy:

> The sole occupation of the authorities at home was to provide the aircraft and equipment demanded by the commander in the field and with the fleet, while Army and Navy authorities formed their policy independently according to their resources or exigencies of the situation.[44]

This approach worked well initially, but aviation technology continued to advance and the introduction into the skies over the Western front of the German Fokker monoplane in the summer of 1915 had devastating consequences for the Royal Flying Corps. The relatively fast and agile German scout was armed with a synchronized machine gun firing through the propeller which annihilated the outdated B.E.2c during a period of losses that became known as the 'Fokker Scourge' and, unsurprisingly, the Royal Aircraft Factory was embroiled in the ensuing controversy.[45]

Although the innovation of the armed 'scout' aeroplane and subsequent dogfights did not manifest on the Western Front until the summer of 1915, in the early months of the conflict opposing aviators had often used rifles and pistols to fight when they stumbled across one another in the air. Even though many of these reconnaissance aircraft already carried small hand-held bombs that could be dropped by either pilot or observer on enemy troop concentrations when the opportunity arose, many believed that the aircraft of the warring powers would remain primarily for observation.[46] A particularly early example of aerial gallantry was reported in the national press on 30 September 1914, which relayed the story of a British aviator who had been wounded during a duel in the air after attracting the attention of an enemy machine whilst dropping bombs on enemy soldiers in the trenches. Flying alone, the airman was unable to bring his rifle to fire upon an enemy aircraft and whilst circling above the two-seater in an attempt to get within pistol range, 'he was hit by the observer of the latter with a rifle'.[47]

Figure 5 Voisin III with Mounted Cannon, Gosport 1915. Author's Collection.

Earlier in September 1914 the Royal Naval Air Service (RNAS) conducted the first air raid of The Great War on the zeppelin sheds at Dusseldorf. Although damage was slight, this and subsequent raids resulted in German civilians demanding better protection against aerial bombardment and Allied nations began to realize the potential effect of aviation on noncombatant morale. Interestingly, Frederick Lanchester had been experimenting with alternative aircraft armament for the purpose of aerial combat before the outbreak of the war. Lanchester designed a special type of duck gun which was loaded with extra heavy pellets, and this had been handed to Farnborough before being forwarded to the Royal Flying Corps Headquarters on Salisbury Plain. Here, it was mounted to an aeroplane for experimentation and had proved somewhat successful. Lanchester noted:

> I think without question the whole subject of firing by heavy charges from aircraft, in place of using a machine gun, when attacking other aircraft, should be gone into as soon as possible and as thoroughly as possible. My own conviction is absolutely against a machine gun in this service, were a quick firing heavy pellet gun available, semi-automatic preferred.[48]

Similarly, some variants of the French-manufactured Voisin 3 and Voisin 4 were the first aircraft armed with cannon rather than machine guns, primarily due to their tubular steel construction, which gave them incredible strength. The cannon itself was an American Hotchkiss, and although useless in terms of aerial combat, it was incredibly effective against ground targets. One wonders what impact such innovations might have had if they had been adopted earlier in the conflict.

National media attention was understandably averted to progress of the conflict and enabled the Royal Aircraft Factory to gain some much-needed breathing space to focus on ensuring research and development, enabling British aviators to remain competitive in the air. However, as production demands intensified on the home-front, questions were once again raised concerning the efficient organization of operations at the Factory. The veteran trade unionist and Labour politician William Tyson-Wilson was concerned in February 1915 that carpentry was being undertaken by piecework at Farnborough in which payment was awarded on quantity produced rather than quality.[49] The financial secretary to the War Office assured Tyson-Wilson that the standard was excellent and that there was nothing to be concerned about, but this question reinvigorated murmurings among the opposition benches. A host of obscure enquiries followed in Parliament as the war progressed, especially as enemy innovations in aviation were reported.

Following the appearance of multi-engined enemy bombers such as Zeppelin-Staaken and Siemens-Schuckert on the Eastern and Western Fronts in 1915, questions were raised as to whether the Royal Aircraft Factory had been similarly foresighted in experimenting with such designs before the outbreak of war.[50] The Under-Secretary of State for War, Harold Tennant, confirmed that this was indeed the case but reminded the House of Commons that the decision concerning the types of aeroplanes constructed at Farnborough was the responsibility of the Director of Military Aeronautics.[51] The Irish Parliamentary Party MP for Clare West, Mr Arthur Lynch, pressed Tenant further and enquired why, if General Henderson, the Director-General of Military Aeronautics, immediatly prior to the outbreak of war, had advocated for the production of multiple-engined machines they were not now available to the Royal Flying Corps. Tennant responded that the provision of other types of aeroplanes was a more urgent requirement and that twin-engined designs were not necessarily more efficient.[52]

Regardless of the outcome, the Factory was once again blamed for a perceived lack of technological innovation and subject to yet further reputational damage which eventually resulted in an official enquiry into its overall management and operation. In fact, Britain relied on French manufactured twin-engined machines in the first instance such as the Caudron G.4 reconnaissance bomber which the Royal Flying Corps and Royal Naval Air Service used throughout 1916 and early 1917 for day and night bombing missions against German Zeppelin and seaplane bases in Belgium.

However, the construction of large multi-engined aircraft was in fact already being considered at Farnborough. In April 1916, O'Gorman presented a paper entitled 'The Design of Large Aircraft' to the Advisory Committee for Aeronautics. The report considered the capabilities of an aeroplane in relation to its size and was based upon preliminary research by Frederick Lanchester. It is testament to the professionalism of the staff at the Factory that one of the principal concerns in new design remained the safety of the aircrew and it was noted that 'the greatest stress which it is possible to put on the machine in flight, will depend almost entirely upon the amount of control which the pilot has on the machine.'[53]

Nevertheless, in the summer of 1915, a Cabinet Committee was formulated to ascertain and examine the resource required for the prosecution of the war until the end of 1916. Writing on 7 September 1915, Committee Secretary Arthur Henderson reported that the present and prospective output of aircraft was satisfactory, and that the Admiralty were hoping to shortly have in possession 2,150 aeroplanes and seaplanes, in addition to about sixty airships and some forty kite-balloons. In parallel the Army were aiming for an estimated strength of 1,418 aeroplanes. Henderson concluded that 'the number of men employed in the actual service, or in the manufacture of aircraft, is not such as to affect seriously either the problem of recruiting or that of munition making, although the proportion of skilled to unskilled workers is probably higher in the aircraft industry than in any other'.[54]

However, the constant distractions of defending themselves against continued allegations of mismanagement and underhand practices had resulted in one significant failure on behalf of the Royal Aircraft Factory administration that threatened the entire output of British aeroplanes and the health of the skilled workforce required for their manufacture. This failure, to conduct the key responsibility for research into 'fabrics, dopes, and varnishes', resulted in an international scandal that extended far beyond the activities at Farnborough.

3

'Mysterious deaths of the liver'

Hazardous materiels and the supply-chain (1912–15)

The manufacture of stable and efficient military aeroplanes was an important preoccupation of the British both immediately before and throughout the duration of the First World War. However, effective designs required not only reliable engines and aerodynamic airframes but also robust fabric coverings that could withstand the demands of aerobatic manoeuvres, aerial combat and the exposed storage conditions experienced on operational aerodromes. The escalating demand for combat aeroplanes conversely increased the demand for individual component parts and materiels which needed to remain in plentiful supply if production demands were to be satisfied. One of the more seemingly innocuous items required in the manufacture of aeroplanes was an adequate supply of cellulose acetate, a critical ingredient in the production of aircraft dope and without which British aeroplane outputs would undoubtedly have been severely compromised.

In November 1912, a Committee of Inquiry was held at the Home Office to determine the precautions necessary in the use of the chemical celluloid, both during its manufacture and in subsequent commercial applications. Celluloid was discovered in the late nineteenth century and heralded the dawn of manmade plastics and was utilized in a variety of applications. However, this new wonder materiel was found to be highly flammable, and the government became increasingly concerned regarding its unregulated storage in the workshops and factories throughout the British Isles.

Consequently, the Earl of Plymouth was appointed Committee chairman and a comprehensive list of witnesses were drawn from a variety of industries in which celluloid was commonly utilized including motion photography, printing and kinematography, to better understand the risks associated with this potentially volatile chemical. During the enquiry Mr Foster Sproxton, chief chemist at the British Xylonite Company, was called as a witness to assist the Committee in determining whether a less combustible alternative might be used in associated manufactures. Sproxton suggested that the most suitable substitute for celluloid would be cellulose acetate, but warned that not only was this substance more expensive, it also had the 'minor disadvantage' of possessing 'a greater stupefying power than chloroform'. This was due to the use of a particular solvent used during its manufacture called tetrachlorethane, which was indeed highly dangerous to human health.[1]

Interestingly, one application for tetrachlorethane was reported in *The British Medical Journal* in June 1916 in the destruction of lice from the bodies of soldiers and their clothing, which rather illustrated just how misunderstood its hazardous characteristics were. It was recommended that the chemical was applied via cotton wool to the human scalp as a most effective means of removing vermin from the hair. Following experiments on patients in hospital, it was concluded that tetrachlorethane 'was very actively insecticidal' and was actually preferred to alternative treatments 'on account of its less irritant properties'.[2] Astonishingly, despite its poisonous qualities being well-known before the outbreak of hostilities, tetrachlorethane remained an active ingredient in British government-approved aircraft dope formula during the early stages of the war with devastating consequences to worker health and production output.

The manufacture of cellulose acetate had originated in Germany, and at the outbreak of the conflict, the only sources of supply available to the British were from either Swiss manufacturers or the Messrs. Usines du Rhône in France. The lack of such an ingredient crucial to the aeroplane production programme resulted in early shortages, and the supply-chain solution adopted by the British government would cause significant scandal later in the war. Originally, dope manufacturers purchased their materiels independently of government procurement contracts, and as such there was no check on the economical use of them. However, by the summer of 1915 the War Department took responsibility for most materiel purchases and managed distribution to both the Royal Aircraft Factory and their growing list of sub-contractors.[3]

The majority of processes involved in the manufacture of aircraft during the First World War consisted of precision carpentry, upholstery and metal work which were no more dangerous to the workforce than any other aspect of wartime production. Nevertheless, there was one procedure in which poisonous substances were initially encountered, and this was during the doping of an aircraft's fabric skin. The process involved the application of dope to the linen fabric that covered the aircraft fuselage and wings. This was often applied via brush and as such the worker was in very close proximity to the chemicals.[4] The dope tightened the fabric, making it impervious to air, close fitting to the aircraft fuselage and waterproof. Consequently, the qualities of a dope suitable for use in aviation were flexibility and durability, whilst ensuring that the fabric became sufficiently taught around the aircraft structure. The official history clarified the origins of the term 'dope' thus:

> Ever since flying became general some means of tightening the fabric has been used: hence the evolution of aeroplane 'dope', a term of American origin, first used because it gave the fabric qualities it did not naturally possess and only subsequently associated with the injurious effects which it was afterwards found to have on the workers.[5]

This process was particularly important during the application of the dope to the aeroplane wings whereby the maximum strength was required for the least weight, and it was found that Irish linen provided the best quality of finish when subjected to the treatment of tautening liquids or dopes.[6] This also enabled the materiel covering the aeroplane wings to endure harsh weathering conditions reducing the risk of stretching and fatal tearing during flight.[7]

The chemical base for aircraft dope was invariably a non-poisonous cellulose compound of either acetate or its associated nitrate. However, the compounds in which the dope was dissolved were particularly injurious to health and poisonous to the central nervous system, liver, kidneys, heart muscles and constituents of the blood. Dr Alice Hamilton succinctly stated the chronology of the effects of aircraft dope on the human body following the results of extensive analysis which was finally published in February 1918:

> It was during the year before the war that physicians first heard of industrial poisoning in connection with airplane doping through reports in German

medical journals. A new and startling form of poisoning had appeared in certain of the Johannisthal airplane works and some of the cases were fatal. Soon after the appearance of these reports, similar cases were published in British medical journals. Dope poisoning continued to be reported from both countries up to the early months of 1915, when information from German sources ceased. The British reports, however, appeared from time to time up to January, 1917, at which time the use of that particular form of dope was largely discontinued in England.[8]

It was true indeed that by the outbreak of war numerous poisonings affecting workers employed in the aircraft industries of several European countries had been reported, but such occurrences continued in Britain long after the use of tetrachlorethane had been banned on the continent.

Upon identification of the condition, medical research was undertaken into the adverse health effects of worker exposure to tetrachlorethane. One of the earliest studies was conducted by Arthur Heffter, a German chemist and pharmacologist, who identified that the inhalation of tetrachlorethane was responsible for increasing amounts of poisoning cases amongst workers in the German aircraft industry. Heffter was a member of a German government commission set up to investigate the illnesses of workers who regularly worked with dope containing high levels of tetrachlorethane. Of the twelve workers he initially examined, two subsequently died and the initial classification of patients afflicted by tetrachlorethane fell into two groups dependent upon physical manifestation and symptoms. The first group predominantly displayed signs of gastrointestinal disturbances, such as enlarged livers and jaundice, whilst the second group suffered from neurological conditions, which included headaches, hand tremors, periodical deafness, parasthesias (acute pins and needles), anorexia and nausea.

Experimentation on animals soon confirmed that the chemical produced similar gastrointestinal and hepatic effects in dogs, although the neurological symptoms were not as easy to determine. Heffter's research resulted in the German commission recommending that all aircraft dopes containing tetrachlorethane be immediately banned. However, before the cessation of hostilities numerous poisoning cases due to tetrachlorethane were confirmed in the aircraft industries of Germany, France, Holland and England although they had decreased substantially.[9]

In England alone there were seventy reported cases and twelve fatalities. Consequently, reports of such poisonings soon appeared in the British press as fatalities began to become more frequent. One of the earliest was entitled 'Mysterious Disease of the Liver' and was printed in *The Times* on 21 December 1914. The report detailed the findings of the inquest into the death of Mr Gilbert Moddy, a 36-year-old French polisher from Queen's Park, Paddington, who had been employed at the government-controlled National Aircraft Factory at Hendon. Moddy had been engaged in the application of aircraft dope to the wings of aeroplanes and had frequently complained of the smell and resulting nausea he experienced from working in close proximity to the quick drying varnish.

Dr Bernard Spilsbury, a pathologist at St. Mary's Hospital, believed that the death was due to an acute and 'mysterious disease of the liver'. Dr William Henry Wilcox, a Home Office expert, also testified that he had carried out experiments on white rats in his laboratory exposing them to quantities of the dope which Moddy had applied during his work at Hendon in an attempt to find the cause of the illness. Wilcox explained that exposure to the dope fumes had not only made the rats drowsy but ultimately resulted in their death and they all demonstrated signs of extensive liver disease during subsequent dissection. The inquest concluded that necessary precautions for the protection of the workforce should be immediately taken at Hendon to prevent future occurrences and the jury accordingly 'returned a verdict in accordance with the medical evidence'.[10] Despite the 'mysterious' nature of the disease which killed Mr Moddy the poisoning was soon attributed to a single ingredient, namely tetrachlorethane, and efforts were undertaken to find a suitable non-toxic alternative.

The primary research into the occurrence of poisoning amongst aeroplane workers was conducted by Dr Willcox, who was not only a physician at St. Mary's Hospital but also a senior scientific analyst to the Home Office. Willcox had first been acquainted with Gilbert Moddy at the out-patient department of St. Mary's on 5 November 1914 and reported that the patient believed that his illness must be associated with his work because ten or so other employees at the Hendon Aeroplane Factory had been similarly affected.[11] Moddy was subsequently admitted to Middlesex Hospital on 14 November 1914, where he died later the same month. Following referral to H. M. Coroner

Clifford Luxmore Drew, a post-mortem examination was ordered, which was conducted by Dr Spilsbury. Following the confirmation of the liver disease, Willcox noted the following in his report:

> A number of animal experiments were conducted by me relating to the possible toxic action of the constituents of the dopes used in the aeroplane factory, and it was clearly demonstrated that one of the constituents – viz., tetrachlorethane – was a powerful liver and kidney poison, causing fatty degeneration of the cells of these organs.[12]

The case also attracted the attention of Dr Thomas Morrison Legge, the Home Office Medical Inspector of Factories, who began an investigation into the health of other workers at the Hendon Aeroplane Works and possible mitigation of the dangerous effects of inhalation of heavy solvents fumes.

Willcox examined a further eleven workers who were also displaying signs of toxic jaundice, many of whom were not directly involved in the application of aircraft dope but were simply working in the same factory in areas adjacent to where the varnish was being applied. Symptoms of nausea, vomiting and jaundice were common complaints but fortunately each of these patients made a good recovery once removed from exposure to the dope fumes. Willcox visited Hendon on 4 December 1914 and reported that the smell of tetrachlorethane was very much in evidence and that the ventilation arrangements were inadequate for the extraction of the heavy dope vapour. During the visit he enquired into the health of some of the workers and reported that several individuals complained of 'nausea, biliousness, drowsiness, constipation, loss of appetite, nasty taste at the back of the throat, headache, and general malaise' and concluded that this was due to the noxious vapours, and the severity of condition was dependent upon proximity to the dope itself.[13]

Cases were soon being reported in other factories where tetrachlorethane-based dopes were present. In early 1915, two fatalities were reported amongst young female employees at the Crayford Aeroplane Works, which was operated by Vickers Limited. The first, a female aged nineteen, began work at Crayford in August 1914 and reported discomfort in the throat on 15 November due to inhalation of dope fumes. By 27 December the patient had become acutely ill, suffering from vomiting and abdominal pain, before falling into a coma and dying on 4 January 1915. The post-mortem examination revealed extensive necrosis of the liver and fatty degeneration of the kidneys. The second fatality from the Vickers' factory was a seventeen-year-old female who had commenced employment in October 1914 but had to give up work on 28 January 1915 due to illness, which included discomfort in the throat, general weakness and jaundice. Medical examination on the 25 February 1915 confirmed intense jaundice, stupor and delirium before the patient passed into coma and died three days later.

By this time interest had been sufficiently sparked for the recent phenomenon of dope poisoning to be raised in the House of Commons. On 11 February 1915, Mr James Rowlands, an advocate of worker's rights and the Liberal MP for Dartmouth, asked the Secretary of State for the Home Department if he had received the report of the inquest held at Crayford and whether any similar cases had been reported. In addition, Rowlands was determined to ascertain what measures the government had taken to ensure the future safety of workers employed in the application of aeroplane dope.[14] The question was answered by Mr Cecil Harmsworth, the Under Secretary of State for the Home Department, who confirmed that several cases of poisoning had occurred at one or two aircraft factories and at the Home Secretary's request a full investigation had been conducted by Dr Willcox, Senior Analyst to the Home Office, and Dr Legge, His Majesty's Medical Inspector of Factories. Upon discovering that effects of the poisoning could be substantially reduced by the provision of effective ventilation, the Admiralty and War Office immediately informed their contractors to carry out such measures as were necessary to improve air circulation in their manufacturing facilities.

The British experience of productivity of war materiel and safeguarding the health of the workforce was later studied in detail in the United States. The British Munitions of War Act of 1915, which resulted in the general control of the munitions industry practices, became of considerable interest to the Americans – in particular, the British decision to appoint an independent Health of Munitions Workers Committee. A 1917 report by the United States Public Health Service chief surgeon stressed, amongst other recommendations, the necessity for an abundant supply of fresh air for factory workers in order

Figure 6 Workers at the Short Brothers Seaplane Works at Rochester, Kent. Courtesy of A.R. Coster/Stringer/Getty Images.

to maintain high production levels and 'physiological stimuli'. Unsurprisingly, guarding against the effects of tetrachlorethane was specifically mentioned:

> Ventilation provisions are particularly important in industries making war materiels because the workers are often exposed to highly poisonous dusts and volatile compounds, of which good examples are trinitrotoluol, in the explosive industry, and tetrachlorethane, which has been extensively used as a solvent in aeroplane varnish.[15]

Even though the health of the workforce appeared secondary to ensuring the maximum output of war materiel, it was obvious that authorities in the United States were determined to learn from the British experience and this undoubtedly benefited American workers.

Nevertheless, back in the House of Commons Rowlands further enquired whether the authorities were now satisfied that the precautions introduced would 'secure the safety of the lives of those engaged' in the occupation of varnishing, to which Harmsworth replied in the affirmative.[16] However, not long after this initial parliamentary exchange a further fatality from tetrachlorethane poisoning was reported of a female worker employed at the Short Brothers Seaplane Works in Rochester. Willcox reaffirmed his recommendation that the prevention of further poisoning by tetrachlorethane vapour was much more important than the treatment of patients suffering from the effects of intoxication and reported:

> Effective measures have been instituted in all factories where tetrachlorethane is used whereby the heavy vapour is removed by powerful extraction fans, which removed the vapour at a low level and rapidly withdraw it from the workers.[17]

The treatment of patients suffering from toxic jaundice due to the inhalation of dope vapour primarily consisted of removing them from all influence of the poison. They were not to return to their place of work until fully recovered and their employers had installed sufficient extraction in accordance with Home Office instructions. However, despite the progress in diagnosis and potential reduction in harmful effects, there was no immediate ban on the use of tetrachlorethane and it was still considered a valuable constituent in the formulation of aircraft dope.

Nevertheless, following Willcox's report this new medical condition was deemed significant enough in Britain to warrant inclusion in the Workmen's Compensation Act, a statute of parliament passed in 1906 that gave working people the right of compensation for personal injury. The following notice was published in the *London Gazette* on 16 July 1915:

> The Secretary of State for the Home Department hereby gives notice that on 7 July, 1915, he made an Order under the Section 8 of the Workmen's Compensation Act, 1906, extending the provisions of the Act to dope poisoning: that is, poisoning by tetrachlorethane, or any other substance used as or in conjunction with a solvent for acetate of cellulose, or its sequelae.[18]

Subsequently in September 1915, whilst serving as Minister of Munitions in the coalition government, Lloyd George appointed the Health of Munitions Workers Committee to examine all aspects of the physical wellbeing of individuals employed in the manufacture of munitions.[19] Listed alongside the manufacture of TNT in the Special Industrial Diseases section was the application of aircraft dope.[20] Tetrachloroethane remained on the list of prescribed diseases at the publication of the National Insurance (Industrial Injuries) Act of 1948.[21]

Despite the obvious recognition by the government of the dangers posed to those working with the substance, questions were still being raised in the House of Commons the following year as to why a non-poisonous alternative had yet to be identified, forcing the Under-Secretary of State for the Home Department, William Brace, to confirm in the House of Commons on 16 September 1915 that a further nineteen non-fatal, and four fatal cases, had been recorded in that year alone.[22] Once again, Rowlands was at the forefront of the parliamentary interest and asked in December 1915 whether Mr Brace's attention had been called to the death of an aeroplane worker at Teddington named Charles Selwood, who had been employed in the waterproofing of aircraft wings.[23]

Brace confirmed not only that he had received reports of the case but also that the cause of Selwood's death was indeed due to the inhalation of tetrachlorethane fumes. The fatality had occurred despite the factory receiving government inspections which had confirmed that although the system of ventilation had been satisfactorily planned, the firm had been unable to obtain fans of adequate strength to ensure that the air was being changed with sufficient frequency. Brace reassured the house that improvements were being made to increase the volume of air passing through the doping room at Teddington and that a new and improved building was being constructed to which the work would be transferred.[24] By late 1915, it would appear the problem was not in the formulation of adequate government safety guidelines, but that there was a shortage of available fans of sufficient strength for incorporation into existing premises to remove the dangerous vapours.

By complete accident, the risk of poisoning from aeroplane dope was almost completely negated by the shortage of materiels required for the purpose of aeroplane manufacture. This was not only the availability of the dope itself but also the fabric needed for the covering of fuselages and wings. By early 1916, the supply of high-grade Belgian Courtrai flax, which was essential in the manufacture of aeroplane fabrics, was entirely cut off following German occupation of the area. This eventually resulted in the War Office requisitioning all the remaining stock of this materiel on 5 January 1917 and issuing a notice reminding anyone in possession of Courtrai flax that should they sell, remove 'or secrete such flax without the consent of the Army Council', they would ultimately be 'guilty of an offence against the said regulations'.[25] Consequently, flax manufacture in the UK once again became a strategic industry, as it had been throughout the nineteenth century, but this time for utilization of both British and Allied aircraft manufactories.

However, it was not just British flax that came under government control. Under the Defence of the Realm Act the purchase and sale of Russian flax was also prohibited on 28 January 1916 as the government became aware of the need to conserve the present and future supply of the materiel for aeroplane construction. The proclamation stated:

> No person shall, from the date of this order, until further notice, buy, sell or deal in dressed or undressed Russian flax or tow at present in stock in the United Kingdom, or hereafter buy, sell or deal in stocks of dressed or undressed Russian flax or tow after they have been imported into this country, accept under licence from the War Department.[26]

The control of a wide variety of materiel stocks increased dramatically as the war progressed and readers were advised that applications for licences could be obtained from the Director of Army Contracts, Raw Materiels Section. Nevertheless, despite the authoritative tone of the original notice, it was obviously deemed necessary to remind those involved in the industry of the conditions of the government emergency powers as it was repeated verbatim under the consolidation regulations on 21 March the same year and reprinted numerous times throughout the following year.[27] By late 1916, the Army Council requested that all those engaged in the cotton, flax and hemp industries registered with the Director of Army Contracts so that such businesses could then be employed directly on the government's behalf.[28]

On 31 March 1917, a joint order by the Admiralty and Army Council was issued with the intention of further exercising direct control over the manufactories producing products of flax, hemp and jute. The order decreed that all factories, workshops and other premises in which the business consisted wholly or partly in the manufacture of flax, hemp or jute work had to adhere to the following directions:

> (a) Priority over all other work shall be given to any work which is either directly or indirectly required for the purpose of any Government Order or Contract;

> (b) Any directions that may be given for the purpose of this Order by the Director of Navy contracts as to work for Naval purposes or by the Director of Army Contracts as to any other work whatsoever, shall be strictly complied with by the owners or occupiers of the said factories or workshops, their officers or servants.[29]

Naturally, the notice included the ubiquitous and obligatory threat of prosecution for those who did not comply and named F.C.T. Tudor and E.G. Pretyman as the two commissioners responsible for the execution of the Orders of the Army Council. Government restriction of the flax industry was rapidly increasing directly in line with the military demand for more combat aeroplanes.

Prior to the outbreak of the war flax had been extensively grown in Ireland and Irish looms were capable of producing linen of adequate quality for aviation use. Conversely, the Scotch mills produced yarns and cloth of inferior quality and the machinery required adaption. This inevitably resulted in the Ministry of Munitions requisitioning the entire Irish flax crop of 1917, in accordance with the Flax Seed (Ireland) Order issued on 12 July of that year.[30] The Ministry of Munitions also assumed direct control of the allocation of raw materiel to spinners for conversion to aviation grade yarn. The official history recorded:

> The administration and control were placed in the hands of the Controller of Aeronautical Supplies, and after consultation with leading members of all the trades concerned, it was decided to form a committee, The Flax Supplies Committee, representative of all the interests involved to act under an Administrator as a purchasing and advisory committee on behalf of the department.[31]

The arrangement resulted in the appointment of professional inspectors and graders, and by September 1917 flax markets opened throughout Northern

Ireland for the purchase of raw materiel. This proved an efficient method of supply, and in the first financial year ending 31 August 1918, it was recorded that 15,017 tonnes of flax were purchased, allocated and sent via rail to spinning mills in both Ireland and Scotland.[32]

Due to the volume of materiel required, a Purchasing Committee was empowered to issue cheques in payment and the product was then passed to the Allocation Committee, which consisted of four spinners, together with a government and deputy administrator. The Allocation Committee were responsible for censoring the stock of materiel apportioned to the spinning mills and also decided to whom the stock would be sold. This required extensive negotiations between the government and flax-spinners in order to encourage them to produce more of the crop and provide greater quantities of materiel of suitable grade for the covering of aeroplane wings.

Incentives were introduced to encourage the growing of flax throughout Northern Ireland, and the Ulster growers were requested to give the benefit of their experience to any farmer wishing to participate in the scheme. Scarcity of seed was negated through importing Canadian flax varieties and the whole process remained heavily regulated from planting to spinning.[33] By 1918, the supply of flax had become so acute that the Dominion Experimental Farms organization issued a special circular in Canada requesting the urgent growth of the crop. The supply of flax for the manufacture of aircraft linen had been severely curtailed and was in increasingly short supply, and consequently Canadian farmers were 'expected to do their utmost to make up the deficiency'.[34] In the UK, the government had already commandeered all flax products entering the British Isles and requisitioned the industry in Ireland.

A good example of the extent of purchasing regulation was the Ministry of Munitions notice of 8 February 1918 which even went as far as to restrict the general purchase of blast furnace dust, a common agricultural fertilizer. The order was issued by the Controller of Potash Production and stated:

> As from the date hereof until May 31, 1918, he hereby licenses the purchase by any person of any blast-furnace dusts to which the Order of the Minister of Munitions, dated the 7 August, 1917, relates, containing potash to an amount exceeding 13 per cent, expressed as potassium oxide ($K2O$), provided that the blast-furnace dusts so purchased are used wholly by the purchaser for direct and immediate application as a fertilizer to the flax

crop in Ireland and to no other crop, and provided that they are purchased from or through an Agent prescribed for that person by the Department of Agriculture and Technical Instruction for Ireland and licensed so to sell by the Controller of Potash Production.[35]

Even the purchase of quality blast-furnace dust was no longer a straightforward transaction as the production of flax assumed authority over the success of any other crop, even those produced for human consumption. By the end of 1917, the operation and administration were such that a more comprehensive organization was formed. The Flax Control Board (Irish Sub-Committee) of the War Office took complete control of the flax-manufacturing industry in January 1918, and from that point onwards spinners were forbidden to manufacture any yarn except those placed under government order. This arrangement continued until the signing of the armistice, but even then, the 1919 flax crop was also appropriated by the Ministry of Munitions. The supply and manufacture of linen and aeroplane dope were indeed intrinsically linked.

Scarcity of resource was such that economy became the order of the day and the dope manufacturers, Messrs. Cellon, Ltd., produced a poster for exhibition in dope shops emphasizing the need for care in handling and application. They recommended that the following seven rules should be enforced at all times in the workshop: drums should always be kept tightly screwed up; materiels were not left in small containers to avoid wasteful evaporation; containers were not to be filled to their maximum limits; brushes should not be full when there was only a small portion of fabric to cover as any drippings onto the workshop floor were considered as a serious source of waste; workers were to be reminded that dope was a thick liquid and that care must be taken to completely empty drums before returning them to the manufacturer; drums should always be turned upside down and allowed to fully drain; brushes were to be kept clean at all times to avoid contaminations; and, finally, workers were expected to check carefully the weight of deposit on fabric so as to ensure the increase in materiel usage called for in the government doping schemes.[36] Such practical steps were indeed logical, but nobody could have foreseen that securing provision of a plentiful supply of aeroplane dope would eventually lead to one of the greatest scandals of the First World War.

4

'Dope poisoning in aircraft factories'

Protecting the health of Munitions workers (1915–17)

In February 1915, a Committee on Production was appointed by the First Lord of the Treasury. This new administration was initially tasked with investigating industrial disputes arising in the shipbuilding and engineering industries then engaged in government war work. Although it was originally recommended that no stoppage of work should take place by either strike or lock-out because of disputes between employers and workpeople, it was soon deemed provident to extend the reference of the Committee and they were further empowered to act as an impartial tribunal in cases whereby parties could not settle disputes 'in-house'.

Amongst the many hundreds of cases referred to the Committee was one concerning the Holborn-based shop-fitters Messrs. F. Sage and Company, who were temporarily engaged in the manufacture of numerous aircraft parts on behalf of the War Office. A claim was made by the United French Polisher's London Society, who argued that employees engaged in the doping of aircraft parts should be paid 10d. per hour, the same rate that skilled painters received from the firm. The parties were unable to resolve the dispute and it was presented to the Committee on 20 January 1916.

Representatives of the firm explained that at the commencement of the government contract for aircraft parts, which required the application of dope to aeroplane linen, the firm originally utilized the services of the painters already in their employ. It was recorded that this measure was largely because they were unable to arrange for the recruitment of sufficient numbers of women at short notice. After some consideration it was decided that the doping work would be better suited to their French polishers, which was already the practice at their Peterborough works, and the change was made accordingly. Upon consideration of the evidence and utilizing their first-hand experience of practices adopted in other manufactories engaged in the same work, the Committee found in favour of Messrs. Sage and Company and the case was dismissed on 24 January 1916. Despite the dangerous nature of the task, the principle of fair payment would appear to have taken precedent.[1]

By March 1916, the Health of Munition Workers Committee had successfully completed four new memoranda for the Minister of Munitions, which included 'Special Industrial Diseases' and the prevention of industrial 'Sickness and Injury'. In regard to special industrial diseases, the committee specifically mentioned the risk to workers engaged in applying dopes containing tetrachlorethane. They concluded that although an 'effective varnish has been found which does not contain the poisonous chemical', the supply of its ingredients was 'at present insufficient to meet the demands' and thus the more poisonous tetrachlorethane-based dopes would be required for some time to come.[2]

By May 1916, debates were once again taking place in the House of Commons regarding fatalities caused by the inhalation of aeroplane dope. The Deptford MP, Mr Charles Bowerman, enquired of the Under-Secretary of State for the Home Office on 11 May 1916 whether he was aware that private manufacturers of aeroplane dope were advertising products which claimed to be non-poisonous, entirely tetrachlorethane-free and available in sufficient quantities to meet military requirements. Furthermore, if the Home Office was aware of such products, why had they not recommended firms involved in the manufacture of aeroplanes to embrace these safer alternatives?[3]

British manufacturers had actually been steadily increasing their production capacity since before the outbreak of war. The Cellon Company, for example, had expanded the Stirling Chemical Works at Stratford in July 1913 and installed modern machinery under the supervision 'of the skilled chemists of Messrs. Thomas Tyrer Limited' to cater for increased demand from the domestic aero-industry.[4] Nevertheless, Mr Brace assured his honourable friend that the Home Office had been in constant communication with all the relevant departments concerned and that the arrangements had already been made for securing an adequate supply of a satisfactory dope product free from tetrachlorethane that could be manufactured in sufficient quantities so as to meet all industry requirements. However, Brace reminded the House that the use of any privately manufactured non-poisonous dope was dependent on its suitability for aviation purposes, which remained a matter for the War Office and Admiralty to decide.[5]

Ultimately, substitute ingredients had to meet not only more stringent safety requirements but also the performance specifications required during combat conditions. Unfortunately, from the perspective of the War Office and aircraft manufacturers alike, tetrachlorethane possessed the best properties of tightening the fabric over aeroplane wings and ensuring the quality of finish required for operational duties. Whilst a substitute was still being sought the Factory Department issued further instructions, in addition to ventilation requirements, for safeguarding the health of the workforce, which included regular alternation of employment for those involved in applying dope and a fortnightly medical examination to identify any symptoms of poisoning as early as possible.[6]

Mr Bowerman was clearly aware of the non-poisonous dope products that were regularly advertized in the British aviation press. Amongst the most prominent were those manufactured by the British Aeroplane Varnish Company, a subsidiary of Holzapfel Limited of Newcastle, which had developed a product called 'Titanine'. The Company had actually openly marketed their product as a non-poisonous aeroplane dope substitute that eliminated all ill-effects on employees since 1915.[7] *Flight Magazine* reported on the 2 April 1915 that due to the strenuous operational conditions in which aircraft were being subjected, the question of quality dope assumed 'even greater importance than is the case in times of peace'.[8]

The manufacturer claimed that the product composition contained neither tetrachlorethane nor any spirit derivative of chlorine or amyl acetate, which were the heavy metals that had previously been employed. The *Flight Magazine* product review recommended that, in light of the fact that 'Titanine' contained no ingredients harmful to workers, this should be in itself sufficient justification for the urgent commencement of official government trials. In addition, the author also quite correctly pointed out that no modification to existing factory ventilation systems was required, and thus the product, if deemed suitably compliant from a performance perspective, could be put into immediate use without the need for acquiring the powerful extractions fans that remained so difficult to obtain.

The article also boasted that in addition to its non-poisonous qualities, 'Titanine' conformed to strict regulations determined by the Royal Aircraft Factory specification and that from examinations of various samples of this dope it was witnessed to possess remarkable degree of flexibility. In addition to these qualities, Titanine, it was claimed, had the ability to sink into the pores of the aeroplane fabric as well as the majority of other dopes and thus manufacturers could be rest assured that they could achieve the tightness required when this product was applied. The article concluded that it was 'almost superfluous to say that Titanine is petrol – and oil-resisting' and that the chemists at the British Aeroplane Varnish Company were convinced that their product could withstand the action of sea-water for very long periods.[9] On paper, this certainly looked like the best possible solution for both the government and the British aircraft industry.

Although the article conceded that detailed tests would have to be conducted to deduce the effect of the air on the dope following long exposures and actual service conditions, it would appear that there was no reason to doubt the manufacturers' confidence in their product and thus a non-poisonous alternative dope was actually available to the British in early 1915. Nevertheless, any approval for the use of a new market product would only follow extensive evaluation to ensure that it performed adequately under service conditions well beyond those of the laboratory. Whilst such tests were being conducted, however, aeroplane fabric and varnish workers remained at risk.

The British Aeroplane Varnish Company was not the only manufacturer dedicated to the development of a product that fulfilled the military requirements for a non-inflammable, petrol and oil-resisting composition for the fabric covering of aircraft wings and fuselages that was also non-injurious to those employed in its application. *Flight Magazine* reported on the 16 April 1915 that the London-based manufacturers of an aeroplane dope sold commercially as 'Novadope' by Messrs. Siebe Gorman and Company were putting a new product on the market known commercially as 'Novellon'. Amongst the advantages claimed for this new dope of British manufacture was that it did not contain any ingredient injurious to health and that it had been manufactured entirely free from tetrachlorethane. In addition, no finishing varnishes were required with this preparation, thus saving both time and money during the manufacturing phase. Alternative options of domestic manufacture, it appears, were indeed becoming readily available.[10]

Notwithstanding that the Under-Secretary of State for the Home Office was quite right to point out to Mr Bowerman on 11 May 1916 that any such new products would require approval from the relevant authorities for use in aircraft manufacture, official government trials of dopes free from tetrachlorethane do not appear to have been sanctioned at either the Royal Aircraft Factory or the National Physical Laboratory. The investigations and experimentation required to ensure the performance of a new product under service conditions would take a considerable amount of time and thus may have proved detrimental to production, but there may well have been another reason for the lack of official appetite to evaluate the manufacturers' claims as to the suitability of their alternative commercially produced dopes.

The situation was once again raised in the House of Commons in June 1916 during an enlightening exchange that insinuated the prolongation of tetrachlorethane-based aircraft dope was due to both Royal Aircraft Factory manufacture of a substance known as D.94 and their insistence that this product was used by all government aviation sub-contractors. It had been reported in *Flight Magazine* following corroboration with members of the trade that this was certainly the case and they demanded to know why such regulation remained:

> Further, it is sought, we understand, even to oblige manufacturers of aeroplanes who are supplying the services with very valuable machines of their own design, to use this particular dope. Nothing could be more reprehensible than this, as, to our positive knowledge, not only is non-poisonous dope being already used in certain directions, but there are several dopes which can be supplied in any quantities required.[11]

Similar answers were sought in Parliament during an exchange between Captain Francis Bennett-Goldney, MP Canterbury, and the Under-Secretary of State for War, Mr Tennant, on 21 June 1916, which centred upon the Factory's manufacture of dope to official specification.

Bennet-Goldney enquired of the Under-Secretary whether either the War Office or the Royal Aircraft Factory had authorized the manufacture of considerable quantities of the D.94 dope compound and subsequently insisted on the sale of such dope to private aeroplane manufacturers. He specifically wanted to know:

> Whether the War Office or Royal Aircraft Factory issued instructions to manufacturers of aeroplanes practically compelling them to use dopes of Royal Aircraft Factory manufacture; whether any manufacturers of aeroplanes protested against the use of such dopes as causing illness and, in some cases death of the women using them; whether such dope proved less efficient than the non-poisonous dope obtainable in the open market; and whether the War Office or the Royal Aircraft Factory are still endeavouring to sell dopes to aeroplane manufacturers?[12]

Such an insightful set of questions required a detailed response, and Mr Tennant recounted to the House that at the end of 1915, competitive tenders had been invited from all trade manufacturers for the supply of 18,000 gallons of dope to Royal Aircraft Factory Formula D.94, and as a result an order was placed for 18,000 gallons. The formula D.94 dope was intended for sale to contractors for the manufacture of aeroplanes as it contained a significantly smaller percentage of poisonous tetrachlorethane than the other principal trade dopes then freely available.

Experience and experimentation at the National Physical Laboratory had also demonstrated that the dope and varnish combinations previously available had not proved satisfactory under service conditions and that a standardized product was required to ensure consistency of finish. Consequently, in October 1915 it was decided to specify the compulsory use in all new Army aeroplane contracts of dope D.94 and varnish V.114, which had been manufactured to both Royal Aircraft Factory specification and under the supervision of the scientists at Farnborough. This decision was believed to have not only reduced the dangers of associated poisoning in aeroplane manufacture but also afforded Royal Flying Corps pilots the best possible quality of aircraft and subsequent chances of survival.[13]

However, contractors were permitted to utilize the stocks of older dope on any existing orders before switching to the new Farnborough-certified product to avoid wastage and delay to the delivery of orders. Tennant conceded that there was no evidence to suggest that the Factory specification dope caused any more significant illness than other products available, but also that the Aeronautical Inspection Department and trade manufacturers were permitted to authorize the use of any dope which ultimately proved satisfactory. An interesting argument was made in the aviation press which surmised that although tetrachlorethane extended the life of the aeroplane fabric, it was effectively unnecessary considering that the life of a combat machine was proving to be so short that preservation of the fabric was academic. Aeronautical commentators questioned whether 'there was any necessity to use such a materiel because the poisonous dope is likely to far outlast the machine itself?'[14]

Ultimately, however, the Under-Secretary of State for War had publicly admitted that, despite the known dangers, tetrachlorethane remained a constituent of D.94, a product manufactured to official Royal Aircraft Factory specification, and that the manufacture of this product had been competitively tendered. Ultimately, although the Aeronautical Inspection Department had started to conduct analytical tests the accusations by Captain Bennett-Goldney had been, effectively, confirmed.[15]

Colonel Mervyn O'Gorman, consulting engineer to the Director-General of Military Aeronautics, and previously superintendent of the Royal Aircraft Factory, also confirmed the presence of tetrachlorethane in aviation dope supplied by the Factory. During the subsequent Air Inquiry O'Gorman was questioned by Justice Clement Bailhache regarding the use of poisonous dopes during his tenure at Farnborough and recounted that complaints had been received from the Home Office that the substance was causing trouble all over the place. He confirmed that the dope issued to manufacturers up until 14 July 1914 contained a substance of a poisonous nature called tetrachlorethane, which kept the consistency soft and prevented cracking when placed on the wings of the aeroplanes.

Nevertheless, O'Gorman also reported that efforts had been made to obtain a less poisonous alternative and that the risks to the workforce of the aircraft industry had been greatly diminished as a result through a combination of these investigations and the adoption of better working regulations in aeroplane factories.[16] Further corroboration by a senior officer in the field of British aviation demonstrates that the continued utilization of tetrachlorethane was officially sanctioned despite numerous claims by manufactories that an alternative product, which was free from poisonous chemicals whilst also satisfied government specification, was readily available.

The better regulations in terms of application referred to by O'Gorman were actually confirmed in the private papers of a factory worker. From January 1916, Miss West worked in the kitchens at the Royal Aircraft Factory and described the nature of the work of the women employed in the manufacture of aeroplanes:

> Then there are the dope girls who varnish the plane with a quick drying very poisonous varnish. It affects the liver. The girls are under medical supervision, have to drink quantities of lime juice and lemonade, may not eat anything in their work room, must wash between meals etc.[17]

The dangers of the work were obviously well known amongst the workforce and the implementation of basic hygiene regulation would have undoubtedly been crucial to workforce safety. In relation to progress into the complete eradication of the use of tetrachlorethane-based dopes, the aviation press continued to voice concerns and questioned why products of a non-poisonous nature had not been officially approved.

The situation was once again raised following the inquest into the death of an aircraft fabric worker at Peterborough in March 1916. Dr Alexander Walker, who made the post-mortem examination, stated in his evidence that he believed the death of James Steele was due to toxic poisoning caused by tetrachlorethane.[18] Walker believed that the death of Steele was due to the heavy tetrachlorethane fumes present in the Peterborough factory despite the firm acting in accordance with the government regulations, following every possible safeguard, and installing the specified ventilation systems. It was reported that although 'the most scientific methods had been adopted to nullify evil effects' of tetrachlorethane, some workers had, unknown to their employers, resumed the old habit of taking their meals in the room where the dope was applied, and it was suggested at the inquest that this was the real cause of the tragic death of James Steele.[19]

Although the inquest conceded that the government regulations, as witnessed by Miss West at Farnborough, had not been adhered to by the Peterborough employees, it failed to address the question as to why such poisonous substances were still causing fatalities when alternative non-toxic products were seemingly available. As part of their argument, *Flight Magazine* reminded its readership that the French had already issued an official decree which prohibited the addition of tetrachlorethane in aeroplane dopes in an attempt to prevent the 'possible sacrifice of human lives'.[20]

James Rowlands, MP for Dartford, actually attempted to raise the decision by the French government to prohibit the use of poisonous dope in the House of Commons on 7 March 1916.[21] However, the Under Secretary of State for Home Affairs was quick to remind Rowlands that such a specific question required prior formal notice and was unwilling to address the subject. Rowlands had initially enquired into the results of a conference between the War Office and the Admiralty into the possibility of obtaining non-poisonous dope only to be reassured that Admiralty experiments were already proceeding. Unsatisfied, Rowlands once again attempted to raise the question of the details of the French government decree only to be informed that enquiries remained incomplete.[22]

However, the *Flight Magazine* article of 30 March 1916 succeeded in securing a response from a representative of the aeroplane trade. D.C. Hutchinson, general manager of the London Branch of the British Aeroplane Varnish Company Limited, wrote an enlightened letter which went some way to satisfy Rowlands' query. Hutchinson wholeheartedly agreed that it was about time the British government followed the example set by their French allies and ban the use of tetrachlorethane-based dopes, particularly as it now appeared that the stringent safety regulations imposed by the Inspector of Factories were incapable of ensuring the prevention of further fatalities.[23] Hutchinson closed with a reminder that 'Titanine', the primary aircraft dope manufactured by his firm, was both non-poisonous and even more efficient than any other product on the market when used as directed. Although one must be wary of the commercial motives attended to such a response from the representative of a manufacturer, he was correct in referring to further fatalities caused by tetrachlorethane poisoning, the victim in question being Miss Ellen Jane Clark.[24]

Rowlands was once again compelled to address the House of Commons concerning the increasing fatalities associated with tetrachlorethane-based aircraft dopes. On 22 June 1916, he enquired of the home secretary whether the government was aware that an inquest had been held on 13 May into the death of Annie E. Baron, who had sadly passed away on 7 May, at Bridlington.

The examining doctor concluded that the illness was due to 'uroenic [sic] poison caused by working in an atmosphere of dope which contained a poison known as tetrachlorethane'.[25] Rowlands further questioned whether the Home Secretary was aware that on 17 May 1916 an inquest had been held at Southampton for Annie Metcalf, who had worked at the Belvedere aeroplane factory on dope varnishing. The post-mortem examination also concluded that 'the continued breathing of the fumes of the varnish which the deceased used at her work had circulated into the system and had set up jaundice which was the cause of death'.[26] What progress had been made, Rowlands insisted, in the eradication of poisonous dope from the factory floor?

The Home Secretary, Herbert Samuel, deferred to the Under Secretary of State for the Home Department, William Brace, who responded that the facts remained as previously stated and that he hoped the arrangement for securing an adequate supply of a government-approved non-poisonous dope would be completed shortly. Interestingly, Brace inferred that the Admiralty and War Office were developing a 'non-poisonous dope for all purposes' when questioned whether all non-poisonous dopes on the market were currently being utilized.[27] Indeed, it would appear from the previous statements in the aviation press that 'Titanine' had yet to be officially approved by the National Physical Laboratory and was not in regular use.

Nevertheless, by August 1916, the petitioning finally began to prove successful. When Rowlands once again queried what progress had been made with regard to the experiments to produce and supply non-poisonous dopes for use in the aviation industry, the Under Secretary of State for the Home Department was able to give the following encouraging response:

> I am pleased to be able to say that not only has there been a considerable decrease recently in the number of cases of jaundice due to dope, but that satisfactory dopes which are free from tetrachlorethane are now available in sufficient quantity, and that the War Office and Admiralty have directed their contractors to use only the approved dopes of this kind. It may be taken, therefore, that the danger from tetrachlorethane poisoning in this class of work has now been removed.[28]

Yet despite the assurance of William Brace, Rowlands diligently enquired of the financial secretary to the War Office the following day in relation to the procurement of aircraft. Specifically, Rowlands was interested to know if any special specification had been issued to aircraft manufacturers which allowed them to use non-poisonous dopes. Additionally, he requested similar answers from the secretary to the Admiralty. The response eventually came from Major Baird, as representative of the Air Board, who reassured Rowlands that:

> Considerable progress has been made in the production of satisfactory dopes of a non-poisonous kind and the Admiralty and the War Office have recently issued instructions to contractors specifying various non-poisonous dopes which meet their requirements. The effect of these instructions is that the use of dope containing tetrachlorethane is no longer permitted for the purposes of either the Naval or the Military Air Service unless the non-poisonous dopes cannot be obtained. Any cases of failure of supply of the non-poisonous dopes will be made subject of special inquiry. Of the eight doping schemes approved, seven are supplied by the trade.[29]

The statement did not rule out the use of tetrachlorethane should alternatives not be readily available, but it at least demonstrated that some progress had been made in relation to governance and industry standards, even if it had taken some eighteen months to become official policy. The trade press was delighted with the decision that any form of efficient trade dope could now be used by government contractors and were quick to offer congratulation upon a 'satisfactory solution of what promised to have unpleasant consequences'.[30] However, those 'consequences' were indeed more unpleasant for some than others.

By September 1916, the use of dopes containing tetrachlorethane was effectively ended but supply of chemical ingredients and associated equipment remained a concern. For example, in a 1918 report for the Ministry of Reconstruction, the Engineering Trades Committee noted the difficulty in obtaining porcelain grinding pans. These had been used for preparing ceramic glazes before the war but were repurposed during the conflict for the manufacture of aircraft colours and dopes. These machines were primarily of German manufacture, and the inability to obtain such equipment was only alleviated once American alternatives were sourced in 1916.[31]

In a letter printed in the *British Medical Journal* in October 1920, Sidney Welch importantly stressed that cellulose acetate as a solid substance comprising cellulose (cotton) and acetic acid was in itself, perfectly safe. Interestingly, Welch was writing from Spondon in Derby, which was where

Figure 7 Female Workers Outside an Aeroplane Factory in Birmingham, 1918. Courtesy of Fotosearch/Stringer/Getty Images.

the British Cellulose factory was located, a site that would later become the centre of what became known as 'the dope scandal'. In its natural state cellulose acetate was not poisonous, but for the purposes of industrial application it was necessary to dissolve the substance with a heavy solvent. Originally, this was where tetrachlorethane was used for the purpose of diluting cellulose acetate for application to aircraft wings and fabrics. When poisonous aircraft dope was finally banned by the Home Office in 1916, tetrachlorethane was substituted with benzyl alcohol, which, despite having mild anaesthetic qualities, was not considered injurious to health.[32]

Following this substitution, W.S. Smith, His Majesty's Inspector for Dangerous Trades, was then tasked with conducting a study regarding the effects of non-poisonous substitutes utilized by the industry thereafter. During the period in which tetrachlorethane-based dopes were in use seventy cases of toxic jaundice, including twelve fatalities and numerous cases of debilitating associated illnesses were reported to the Factory and Workshops Department. Following the first reported case of toxic jaundice the Department raised their recommendations for minimum ventilation in aircraft factory doping rooms from fifteen to twenty changes per hour to thirty changes per hour. Whilst the increased air changes resulted in a marked reduction in instances of acute poisonings, data collected following the introduction of the non-poisonous substitutes suggested that the standard of ventilation needed to be maintained even when using products free from tetrachlorethane.

Despite the substitution to non-poisonous alternatives, complaints were soon received that the effects from the fumes of these new formulas were more noticeable than those experienced from the older poisonous dope compounds. Consequently during 1917, two Home Office doctors carried out an investigation into the blood condition of workers in the immediate vicinity of the doping rooms. Following the examination of thirty-seven female workers it was concluded that their blood condition was below proper standard, although not to such an extent as to be considered dangerous to life. In addition to symptoms of headaches these women were found to have developed a mild anaemia which suggested that any relaxation in ventilation requirements would result in the development of more serious illnesses.

In 1917, only eleven cases of symptoms attributable to dope application were reported to the Department, despite a 300 per cent increase in the number of firms engaged in the process. The improvement in ventilation, coupled with the removal of tetrachlorethane-based solvents, undoubtedly improved the working conditions of thousands of individuals employed in the British aircraft industry. Smith concluded that following comprehensive surveys of new aircraft factories and approval and testing of ventilation systems:

> With very few exceptions these have been found satisfactory and in compliance with the requirements of the Department. Systematic inspection and testing of all new plant has been undertaken by my staff; and I am glad of the opportunity of putting on record the willing cooperation shown by occupiers, architects, and heating and ventilation engineers in accepting our advice and complying with our suggestions.[33]

On 5 November 1917, His Majesty's Principal Lady Inspector of Factories, Miss A.M. Anderson, addressed the Royal Institute of Public Health concerning the health of women workers employed in wartime industries.

Anderson praised the government's regulative control procedures in relation to the management of dangerous and injurious trades and the processes which had been progressively developed under successive Factory Acts. She believed that the pre-war experience of industrial disease, such as instances of 'plumbism' in the ceramic industries, meant that new kinds of industrial poisonings could be controlled relatively swiftly. She used the following examples to illustrate her point:

> Having this body of knowledge and experience it was a comparatively simple matter, when serious new kinds of industrial poisoning arose in connection with the rapid development of aircraft and explosive manufacture during the War, to apply the same methods of control. Cases of toxic jaundice, popularly known as 'Dope Poisoning', where the arose (a) in varnishing the wings of aeroplanes to make them impervious to moisture and air, by means of a varnish containing tetrachlorethane, and later, more numerous in (b) the manufacture and use of trinitrotoluene for high explosive, known as T.N.T., could thus be quickly studied and the causes regulated.[34]

Despite the improvements in working conditions and productivity, the subject of the adequate supply of aircraft dope would remain a controversial subject for the remainder of the war and the British Cellulose Company would find itself at the very heart of the ensuing scandal.

5

'The Air Committee fiasco'

Managing the conduct of the air war (1916–18)

The Committee of Imperial Defence was originally uninterested in military aviation and only begrudgingly authorized the establishment of a Sub-Committee on Aerial Navigation in 1908. By November 1911, this committee had recommended the creation of a single flying corps, but the Admiralty resisted, and eventually developed its own air capability called the Royal Naval Air Service on 1 July 1914.[1] This was in spite of the fact that an Air Committee had been established on 13 April 1912, just shortly after the inception of the Royal Flying Corps.

The Air Committee had been intended to act as mediator between the War Office and the Department of Admiralty in all matters relating to the development of military and naval aviation. Unfortunately, the new entity lacked any executive authority, despite being made up of representatives from the two war ministries and thus became increasingly and frustratingly ineffective. The major problem lay in the fact that any recommendations made by the Committee required ratification by both the Imperial General Staff and the Board of Admiralty, a consensus that became more and more difficult as the aeronautical prerequisites of the army and naval diverged. Ironically, the inter-service rivalry was such that the Committee was effectively redundant by the outbreak of war and failed to hold any further meetings during the very time it was most needed.

By 1916, the continued lack of cooperation between the Army and the Admiralty was causing not only serious component supply problems but also a complete lack of aerial strategy, particularly in relation to the air defence of the British Isles. To address the problem, the War Office then established the Joint

War Air Committee in an attempt to further coordinate the demands of the two services in terms of aircraft design and the supply of the components and materiel required for aeroplane manufacture. This new agency was chaired by Edward Stanley, Lord Derby, but once again lack of executive authority thwarted any attempt to effect positive change before the chairman himself resigned after only eight sittings and the oversight structure was once again revised. *The Times* concluded that 'inter-service jealousies proved too much for Lord Derby' and were anxious to see if the government could make any meaningful intervention. It was reported that when John Walter Edward Douglas-Scott Montagu, Lord Montagu of Beaulieu, and Lord Derby had realized that the Committee was 'doomed to sterility' by the nature of the stringent regulations controlling it, they both decided to resign in order to draw attention to the government's catastrophic mismanagement of the conduct of military aviation.[2] Both Lord Montagu and Lord Derby remained vocal opponents of the British air policy for the remainder of the conflict.

The next iteration of the executive administration of British aerial policy was created on 15 May 1916 and was entitled the Air Board under the chairmanship of George Curzon, Lord Curzon. Curzon also held a cabinet position, and it was hoped that his additional political status would give the Air Board the authority required to streamline the development of British military aviation into one amalgamated service.[3] Nevertheless, it was concluded in October 1916 that although the Army were willing to cooperate on future developments the Admiralty remained fundamentally opposed to any serious collaboration. Unsurprisingly, the Air Board consequently stagnated following the collapse of the Asquith government at the end of the year, and it was not until the creation of the Air Ministry on 2 January 1918 that any real progress was accomplished.[4]

Nevertheless, despite management frailties, numerous recommendations were enacted that had significant consequences for the future of the Royal Aircraft Factory and subsequent placing of government aviation contracts. The situation also attracted significant attention in Parliament which only served to further complicate an increasingly fragile relationship between the two senior services. One individual was so determined to champion the military requirements of the Naval Air Service to the government that he retired as a naval aviator expressly to gain election to Parliament and argue the cause on the political stage.⁵ In March 1916, Noel Pemberton-Billing won the Hertford by-election and entered the House of Commons as an independent politician. He was often referred to by his contemporaries as the 'First Air Member', and, with his personal experience of combat aviation and aeronautical engineers, Billing had manufactured aeroplanes to his own design.⁶ The newly elected politician became an outspoken opponent of the Royal Aircraft Factory and government aviation policy and announced thus to Parliament on 14 March 1916:

> I left the Royal Naval Air Service because I felt that, unless someone came to this House with a weight of authority which only a constituency can give him, the Air Service would continue to be a byword among its members and a subject of almost tragic mirth in its efforts to defend this country. I have listened with considerable interest to the Right Honorable Gentleman the Under-Secretary for War and to what he has said in regard to the Air Service, and I have but one remark to make now. I fancy – indeed, I am sure – he is most grievously misinformed.⁷

He immediately voiced his concerns regarding the real position of military aviation and urged the prime minister, in view of growing public anxiety, to fix a date for the resumption of the debate into the future management of the Air Service.⁸

Billing was undoubtedly well connected, and his queries were formed through a combination of practical and technical knowledge that was often uncomfortable for the government. On 11 May 1916, in an attempt to portray the Farnborough administration as incompetent, he questioned whether orders had been placed for 2,500 engines of their own design and asked the Under-Secretary of State for War to confirm that since placing this order in excess of 500 modification drawings had already been issued to manufacturers.⁹ Billing was also doggedly eager to know if the Factory engine design was based on the successful French Renault and, if so, why alterations made at Farnborough had resulted in a reportedly wholly inefficient and unreliable motor.

Mr Tennant kindly reminded Billing that the Directorate of Military Aeronautics was responsible for placing orders for engines and that one of those in question was indeed based on the French design. However, Tennant also quite correctly stated that alterations to specifications were indeed part of the development process, but this did not quell the political and public misconception that revised drawings automatically meant inefficiency rather than improved performance.[10] Billing even directly questioned the prime minister, Herbert Asquith, about why a forthcoming board of enquiry into the conduct of the air war was constrained to the Royal Flying Corps with the experiences of Royal Naval Air Service strictly omitted. Asquith replied:

> It is clear that this inquiry was to be made into the relation between the casualties in the Royal Flying Corps and the character of the machines with which the Army pilots had been provided. The charges of murder were made against the Army, not the Navy. In any case, after consulting the First Lord of the Admiralty, I do not propose to extend the scope of the judicial investigation.[11]

In fact, the board of enquiry was a direct result of Billing claiming that sending Royal Flying Corps pilots into combat in outdated British aeroplanes of government design was tantamount to corporate murder.

Billing was often supported in his criticism of British aviation by Arthur Lynch, who had also experienced active service whilst fighting as a colonel for the Boers in South Africa. Lynch shared Billing's belief that the management of British aviation was being mishandled and on 8 May 1916 asked the Under-Secretary for War whether the government would take advantage of the services of private aircraft factories in the production of fighting machines, that would assist the manufacturers which comprised the British aircraft industry and 'render and stimulate their efforts by suitable orders'.[12] Naturally, the response was in the affirmative but the veiled references to Farnborough stifling the development of private industry were once again brought into the spotlight.

By this stage of the war, however, even Liberal politicians were expressing concerns about the effectiveness of the military aircraft programme and Sir Arthur Markham asked the prime minister if he was aware that there had been a delay in deliveries owing to the fact that government contractors had been told to prioritize the manufacture of 'large numbers of motor cars for the use of the staff' over the construction of aeroplanes.[13] The question was rebuffed by the financial secretary to the War Office, who politely requested that if more details could be supplied, he would personally investigate the allegations, but it was clear that there was indeed unrest across the political spectrum in relation to the direction of the air war.

On 30 March 1916, the War Office formally commissioned an independent report into the affairs of the Royal Aircraft Factory following criticisms previously raised. The terms of reference of the Committee were:

> To enquire and report whether, within the resources placed by the War Office at the disposal of the Royal Aircraft Factory and the limits imposed by War Office orders, the organization and management of the factory are efficient, and to give the Army Council the benefit of their suggestions on any points of the interior administration of the factory which seem to them capable of improvement.[14]

The report was issued on 12 May 1916 by the Committee chairman, Richard Burbidge, who was a famous businessman and the managing director of Harrods. Burbidge started by expressing his gratitude for the assistance afforded the Committee in their investigations from Lieutenant-General Sir David Henderson and the Staff of the Military Aeronautics Directorate; Lieutenant-Colonel M. O'Gorman, factory superintendent; Major Smitheyt Heckstall-Smith, assistant superintendent; and the Staff of the Royal Aircraft Factory. The report then proceeded to offer a detailed and impartial summary of the workings of the Factory.

Burbidge and his two experienced fellow investigators, Sir Charles Parsons and Sir Hay Frederick Donaldson, were quick to realize that the Royal Aircraft Factory could not be regarded as an establishment working on strictly commercial lines but instead concluded that it was more fitting to describe the facility as probably the largest experimental laboratory in the UK. The Factory was indeed required to conduct full-scale experiments in order to prove or disprove the viability of the trials conducted on aircraft models at the National Physical Laboratory.

Consequently, development work at Farnborough was not only expensive but also required the issue of modification drawings as and when improvements were determined as a natural part of the research and design process. It is important to remember that aviation technology was in its infancy and thus modification did not necessarily mean procedural oversight. More important, however, was the fact that the Committee were able to independently confirm that the only manufacturing undertaken at Farnborough since the outbreak of war was 'an output of about 50 non-experimental machines and the manufacture of spare parts to meet urgent demands'.[15] This should have silenced those who argued that the existence of the Factory was in direct competition to private enterprise once and for all. It was considered that orders for spare parts were a significant aspect of the Factory's responsibility and that it was essential that once received, the manufacture and despatch of any such replacement components was both rapid and economical.

Major Heckstall-Smith had supplied details of all the work undertaken at Farnborough, which enabled the Committee to calculate the percentage of time and resource allocated to individual tasks. They concluded that 22 per cent of the Factory's activities were dedicated to experimental work, 35 per cent to the construction of aeroplanes, 33 per cent to aircraft repairs and the manufacture of spare parts and 10 per cent of time was taken in the repair of engines and the manufacture of associated spares. Colonel O'Gorman confirmed these figures but was also keen to emphasize that the time dedicated to the construction of aeroplanes included the manufacture of experimental machines which were required as proof of design and were not necessarily destined for production.

The Committee also reported that the preparation of an entirely new aeroplane design could take anything between six and nine months before any physical construction in quantity could commence, a remarkable amount of time in comparison to the gestation period of later aircraft designs. In order to design and manufacture aeroplanes and engines swiftly in the quantities required, experimental machines had to be produced at Farnborough whilst the working production drawings were prepared concurrently. The demands of the services for replacement parts, aeroplanes of improved performance, and more powerful engines often resulted in orders being placed with sub-contractors for complete machines before the designs and construction drawings had been fully completed. Naturally this resulted in the issue of modification drawings. But once again, it must be remembered that this technology was entirely new and previously unproven – something that was often overlooked by the main detractors of the Factory and its methods.

The Committee did, however, conclude that the system of administration adopted at Farnborough was unnecessarily elaborate. Although the members unanimously agreed that such an experimental facility should exist, they also wished to see operations streamlined and reorganized on a more commercial basis with a clear line of demarcation drawn between experimentation and manufacture.[16] Their belief that the Factory should focus primarily on experimentation was even widely reported in the media and should have served to reassure those private manufacturers that the work at Farnborough was to their benefit rather than any form of competition.[17] Nevertheless, the general consensus amongst the members of the Committee was that the standard of efficiency required by the War Office in both design and construction had been satisfied and that essential data had been placed at the government's disposal for the purpose of making informed decisions regarding strategy and the conduct of the air war.

Despite recognition 'to the ungrudging work done under the trying conditions of war pressure by the Superintendent and Staff', numerous suggestions were made for the implementation of improvements in terms of general management and organization. Amongst these was the recommendation that the management structure should be revised to comprise a director of the Royal Aircraft Factory, a superintendent of Designs, and a superintendent of Manufacture, who should all be suitably qualified civilians dedicating their entire time to the affairs of the Factory. It was not believed that these senior management positions required intimate knowledge of aviation but that each individual should be recognized for their abilities in general business administration and operational management.

The Committee suggested that the revised board should also include a military adviser without specific executive duties who would ensure the needs of the services were satisfied and translated into a suitable format of design specifications. In addition, the report advised the appointment of a civilian as Controller of Aircraft Supplies responsible for direct communications between the Factory and contractors in order to remedy the ill feeling that still existed within the private aeroplane industry:

> We think it would be better that direct contact with contractors, including the issue to them of drawings, should be made through a third party, *e.g.*, the Controller of Aircraft Supplies and not by the Royal Aircraft Factory. It is, of course, undesirable to cut off all communication between the Royal Aircraft Factory and the Trade, but we think it would be preferable that enquiries should first of all be made to the officer issuing drawings,

presumably the Controller of Aircraft Supplies, and that he should put any particular contractor into touch with the Royal Aircraft Factory in order that any desired information, data, or explanations, may, when required, be afforded direct. This course would also keep track of alterations, if any, from the original approved designs. Of course, the Controller of Aircraft Supplies and the Director of the Factory would, in fact, be in reasonably close touch.[18]

Unfortunately, the pragmatic recommendations of Burbidge's committee were not met with enthusiasm by Lord Curzon's Air Board, who reported their observations to the War Committee in June 1916. A key element of fact that they wished to firstly qualify was the percentage of the Factory's time dedicated to the 'construction of aeroplanes'. Although the 35 per cent figure remained the same the Air Board disputed that it represented the construction of new aeroplanes, which they believed to be less than 10 per cent. The response insinuated that the blame for this error lay with Colonel O'Gorman as he had checked the figures and argued that majority of that allocation was dedicated to experimental investigation. This, Curzon believed to be 'very desirable to correct'.[19]

Unsurprisingly, the Air Board also disagreed with the proposals concerning the administration of the Factory. Following consultation with Sir David Henderson, the Director-General of Military Aeronautics, the Air Board adopted a simple strategy that resulted in the replacement of the incumbent Superintendent. Curzon believed that a Board of Management was an instrument of private business unsuited to the exigencies of a military organization and that the overall direction of Farnborough should remain in the hands of a single suitably qualified superintendent assisted by a head of design and head of production. In regard to Colonel O'Gorman, the Air Board made the following reference:

> Colonel O'Gorman has, in their opinion, rendered eminent public service in the design and construction of aircraft, and they think that these abilities can best be employed in the future in the capacity of consulting engineer to the Director-General of Military Aeronautics at the War Office.[20]

Ultimately, O'Gorman was replaced by Sir Henry Fowler in September 1916 and became consulting aeronautical engineer to the Director-General of Military Aeronautics until 1919. In his memoirs Geoffrey de Havilland stated that O'Gorman was an exceptional administrator and instrumental in the development of British aeronautics. De Havilland attributed his eventual downfall to his strength of character which did not sit well with War Office officials who believed that scientists should be subservient to their demands, no matter how ill-informed those demands may be.[21] Nevertheless, O'Gorman's forthright nature was not the only reason for his premature departure as superintendent at Farnborough, and de Havilland specifically noted that Pemberton-Billing was instrumental in convincing senior officials behind the scenes that he was no longer suited to lead the experimental establishment.

The Air Board did at least support Burbidge's recommendation that communication between the Royal Aircraft Factory and the private contractors with which the War Office had business relations be reduced to a minimum. However, they did not endorse the creation of a Controller of Aircraft Supplies and believed that such functions could be adequately discharged through the Department of Military Aeronautics at the War Office. The Air Board reported that they were exploring the means of increased output of aeroplane engines by private manufacturers, a key area of improvement identified by Burbidge, and believed that the present situation had not been caused by a lack of financial assistance but want of available skilled mechanics. In the meantime, the role of the Factory in aero-engine experimentation and design would through necessity remain paramount. On 1 August 1916, Curzon further qualified his desire to encourage the increased output of aero-engines by private manufacturers explaining that he had invited industry representatives to present themselves to the Air Board in order to hear their thoughts. Curzon reported:

> They attended in force. We listened to everything they had to say, and I myself was rejoiced to hear how small was the area of complaint over which they travelled. Really what it came to in the last resort was, not that they were jealous of the Air Factory or that they had any complaint of unfair competition, but that they wanted more skilled labour to enable them to carry out a larger programme. We entered at once into communication with the proper Department to arrange for the release of more skilled labour from the Army. But everybody is dipping their hands into the same bin, and it is exceedingly difficult to get what you want.[22]

Despite the obvious improvement in relations between the industry and the scientists and engineers at Farnborough, the Air Board did not propose to comment on the allegations of defective internal administration and preferred to wait until the new superintendent was appointed before investigating them further.

Nevertheless, the scandal continued to mount in the public realm and government investigations were not simply restricted to analyses of efficiencies at Farnborough as the entire air policy was soon subject to debate. Following a series of spectacular claims in Parliament of corporate maladministration, even extending to murder, a committee was formed to scrutinize the administration and command of the Royal Flying Corps in its entirety. The Committee was chaired by Justice Clement Bailhache and produced an interim report in August 1916.

Billing was at the heart of the debate throughout the ensuing investigation and remained vehemently critical of the government's policy towards the conduct of the air war. He was particularly disparaging towards machines designed and produced at Farnborough and made the following provocative statement in the House of Commons on 22 March 1916:

> I do not intend to deal with the colossal blunders of the Royal Flying Corps, but I may refer briefly to the hundreds-nay, thousands-of machines which they have ordered and which have been referred to by our pilots at the front as 'Fokker Fodder.' Every one of our pilots knows when he steps into them that if he gets back it will be more by luck and by his skill than by any mechanical assistance he will get from the people who provide him with the machines. I do not want to touch a dramatic note this afternoon, but if I did I would suggest that quite a number of our gallant officers in the Royal Flying Corps have been rather murdered than killed.[23]

As the debate intensified toward the end of the month Billing made further accusations against both the administration and higher command of the Royal Flying Corps, declaring on 28 March:

> It is extremely difficult, even in law, to draw a hard-and-fast line between murder and manslaughter, or between manslaughter and an accident caused by criminal negligence. When this negligence is caused by the official folly of those in high places, coupled with entire ignorance of the techniques which

in this case can alone preserve human life, official folly becomes at any rate criminal negligence. When the death of a man ensues, the line between such official folly and murder is purely a matter for a man's conscience.[24]

Unsurprisingly, the government were forced to respond to such explosive allegations through the formation of the Bailhache Committee, who were tasked with scrutinizing the efficiency of the Royal Flying Corps 'with particular reference to the charges made in Parliament and elsewhere against the officials and officers responsible for that administration and command'.[25] The Committee of Inquiry heard extensive evidence from serving officers and officials and were assured by the War Office that they would be furnished with any information they required that may be used to corroborate, or indeed disprove, ensuing testimonies.[26] Subsequently, a complicated series of evidence was presented throughout the remainder of 1916 that not only tied up important human resources but often became difficult to disentangle in a muddled chronology of events. However, it is certainly worth persevering with these extracts as they present a fascinating insight into the contemporary mechanics of the British aircraft industry.

The ensuing debates surrounding the air services were simultaneously championed by Joynson-Hicks in the House of Commons and Lord Montagu in the House of Lords during May 1916, and both men passionately believed that the matter was of incalculable importance to the future conduct of the war and the security of the British Isles. The press was also eager to bring the discussion into the public domain and assist in pushing government reform of the air policy and its future relationship with the British aircraft industry. *The Times* remained at the forefront of the media scrutiny and argued that the first and greatest need was to put a stop on the 'cut-throat competition between the naval and military air services'.[27]

It was certainly evident that by the middle of 1916 the two air services had developed independently and that a more unified approach was necessary to maximize the efficient use of resource required in the design and construction of British aeroplanes. Commentators argued that in order to achieve this aim a single independent air service was required and warned the government that the public would no longer stand for half-hearted political compromise or another white-washing committee. This could not be achieved by simply amalgamating the existing inefficient institutions under one elaborate title and needed to be an instrument that was capable of doing justice to the brave pilots of the Royal Flying Corps and Royal Naval Air Service serving their country on the front lines. There was a genuine belief that the organization of the flying services at home still failed to grasp the vast scale on which the phenomenon of aerial warfare in the future would be conducted and that orders for aeroplanes needed to be placed in their thousands as a matter of urgency rather than in the modest procurement quantities still prevalent in early 1916. This lack of foresight, it was argued, meant that British designs were only ever as good as the last captured German machine when they should really be 'thinking ahead of the next imaginable German invention' as the benchmark for future designs.[28]

The fear that the administration was inadequate and that resources were unnecessarily wasted due to inter-service rivalries and competing government departments was very real indeed and inspired a host of concerned individuals to continue to publicly question government policy. With the war entering its second full year there can be little doubt that the public required some reassurance that their sacrifices, both materiel and financial, were being wisely managed by the government and 'that the organization at the back' was ultimately 'worthy of the men at the front'.[29] It was also during May 1916 that Billing failed to appear before the Bailhache Committee, which naturally caused a stir considering many of the accusations that the Committee had been tasked with investigating had been made directly by him.

When challenged on this fact, Billing was naturally defensive and reminded the Commons that he had entered House with the sole intention of effecting reform in the air services and that 'no amount of slur and insults from the Treasury Bench, and no amount of attack in the newspapers' could deter him from his goal. Billing made his opinion of the Committee perfectly obvious:

> It has been suggested that, either through cowardice or some other reason, I have refused to appear before this Committee of Inquiry. I do not want to deal with this Committee: it has dealt with itself: its fallacy is so perfectly obvious to any right-thinking man that there is no occasion in the public interest to discuss it.[30]

Billing argued that the members of the Committee did not possess the military or technical qualification to discuss the charges of negligence and maladministration made against the government and were thus effectively a public relations exercise.

In truth, the situation had indeed become increasingly confused in terms of the accusations made against the Royal Flying Corps because that service could not be disaggregated from the Naval and Military Wings of which it was comprised. Billing had served in the Royal Naval Air Service and most of his charges were made against that service even though, through the necessity of the Army List, it could not be sufficiently isolated from its wider administrative body. Billing attempted to further explain the reasoning for his allegations concerning the quality of British aeroplanes produced under government instruction in order to clarify his own position as the self-appointed representative of British military aviation:

> If we have in this country, and we have in this country, the best machines, and some of the best engines, and if we continue, on the other hand, to build machines of design which the Government officially decides, and if we continue to order in large quantities engines which are in the opinion of experts in this country inefficient, then I say we are guilty of supplying our officers with machines that are inefficient, and if they meet their death in consequence of not having the best materiel, it is very difficult to find a word with which to describe the behaviour or the conduct of those people who are primarily responsible.[31]

Effectively, Billing believed that the Bailhache Committee had not been properly constituted nor given the independence, expertise or terms of reference necessary to conduct a thorough investigation against the government. However, due to mounting political pressure Billing would soon be forced to attend the enquiry in person.

The judicial Air Committee resumed their enquiries nevertheless, and on 26 May 1916 Lord Montagu was asked to give evidence regarding his experience as a member of the Joint War Air Committee. Montagu proceeded to give an account of the early British experimentation with heavier-than-air machines and reminded the Committee of the fact that the Wright Brothers had originally offered their invention to the War Office in 1909 only to be told that their services were not required.[32] This was in spite of the Wright Brothers being recently presented with the Aero Club Gold Medal for 'solving the problem of flight' by President Taft at the White House on 10 June the same year.[33] Montagu, who was admittedly an aviation enthusiast, explained that he was dismayed at the government's initial apathy to the advent of powered flight and raised the issue on numerous occasions before the outbreak of war in the House of Lords:

> But my warnings fell on deaf ears; I was assured by the Government that everything possible was being done, but it was with the greatest difficulty, as Sir David Henderson knows, that proper provision for the R.F.C., small as it was in those days, could be secured. I would remind the Committee that it was originally only one corps, with naval and military branches.[34]

The British also failed to grasp the potential of rigid airships, and it was not until 5 October 1907 that the first army airship, Nullis Secundus, made any significant voyage during a flight from Aldershot to the Crystal Palace.[35] An event that quite literally, brought London traffic to a standstill.[36] The naval airship programme developed even more slowly and the No. 1, commonly known as the Mayfly, was not ready for trials until 1911 when she was completely wrecked during trials at Cavendish Dock, Barrow, on 24 September.[37] Unsurprisingly, Montagu concluded that Britain was 'wholly unprepared for a big or even a small war' involving military aviation in August 1914.[38] The same concerns had also inspired Britain's first air correspondent, Harry Harper, to collaborate with Claude Grahame-White in the publication of a book warning the British public of the perils that lay ahead if the government continued to neglect the development of the 'flying machine as a military weapon'.[39]

Following the pre-war appraisal on the British experience, Montagu had nothing but praise for the personnel of the Royal Flying Corps and their equipment during the first year of the war. Although it was true that they were small in number, they were certainly more than equal in terms of quality and had enjoyed significant success flying the Factory designed B.E.2c in combat on the Western Front. Montagu argued that during the early stages of the war the B.E.2c had undoubtedly proved its superiority and 'hardly any German machine dared fly over our lines, for we had attained a certain amount of ascendency, chiefly due to our pilots' skill and pluck'.[40] However, the introduction of more powerful German aeroplanes during 1915 had certainly turned the aerial advantage in their favour but Montagu's opinions concerning the Royal Aircraft Factory were particularly interesting.

Montagu informed the Committee that, in his experience, the majority of the British aeroplane manufacturers continued to regard the Factory with both suspicion and dislike. There was a genuine concern that private constructors would not be willing to give evidence for fear of victimization and potential loss of government contracts. Nevertheless, he did concede that Colonel O'Gorman and the staff at Farnborough had been placed in an impossible position, whereby they were expected to not only operate as the government's chief aeronautical scientists and manufacturers as required but also critique the designs and performance of private industry.

Consequently, should a private design prove to be of superior performance, the Factory was in the ridiculous position whereby it was expected to officially acknowledge the inferiority it its own, and by association, the government's work. Naturally, this could also occur the other way around, which invariably only served to further fuel suspicions of institutional foul play amongst private enterprise. The Navy system, on the other hand, was more dependent on private manufacturers who supplied a design which was modified accordingly based upon the operational requirements. With such divergent approaches to the same problems, it is easy to see why there was mounting confusion and resentment on all sides. However, the British were not averse to using foreign-manufactured machines to ensure the Royal Flying Corps pilots maintained the best possible advantage. The French-manufactured Spad S.VII was used extensively throughout 1916 to redress the balance on the Western front but this would no doubt have only increased the dismay of British aircraft firms.

On 2 June 1916, Sir Alfred Mond, Liberal MP for Swansea, gave evidence to the Committee and made particular reference to the Fokker monoplane which was believed to have inflicted such casualties on the Royal Flying Corps during the summer of 1915.[41] Although Mond had a point, subsequent analyses by aviation historians have questioned the effectiveness of the Fokker monoplane and even suggested that its performance was inferior to British machines, its only advantage being the virtual monopoly of airborne armament that was swiftly addressed by the Royal Flying Corps and Allied air forces.[42]

In fact, the story could easily have been one told in the Allies' favour as innovation in aircraft armament was not simply restricted to the Germans. The Vickers F.B.5 'Gunbus' was the first British aircraft design specifically manufactured to mount a machine gun. The first of these machines entered service with the RFC in 1914 and served on the Western Front the following year, enjoying an early advantage before the introduction of the German Fokkers. The adoption of armament was not a universal requirement until later in 1915 and many of the aeroplanes operated by the RFC remained unarmed. Although the Royal Aircraft Factory continued to produce tough and stable designs such as the R.E.5, many were slow and not particularly manoeuvrable, which meant they were easy prey for the early German armed scouts.

Nevertheless, Mond also believed that the Fokker machine had originally been offered to the British government by its Dutch inventor, who had failed to make the acquisition and used this as a further example of government mismanagement.[43] General Henderson, representing the Royal Flying Corps, enquired as to whether Mond really believed the German-operated machine was superior to Allied aeroplanes before reminding members of the enquiry that the threat had been dealt with swiftly once the utilization of the synchronized machine-gun firing through an aeroplane propellor had been discovered.

Henderson was indeed right to point out that it wasn't necessarily true that the British did not operate aircraft of their own that could have stolen the advantage later enjoyed by the German Fokker. Some private designs such as the Bristol Scout designed by Frank Barnwell, which entered service with the Royal Flying Corps in 1914, would have undoubtedly made an excellent early fighting aeroplane if it had been armed earlier in its service career. Although this type was the first British aeroplane to be armed with a synchronized forward firing machine gun in 1916, by this time its performance was already obsolete and a real opportunity to gain early aerial supremacy had been missed. Nevertheless, it would be wrong to assume that mounting a machine gun to an aeroplane was an easy task, and stability could be severely compromised by the additional weight of armaments and invariably more powerful engines and stronger airframes were required to cope with these additional demands.[44]

Arthur Lynch also wished to clarify some evidence that he had previously submitted before the Committee concerning the experiences of an informant inventor who had proposed a new flight principle to the War Office. The inventor in question had been advised that in order to obtain a hearing an aeroplane had to have been physically constructed to prove the theory and Lynch argued that this was not the way to deal with scientific minds. However, at the risk of somewhat undermining his own argument, Lynch also conceded that he had recently come to the conclusion that inventors might easily be divided into three categories: inspired men, inspired idiots or those to which the word 'inspired' did not apply. In reality, it would have been hugely irresponsible for the government to finance the investigation of every unsolicited theory with public funds, but the day's hearing did serve to illustrate some of the more nonsensical elements of evidence the Committee was required to give consideration.

The previous day, 1 June 1916, Lord Montagu had taken the opportunity to address an audience in Manchester regarding the need for an Imperial Air Service and formally pledge his support for the appointment of Lord Curzon as chair of the Air Board. However, he stated his dismay at the jealousies that existed between the services and even argued that their continued destructive relations put the very defence of the United Kingdom at risk. Curzon wanted the nation to wake up to the basic fact the British people were no longer living on an isolated island and that their industrial heartlands, the very engine room of the war effort, was liable to attack by enemy aircraft by night whilst coastal towns and dockyards remained vulnerable by day. Curzon believed that the lack of a coordinated air policy left the British inadequately prepared in terms of aerial defence and warned that unless the authorities were put under constant pressure to act there 'was always a tendency to slacking on their part'.[45] Such vocal criticism by a Lord of the Realm provided additional urgency to the Air Inquiry, and the government, determination to indeed do something to save face. The easiest target for government intervention was to focus their attention on something in their control such as the administration of the Royal Aircraft Factory, and, at Lord Montagu's insistence, this soon became the main target of the Committee's attention.

On 4 July 1916, the Committee resumed its hearing, and evidence was received from Royal Flying Corps pilots, mechanics and workmen but not before Lord Montagu had sought reassurance from General Henderson that he had no objection. Henderson duly gave reassurance that no member of service personnel would suffer victimization but asked that the evidence should be heard in his absence and insisted that he would merely ask what was said and not individual names. Billing was also present at this hearing and was eager to know from General Henderson the circumstances surrounding recent accidents during pilot training at Netheravon.

One fatal incident in question involved the wings folding up on a B.E.2b machine due to cables breaking during a diving manoeuvre. Henderson, when questioned, did not believe that the maximum tolerances of such cables had been re-calculated since the accident but confirmed that should it reoccur then this would require attention. Billing seized upon the opportunity to demonstrate the response as evidence of negligence enquiring of Henderson, 'do you always wait until two men are killed before you take precaution?'[46] However, Sir Charles Parsons, a member of the Committee and an eminent engineer, came to Henderson's assistance by advising those assembled that no scientific mind would make such an insinuation and that there was no evidence that cables were overstressed concluding that there was nothing, to his mind, 'to show anything wrong with it at all'.[47]

However, it was the session on 11 July that proved to be the most damning concerning the activities of the Royal Aircraft Factory. The Committee were first presented with a tabulated document that suggested aero-engines designed at the Factory were the least economical when compared with privately manufactured types. Despite this fact, evidence suggested that orders had been placed for the Farnborough designs before sufficient reliability tests had been completed. This, in turn, raised the subject of the effective use of labour

Figure 8 Royal Aircraft Factory Planning Department. Author's Collection.

at the Factory despite this being an area of enquiry that was not technically within the jurisdiction of the Committee. Nevertheless, Lord Montagu called an unnamed witness employed at Farnborough to give evidence concerning work ethic and professionalism. The justification, Montagu argued, was that ensuring workers were effectively employed and the continued production of substandard designs were intrinsically linked, and the witness was allowed to present their evidence.

The witness claimed that everybody was kept busy when official visits were being undertaken, but this was simply window dressing as the majority of the time workers had very little to do and the supervision of hours had only very recently been introduced. The witness believed that there was a large proportion of incompetent men employed at Farnborough whilst many were actively seeking to avoid being called up for active military service. There were also unnecessary tiers of management, and it had become a standing joke that there was 'one man, one foreman'.[48]

> Continuing, the witness said he did not get enough work, and he met a man who had been at the factory for two years and was leaving because he was 'fed up'. Until recently men were paid for bad work as well as good, and he had heard that some of the materiel that had been scrapped had been buried. It was reported that one man, who wore a bog coat which had big pockets, had taken away enough parts to put an engine together. The works were fine, and the machinery was tip-top – could not be better – and there were good men there, but they were not fully employed, though they often worked overtime.[49]

Following this damning statement, the chairman reminded Lord Montagu that the Committee were not enquiring into the internal administration of the Factory, and they would not hear any further evidence on that matter. Nevertheless, the insinuation of maladministration and poor working practices had already been clearly made.

Colonel O'Gorman was asked to respond and stated that it was untrue that engines had not been tested and denied that Factory designs had been copied from the endeavours of private manufacturers. Furthermore, O'Gorman maintained that he did not know Lord Montagu's witness and reassured the Committee that he was allowing every fit man he could spare to go to the front whilst continuing to function with the best operatives available. Inevitably, however, such sustained criticism only reinvigorated previous suspicions within the British aircraft industry concerning over-resourced government monopoly.[50]

The issue of personnel was once again raised in Parliament on 16 August 1916, when the MP for Barrow-in-Furness, Mr Charles Duncan, enquired of the financial secretary to the War Office whether he was aware of the rumour that married men were being discharged from Farnborough at the expense of retaining single unskilled men. Mr Henry Forster assured his honourable friend that single unskilled men were only being retained in a few cases due to labour shortages and that these would be replaced as soon as suitable substitutes could be obtained.[51] Even following the enquiry, suspicion regarding the practices at Farnborough remained.

The Committee also heard evidence from Dr Richard Tetley Glazebrook, director of the National Physical Laboratory and chairman of the Advisory Committee for Aeronautics, who presented technical detailed evidence regarding the design and stability of aeroplanes. Glazebrook had written the 1912 report on the accidents to monoplanes and was regarded as one of the pre-eminent aviation authorities within the United Kingdom.[52] His obituary contained the following tribute:

> It is for the services which he rendered in this manner in the early progress of flight, as well as for his work as the first Director of the National Physical Laboratory, that Sir Richard Glazebrook will be remembered in the history of science and of this country.[53]

The Committee were particularly interested to ascertain whether the B.E.2c was, in his opinion, an efficient and satisfactory machine, to which the witness unhesitatingly replied, 'thoroughly'. Glazebrook reminded the Committee that it was incredibly difficult to combine 'all the qualities that were required in an aeroplane in one design' but the B.E.2c had successfully amalgamated those requirements and was the result of applied scientific study concerning the problems associated with aviation.[54] It was certainly true that the aircraft could not have been designed without the application of considerable government resources available at both Farnborough and the National Physical Laboratory.

A fellow Aeronautics Advisory Committee member, Professor Petavel of Manchester University, corroborated Glazebrook's evidence by stating that

Figure 9 B.E.2e, 140 Squadron, Royal Air Force, March 1918. Author's Collection.

the B.E.2c was more easily controlled than other types of machines and thus inherently safer for pilots to fly. In light of this evidence from leading aviation scientists, the accusations of negligence on behalf of the government started to appear rather thin, and neither the Royal Aircraft Factory nor National Physical Laboratory could be blamed for obsolescence as a result of an increasingly fast paced technological conflict.

In fact, by this stage of the war both the Royal Flying Corps and Royal Naval Air Service had become early adopters of aeroplanes designed by Herbert Smith, chief designer at the Sopwith Aviation Company. The Sopwith 1½ Strutter fighter bomber and the Sopwith Pup fighter entered service towards the middle of 1916 and heralded the introduction of a variety of successful aeroplane designs from private manufacturers, the British aircraft industry having finally overcome the initial challenges of producing competitive design of consistent production. By the end of the conflict, machines from firms that would later become household names such as Handley-Page, Armstrong-Whitworth, Blackburn, Martinsyde and Shorts were successfully employed in British military service.

O'Gorman was recalled before the Committee at Westminster on 12 July 1916 to explain the continued use of poisonous dope at the Factory and he recounted that the products used up until 1914 contained a poisonous substance, namely tetrachlorethane, which kept the varnish soft and prevented it from cracking. Efforts continued to be made to obtain a less poisonous compound and he believed the dangers had been greatly diminished since better regulations had been adopted under Home Office guidance. He was also questioned regarding the functions of the Royal Aircraft Factory and was asked to respond to a statement by Lord Montagu which regurgitated the old argument that the Factory had attempted to keep a monopoly in the manufacture of aeroplanes and aero-engines instead of encouraging the development of British manufacturers. The superintendent confidently stated before the Committee that there was absolutely no shadow of truth in the statement and that no more than four experimental engines had been constructed at Farnborough. In order to highlight his assertion that there was no monopoly at the Factory, O'Gorman reminded the Committee that they had produced less than 2 per cent of the entire total number delivered and that if they had indeed attempted to secure the control of engine manufacture they would have been 'cutting our own throats, seeing that we could not produce anything like the number required'.[55]

However, it would be wrong to assume that private aircraft manufacturers had no reason to complain about the conduct of the air war, and there certainly was one machine produced at Farnborough that represented a technological step backwards rather than evolution. The B.E.2e was introduced into front-line service with the Royal Flying Corps in 1916 and was the last model in the series. Ironically, it was slower and less well armed than its predecessors, but despite the retrograde performance, over 1,800 were manufactured but were soon realized to be obsolete and were relegated to a training role.

Back at the enquiry Justice Bailhache was interested to ascertain the number of personnel employed at Farnborough and questioned in what work the 4,000 employees were engaged if the Factory was not intended for production. O'Gorman once again had to state the case that Farnborough was effectively the sole workshop of the Royal Flying Corps and was also responsible for providing spares for the machines at the front. Wastage was increasing all the time, and many components had to be made by hand and could not be easily manufactured by industrial processes. He conceded that 'the word "factory" was a little misleading: it was a laboratory on a full scale', and the various engineers belonging to manufacturing firms that continued to make countless visits there knew there was no commercial competition.⁵⁶ Ultimately, the functions of the factory were best described as experimental and jobbing whilst programmes of work were thus necessarily determined to meet the technical and tactical demands of combat at the front. Following this statement, the Committee adjourned *sine die* to consider the extensive evidence collected and did not take any further testimonies in public.

Due to the scale of evidence the Committee produced an interim report on 3 August 1916 primarily in response to the accusations Billing had previously made before the House of Commons in order to protect the reputation of the government. Each allegation and incident of supposed negligence was methodically assessed which resulted in the following appraisals. The Committee stated that they would not have blamed Mr Billing if he had enquired into flying fatalities from the perspective of a concerned aviator or as a professional experienced in aeronautics who was eager to satisfy himself that the utmost was being done to secure the safety of British pilots. However, they considered that to portray such tragedies as 'charges of criminal negligence or murder' was 'an abuse of language and entirely unjustifiable'.⁵⁷ The report concluded with the final reminder:

> There has been an enormous expansion in the Flying Service since the war and all the critics of the Service without exception have borne testimony to the great progress made in its efficiency – a progress which although most noticeable since the beginning of this year is in the opinion of the Committee the result of many months of strenuous work.⁵⁸

There is no doubt that progress had been made, but the energy expended on proving or disproving allegations was to result in other areas of supply, more crucial to the success of British aviation, not receiving the care and attention required.

This intense period of judicial process throughout 1916 comprising enquiry, report and recommendation regarding Britain's past and future conduct of the air war ultimately resulted in some confusion as to the real point at issue. Nevertheless, the result was that the government pinned their faith firmly on the judgement of the Air Board in relation to the Royal Aircraft Factory Committee Report. Although, the aviation press was inclined to agree with Richard Burbidge's suggestions of increasing the responsibilities of civilian aeronautical experts *Flight Magazine* reassured its readership that 'the country may rest assured that after this shake-up the re-organization of the Farnborough factory will be based on a very solid foundation of honest endeavour' in order to get the best results on behalf of the nation.[59]

Ultimately, both the Burbidge report and Air Board response recognized the disconnect between the general organization at Farnborough and the conduct of the functions for which it had originally been created. Taking a broad view of the Committee's report, it is evident that, as was generally conceded, there had been considerable looseness in the organization and in the carrying out of the functions for which the Factory was originally created. However, the Air Board still did not possess the executive powers necessary to approve any such reorganization, and once again the best had to be made in a compromise that continued to hinder the development of the British aircraft industry.

The lack of progress was sufficiently frustrating to prompt Lord Montagu to write to the War Cabinet in September 1916 concerning the future supply of military aeroplanes. Montagu argued that a separate organization, in intimate touch with the Air Service, should be responsible for the supply of aeroplanes so that operational requirements could be incorporated as early as possible during the design stages and reasoned that such an approach would have numerous advantages:

> It would prevent the loss of time which at present results when a firm takes orders from two Government Departments, and being unable to deal properly with both together, devotes itself mainly to the one which will pay it best. It would make for the saving of money which results when all the arrangements with a firm are in the hands of one negotiator. It would prevent the waste of labour which results when a firm can play off the needs of separate Departments against the Labour Officers of the Ministry. It would make for economy in the supply of materiels and machinery from our limited stocks. It would increase output, lessen cost, and obviate the overlapping and friction which must occur more and more frequently if the present system is allowed to continue.[60]

Ultimately, Montagu objected to the fact that the supply of aeroplanes to the Admiralty and War Office remained independent of one another and suggested that the Ministry of Munitions should take control and devise an efficient method of satisfying the aeronautical requirements of both services simultaneously.[61] Although generally pragmatic, there was still significant ground to cover before the creation of an autonomous Air Ministry.

Reports were also being received of the dissatisfaction of workers employed within the industry itself. In August 1916, James O'Grady, MP for Leeds East, asked the prime minister if he was aware of the growing discontent amongst woodworkers in the aircraft industry relating to wages and enquired whether a small committee might be appointed to review the matter. The question was answered on behalf of Asquith's government by Mr Harcourt, First Commissioner of Works, who explained that the Committee on Production had recently considered claims on behalf of aircraft industry woodworkers in the London and Glasgow districts and concluded that they should be paid the highest rates of wages comparable to men in the building trade. However, the Committee did not believe a direct pay rise was necessary in this instance due to the practice of advancing wages in the form of war bonuses. Mr O'Grady responded that despite the specialist nature of their employment, aircraft woodworkers were only receiving 2d. an hour which was less than they would earn for the menial task of making ammunition boxes.[62] Such disparity in wages resulted in strike action during 1917 and is clear evidence that dissatisfaction was not simply restricted to the public facing spheres of the aircraft industry.

By October 1916 serious concerns were being raised with regard to the position of the Air Board following continued Admiralty indifference to its very existence. Lord Montagu addressed an audience in Brockenhurst, Hampshire, and publicly questioned, 'How long was Lord Curzon going to tolerate this somewhat absurd position?'[63] Recent Zeppelin raids on the British Isles had once again brought the spotlight onto the conduct of the air war and reinvigorated public and political interest. Aviation was becoming an increasingly important aspect of the conflict and it had been believed that the Air Board was the key to the future development of an autonomous air service. However, it was becoming clear that it had no real power and was thus unable to achieve a status as the de facto authority on British interest in the air.

The Air Board effectively had no more influence than its unfortunate predecessor, and although Lord Curzon was also a member of the War Committee, he could do little more than attempt to influence policy and answer the increasingly vitriolic questions raised in Parliament. Feelings were also running high in the press, and *The Times* reported on the 6 November 1916 that another crisis in the history of national aviation was looming if the Air Board were not given more meaningful powers than those afforded by their current advisory nature. The correspondent argued that the government would find it incredibly difficult after the previous two failures 'to appease the nation or Parliament by suggesting the appointment of yet a third body with no real powers, merely as a sop to clamour and as an excuse for delay'.[64]

In fact, beyond this point the government itself was in far greater turmoil. Herbert Asquith's coalition finally collapsed on 6 December 1916, resulting in his resignation and David Lloyd George becoming prime minister. This had a profound impact on the organization of British air policy and Lord Curzon was swiftly replaced by Weetman Pearson, Lord Cowdray, in January 1917. A more fundamental change, however, was the appointment of Rear Admiral Godfrey Paine to the Air Board whilst the responsibility for design and procurement of aircraft passed directly to the Ministry of Munitions. Paine was the director of Naval Aviation and his willingness to serve on the board greatly improved inter-service cooperation.

However, upon appointment the Second Air Board wished to clarify the relationship between themselves and the responsibility of the Ministry of Munitions for both the design and supply of aeroplanes. In a letter to the War Office dated 1 February 1917 the following conclusions were summarized:

> The decision of the Cabinet to entrust the design as well as supply of aircraft to the Ministry of Munitions was found to give rise to certain difficulties. That department, constituted primarily as a manufacturing or supply department, did not consider itself well adapted to dealing with the highly specialized duty of selecting and approving designs of aircraft. The science of aeronautics is at present in a state of such rapid and constant growth that it appeared expedient that its application to questions of design should be in the hands of a body on which the Naval and Military Flying Services were directly represented, and an agreement was arrived at accordingly that the Air Board should be charged with this duty.[65]

The Air Board ultimately assumed responsibility for these functions from both services, enabling Farnborough to focus on practical scientific investigation and paving the way for the establishment of the independent Air Ministry in January 1918.

Following the seemingly endless turmoil of scrutiny committees, witness evidence, claims and counterclaim, there was a period of reflection upon the events 1916 and the relationship that then existed between the Royal Aircraft Factory and private British aircraft manufacturers. One of the principal accusations against the Farnborough management was that it had purposefully delayed ordering aircraft engines from private firms whilst they perfected their own designs to achieve a market monopoly. The underlying allegation that the Royal Aircraft Factory was a competitive manufacturer was effectively dispelled by simple analysis of the output and it was clear that the work was primarily experimental in nature. The criticisms that Factory designs, whether of aeroplanes or engines, were not efficient or effective had also been largely dismissed.[66] Nevertheless, the Royal Flying Corps required more capable machines than ever before and in larger quantities and configurations than the Factory could ever hope to provide but crucially private industry was now sufficiently established to provide the solutions.

On 15 February 1917, Field-Marshal Haig, commander-in-chief of British Armies in France, wrote to the War Cabinet expressing his dismay at the state of the Air Service on the Continent. In September 1916, Haig had been promised a substantial increase in the number of technologically up-to-date fighting aeroplanes but these had failed to materialize prompting Haig to deliver the following stark warning:

> The position as regards fighting squadrons in particular is most serious. Our fighting machines will almost certainly be inferior in number and quite certainly in performance to those of the enemy. In view, therefore, of the marked increase in number and efficiency of the German aeroplanes, it appears that we cannot expect to gain supremacy in the air in April, and it is even possible that it may pass to the enemy.[67]

Contrary to contemporary popular belief, Haig himself was an early adopter of the potential of airpower to turn the tide on the Western Front and he gave every support possible to Hugh Trenchard's 1916 paper entitled Future Policy in the Air. In this document, Trenchard set out his doctrine of offensive fighter operations in German-occupied territory to prevent them from flying over British lines. Although costly in terms of machines and pilots, both men thought the price worth paying to establish military ascendancy on the

Western Front. However, the policy invited criticism that losses were due to the fact that British designed aeroplanes were technologically inferior to their opponents when, in reality, they were simply flying more sorties and operating at the limits of their endurance which ultimately increased the odds of fatalities.[68]

The War Office responded to Haig, on behalf of the Army Council, on 24 February 1917 acknowledging the delay but reminded the field-marshal that the programme of September 1916 was 'based to a considerable extent on the estimated value of unproved types of aeroplanes and engines', some of which turned out to be complete failures which resulting in delivery being approximately one month late.[69] The delay was deemed to be the result of difficulties of supply but also, rather intriguingly, the delivery method of aeroplanes to the Front. This was principally that the General Officer Commanding, Royal Flying Corps, Expeditionary Force, Hugh Trenchard, had insisted that aeroplanes should be sent to France by air instead of in packing cases:

> The result of compliance with this result has been that during every period of bad weather there has been congestion at the manufacturer's works, and consequent slackening of output. If more aeroplanes could be received by sea, supply would be more regular.[70]

The War Office concluded that it was hoped that the situation would be remedied in future following recent priority given to aircraft construction and the amalgamation of Naval and Military requirements in aeroplane supply. The Air Board believed it was necessary to add the following caveat regarding future aeroplane supply and wrote the following on 1 March 1917:

> The Board and the Ministry of Munitions are gradually taking over the duties; in connection with the design and supply of aircraft which have recently been assigned to them. It will be readily understood that the transfer of functions involved, and the amalgamation of certain Naval and Military Departments are processes which must be carried out with considerable care and deliberation if a breach of continuity in the supply of aircraft is to be avoided.[71]

Although the situation was indeed improving, there was still rather a long way to go to meet the military requirements and performance expectations for combat aircraft.

The British also relied heavily upon French manufactured aero-engines for the production of their own aeroplanes and there was an intricate interdependence between the Allies in relation to materiel supply. The British government had to place large orders for French-manufactured Clerget and Hispano-Suiza engines due to an inability to produce sufficient quantities under license in the UK. This was a situation for which Farnborough had been wrongly blamed.

In reality, the Air Board under the guidance of Lord Cowdray now considered the Royal Aircraft Factory in the same light as any private contractor. Designs prepared at Farnborough were under the same technical scrutiny as those from private concerns and work schedules were allocated through the Technical Department of the Air Board. In addition, repair work was also carried on together with miscellaneous urgent requirements. Major Baird, parliamentary secretary to the Air Board, reassured the House of Commons on 26 April 1917 that should it 'suddenly become necessary to produce one particular type or any of the hundred and one standards or things required for manufacture' time was saved by having this done at the Factory.[72] The perceived rivalries between Farnborough and the industry had finally been settled.

At a conference between the Air Board and representative of the French Aviation Services during February 1917, delays in delivery by French manufacturers were deemed to be largely due to the inability of the British to supply the raw materiels necessary to satisfy the contracts and enable production.[73] The supply situation was such that when new aircraft designs were ready, they were rushed to the Front to replace the out-of-date aeroplanes, but the pilots often did not have sufficient time to become accustomed before flying them in combat. The pace of technological development was such that it became increasingly difficult for military hardware to remain up-to-date. In reality, the problems associated with the production of new types of aircraft were of an extraordinary complexity that had never been previously undertaken or perfected, let alone during the pressures of wartime conditions. However, engines were still considered the greatest challenge to the progress of British aviation and the Air Board noted the following on 17 April 1917:

> The root difficulty to be overcome is that of the production of engines of the increased power required by the constant developments of aviation. It cannot be too clearly appreciated, for the purpose of understanding the

present situation, that with the exception of the Rolls-Royce engine, and in a lesser degree of the Beardmore engine, it is only to-day that we are reaching the stage of the production in substantial quantities of an engine, suitable for Fighter and Fighter-Reconnaissance aeroplanes, of British design and manufacture.[74]

The situation was not only further complicated by the diverging demands of the two services but also the realities of the time required between the submission of general performance requirements and the physical manufacture of an aero-engine.[75]

Nevertheless, although engines were indeed rightly recognized as an essential aircraft component, there was also a similarly critical, if far less glamourous materiel requirement that had failed to receive the necessary attention amongst the endless debates of 1916 and the reconstitution of the Air Board in early 1917.[76] The inability to secure the supply of high-quality aeroplane dope would threaten not only Britain's capability to retain the ascendency in the air war but also the future of Lloyd Geroge's coalition government.

6

'British Cellulose & Colonel Grant Morden'

Procurement practices (1915–18)

As the global conflict intensified, the science of supply, procurement and logistics became so increasingly intertwined as to render military and political success inseparable – a phenomenon Herbert Asquith and his Liberal government found out to their cost in May 1915. Although historians remain undecided as to the precise causes that resulted in the fall of Asquith's Liberal government and the subsequent creation of the first coalition, the Shell Crisis, in which a shortage of high-explosive artillery shells reduced British military combat effectiveness, undoubtedly played an important part. However, it also had a significant effect on the British aircraft industry and the future conduct of the air war.[1] By June 1915, the British government had created the Ministry of Munitions, which assumed responsibility for all pending and existing armaments contracts. David Lloyd George was appointed Minister of Munitions with responsibility for the effective coordination of the production and distribution of all ordnance critical to the war effort.[2] The powers of the newly appointed minister, as stated in the Ministry of Munitions Bill of 3 June 1915, were as follows:

> The Minister of Munitions shall have such powers and duties in relation to the supply of munitions for the present war as may be conferred on him by His Majesty in Council, and His Majesty may also, if he considers it expedient that, in connection with the supply of munitions, any powers and duties of a Government Department or authority, whether conferred by statue or otherwise, should be transferred to, or exercised or performed concurrently by, the Minister of Munitions, by Order in Council make the necessary provision for the purpose, and any Order made in pursuance of

this section may include any supplement provisions which appear necessary for the purpose of giving full effect to the order.[3]

The new Ministry effectively enabled the war to be conducted on an ever-increasing industrial scale. A Parliamentary Bill had already passed on 10 March 1915, whereby manufacturers, deprived of their usual markets, were compelled under the Defence of the Realm Act to adapt their factories to satisfy the materiel demands of the war effort, but the Munitions Bill was a step still further in the government control of production.[4]

However, the influence of the Ministry of Munitions was not just confined to the UK. Branches were also established throughout the dominions to exploit the manufacturing capabilities of the British Empire and optimize production output. In Canada, for example, the Shell Committee, which had been responsible for placing contracts in North America on behalf of the British government, was superseded by the Imperial Munitions Board in November 1915. Following reports of ongoing inefficiencies in the production of munitions in Canada, Robert Brand, First Baron Brand of Eydon, was tasked with the critical role of coordinating and improving Anglo-Canadian relations.[5]

The adverse criticism within Canada itself pertaining to contract procurement practices had resulted in demands for a parliamentary enquiry into the method of operation and administration even before the Ministry of Munitions had been established. The Imperial authorities believed that such an investigation would only serve to hinder the progress of the newly created administration, and on 7 March 1916 the Canadian prime minister, Sir Robert Borden, refused a motion by the leader of the opposition, Sir Wilfred Laurier, for the appointment of a Parliamentary Committee to enquire into alleged malpractices in the awarding of contracts in both Canada and the United States. Borden justified his refusal by arguing that the Shell Committee were acting on behalf of the imperial government and that the funds involved were also Imperial and not solely within Canadian jurisdiction.

The demands for a parliamentary enquiry were reinvigorated later that same month when definitive charges were made involving the award of certain contracts by Colonel Allison. The first was a contract for the supply of fuses issued on 19 June 1915 to the International Arms and

Fuse Company, the second fuse contract was issued on the same date to the American Ammunition Company, the third contract for cartridge cases was issued on 16 July 1916 to the Edwards Valve Company of Chicago, and the final contract was issued to the St. Louis-based Providence Chemical Company for the supply of petric acid. The evidence became impossible for Borden to continue to ignore, and he authorized the appointment of a Royal Commission, which began hearing evidence on the 19 April 1916. The Royal Commission split the charges into four separate categories upon which to base their forthcoming investigation:

1. A general accusation that Canadian manufacturers had not received sufficiently preferential treatment in the placing and award of contracts.
2. An indictment of the companies to which the fuse contracts had been awarded which stated they were of 'mushroom' growth and both financially and commercially unsound.
3. The accusation that excessive prices had been paid.
4. Contracts had been awarded for which commissions had been received and there was an insinuation that General Hughes had intervened in the work of the Shell Committee to influence the award of said contracts.[6]

Of the first three charges it was concluded that the Shell Committee could not be subject to adverse criticism, and that although minor errors were believed to have been made, these were considered acceptable in relation to the pressures of ensuring deliveries were made on time.

In relation to the fourth charge the Commission considered that they had established beyond all doubt that neither General Sam Hughes, the Canadian Minister of Militia and Defence, nor the Shell Committee received any commission or unduly influenced the awarding of contracts. Hughes himself had reminded the Commission that he was not responsible to the British War Office for what occurred in relation to the Shell Committee nor accountable to the Canadian Parliament for expenditure, a loophole through which all responsibility for ethical governance could be both conveniently and technically relinquished.[7] The Canadian war budget was introduced by Finance Minister William White, on 5 February 1916 and levied a 25 per cent tax on war profits. Although the new taxes were naturally unpopular with industrialists, they were only expected to yield about $50,000,000, whilst the ordinary revenues were still inadequate to meet a growing war expenditure in excess of $250,000,000. Demand for munitions necessitated rapid expansion of the war department and consequently opportunities for those tempted by corruption became almost inevitable.[8]

As such, the Commission were scathing of the conduct of Colonel Allison, who in two instances had either received commissions or promises of commissions, and this reflected badly on General Hughes as he was his close personal friend. It also came to the attention of the media that Hughes had recommended to Lord Kitchener on 21 September 1914 that a special purchasing committee, comprised of both him and Allison, should be established representing the interests of the British government in Canada and the United States. This suggestion was ultimately not acted upon, but aroused speculation that the two officers were planning to benefit directly from the awarding of munitions contracts.[9]

Nevertheless, whilst the manufacturing powerhouse of the United States remained neutral, the Allied powers were effectively in the absurd positions of bidding against each other in the North American market and thus creating plentiful opportunities for former businessmen like Allison to take advantage and improve their personal financial position. As early as October 1914 Allison's activities had drawn the attention of Sir Cecil Spring Rice, the British ambassador to the United States, who warned Lord Grey, the British foreign secretary, of corrupt purchases and rumours of collusion between Allison and Hughes. This prompted Borden to telegram George Perley, the acting Canadian high commissioner in London, to 'unofficially' warn the British Foreign Office against any business dealings which involved Allison. The 'off-the-record' correspondence was primarily due to the awkward and potentially damaging nature of disturbing the special relationship that existed between Allison and Hughes and subsequent effect upon recruitment of Canadian troops for deployment overseas.[10]

Allison was also involved in the procurement of explosives for the Russian military, but Borden's warning appears to have been headed by the British, who were highly suspicious of his activities surrounding North American contracts. On 25 January 1915, Walter Long, the Secretary of State to the Colonies, sent an encrypted cypher to Prince Arthur, governor-general of the Dominion of Canada, following concern by the Russian government regarding the validity of recent contracts placed with Allison's Canadian syndicate for the manufacture of explosives. Long concluded:

> War Office will in future place contracts for munitions of war on behalf of Russian Government in United States, and as regards Canada orders will be placed through Purchasing Commission here.[11]

The acquisition of Russian contracts, without first passing through the scrutiny process of the authorized purchasing committees, raised concerns amongst the Allies and encouraged the British in particular to closely monitor Allison's activities. Foreign Office correspondence even expressed regret that there was not a method to 'extinguishing him permanently' once they were convinced that Allison was taking personal commission on behalf of the Russian government.[12]

The Canadian Commission of Inquiry eventually proved that Colonel Allison had negotiated a half interest in the shares of a promoter in an investment organization called the American Ammunition Company Group. Mr B.F. Youkum, with the assistance of Allison, had secured a commission of £200,000 in a fuse contract which was granted to an American Ammunition Company by the Shell Committee. *The Times* Canadian correspondent reported that the facts:

> Partially substantiate the charges made in Parliament, and involve Colonel Allison, whose close personal relations with Sir Sam Hughes, Minister of Militia, are the subject of criticism. There is not a tittle of evidence, however, that the Shell Committee or Sir Sam Hughes had any knowledge of these transactions.[13]

Nevertheless, confidence in the transparency of the institution had been greatly shaken, particularly regarding war profiteering and the capabilities of such syndicates to be able to physically manufacture and deliver the promised products in the quantities that were ordered. Despite the disgrace of Colonel Allison, subsequent Canadian interest in the manufacture of aeroplane dope and preferential contract agreements were to result in a scandal of even greater magnitude.

At the beginning of the conflict, it was brought to the attention of the War Office that Britain did not possess a domestically produced supply of cellulose acetate, the essential ingredient required in the manufacture of aircraft dope. British aircraft manufacturers had to obtain the dope from either the Usines du Rhône factory in France or from the Cellonite Company at Basel in Switzerland, and securing supply became increasingly difficult as the war progressed. The War Office only began to obtain larger quantities from the Usines du Rhône in late 1915 despite reports that the French product was of quality compared to that manufactured by the Swiss.[14]

Although the shortage of dope supply was obvious before the outbreak of war, the Directorate of Military Aeronautics did not issue tenders for the domestic manufacture of 100 tonnes of cellulose acetate until July 1915, which specifically stipulated that production should be undertaken in England. The official history states that the only tenderer for the contract was Dr Dreyfus of the Basel-based Cellonite Company and upon the award of contract he reserved the right to manufacture the first fifty tonnes in Switzerland before transferring production to the UK.

Dreyfus was awarded the tender and opened negotiations for the purchase of the Safety Celluloid Company's Work in Willesden, but the capacity of that factory proved to be insufficient. Following formal signature of contract, Dreyfus suggested that it would be difficult to raise capital for the enterprise unless it was guaranteed against war taxation. After failing to secure adequate reassurances of loans from the government for the new enterprise, Dreyfus returned to Switzerland, where he was approached by a variety of potential financiers who had previously failed in the manufacture of cellulose acetate in the UK.

Following negotiation, and amidst all the controversy surrounding the conduct of the air war and the administration of the Royal Flying Corps, the British Cellulose and Chemical Manufacturing Company was quietly incorporated on 18 March 1916 and the government finally committed themselves to the erection of a manufacturing facility for the production of cellulose acetate by means of the Dreyfus process. A site was eventually chosen at Spondon, Derbyshire, and construction began in August 1916 much to the delight of the local press who confidently proclaimed the new factory would 'give employment to some thousands of workpeople'.[15] The huge expansion in the aeronautical programme also necessitated the construction of other specialist factories for the manufacture of ball-bearings and machine-guns and these were appearing in towns and cities all over the country.[16]

With the government now committed, the promoters of the new company once again approached the War Office to secure exemption from excess profits duty, a clause that Dreyfus was particularly adamant upon. Consequently, as the production of cellulose acetate was now recognized to be of such crucial importance to the air war, the government reluctantly agreed to provide assistance in November 1916 following prolonged negotiations that had already further delayed production. The War Office agreed that the capital expenditure incurred upon the new factory during wartime was to be refunded to the company 'up to a maximum equal to excess profits duty actually charged in respect of each year's working during five years from the company's foundation.'[17] This was on condition that reasonable prices were quoted, orders during the war would be exclusively taken from the government, and that the government would retain priority over manufacture as required even after the war.[18] In effect, British Cellulose would benefit from an excellent arrangement, wherein they would receive public funds through priority contracts no matter how they chose to operate the company, safe in the knowledge that they were guaranteed exemption from any excess profits.

No doubt aware of the preferential treatment received by British Cellulose at Spondon, other chemical manufacturers such as the Cellon Company and the United Alkali Company offered to erect factories in England at their own expense for the purpose of manufacturing cellulose acetate. The Admiralty were particularly anxious to extend the potential sources of supply, not only to ensure sufficient competition but also for quality control purposes due to concerns with the performance of the Swiss product manufactured in Basel. Nevertheless, the War Office persisted with the policy of providing exclusivity to British Cellulose despite the fact that the new company was unable to deliver any domestically manufactured acetate at all until April 1917 and nothing in sufficient quantity until July 1918.[19]

This frustrating delay no doubt influenced the government's decision to transfer responsibility for the administration of the new concern to the Department of Aeronautical Supplies at the Ministry of Munitions, who took over responsibility for the new company. One of their first interventions was to cancel the original financial agreement whilst raising loans on account of capital expenditure and placing direct contracts with the company in the region of three million pounds sterling. *Flight Magazine* reported:

> Further than this, the Ministry took what appears to be the extreme step of prohibiting the import of cellulose acetate by other companies who were under contract to supply it, and refused all offers made by others to manufacture it in England. This amounts to presenting the British Cellulose Company, which is the child of Basel concern, with a complete monopoly of the manufacture of cellulose acetate, a monopoly which has not the saving grace of a monopoly that shall be able to supply the needs of the State.[20]

Aircraft industry demand for cellulose acetate was indeed acute but such extreme favouritism on behalf of the government naturally aroused suspicion. The process was openly criticized in the Fifth Report of the Select Committee on National Expenditure, which ultimately brought the situation to the attention of the public and politicians.

The National Expenditure Committee was appointed on 19 February 1918 to scrutinize how efficiently public funds authorized by the government were allocated in the pursuance of national priorities, in particular those linked to the success of the global conflict. The jurisdiction of the Committee was as follows:

> To make recommendations in regard to the form of Public Accounts, the system of control within the Departments and by the Treasury, and the procedure of this House in relation to Supply and Appropriation, so as to source more effective control by Parliament over Public Expenditure.[21]

In October 1917, the Sub-Committee attached to the Ministry of Munitions had become intrigued to find that the supply of cellulose acetate had been entrusted to a single manufacturer. This firm had also been guaranteed a refund from excessive profit duties on their entire, and not inconsiderable, capital expenditure throughout the duration of the war. Even more startling was the fact that their deliveries had proved unsatisfactory, and all other offers of manufacture from private concerns had been refused. There were definitely, in the opinion of the Expenditure Committee, serious questions that needed to be answered.

Unsurprisingly, the peculiar circumstances surrounding the incorporation of the British Cellulose and Chemical Manufacturing Company was soon discussed in the House of Commons on 1 August 1918, immediately following the publication of the Report of the Committee on National Expenditure the previous month. The Conservative Member for the City of London, Sir Frederick Banbury, conceded that cellulose acetates were 'not words which would attract a considerable audience in the House of Commons', but he implored the members present to scrutinize what he believed to be a grave misappropriation of public finances.[22]

Sir Frederick, a successful stockbroker and businessman in his own right, noted that any essential ingredient required in the manufacture of aeroplanes would be most attractive to potential investors who would have undoubtedly recognized the potential of this new technology in securing profitable returns. He was particularly keen to draw the attention of the House to the involvement of Sir Trevor Dawson, managing director of Vickers Limited, and Colonel Walter Grant Morden, on the Staff of the Canadian Minister of Militia, Sir Sam Hughes. Colonel Grant Morden was a Canadian financier and shipping magnate of dubious reputation and was responsible for making the initial approaches to the Assistant Financial Secretary of the War Office.

Characteristically, the proposal to exclusively manufacture cellulose acetate by the Dreyfus method on behalf of the government was on the proviso that the company was guaranteed exemption from excess taxation for a period of five years.[23] Banbury explained:

> Sir Trevor Dawson contemplated raising capital to the extent of £120,000, and that is a figure which ought to be borne in mind, because the Report goes on to show that something more than £3,500,000 represented the share capital of the company. We are accustomed here to talk of millions as if they meant nothing at all, but as the Chancellor of the Exchequer told us earlier this evening, they are a very important matter, and when you have a company which states that all that is needed to meet the requirements of the War Office is £120,000, and, afterwards, its demands go into millions, it surely is desirable there should be some explanation.[24]

For reasons unstated, the War Office then applied to the Treasury on behalf of the new concern for permission to refund the capital amount expended on machinery up to a maximum equivalent to the excess profits duty. Banbury was at a loss to ascertain what authority any government department had to put forward such a request to the Treasury on behalf of any individual or company seeking direct exemption from a taxation that had been approved by the House of Commons. Despite the irregularity, the request was subsequently granted on 3 June 1916 following assurance from the War Office that such measures were essential to the war effort.

The Sub-Committee on National Expenditure were convinced that the influence of Sir Trevor Dawson was instrumental in securing this exemption and that correspondence between Vickers and the Chancellor of the Exchequer, Bonar Law, had been such that the Contracts Branch considered the application for exemption on the basis of *jose jugée*.[25] But if the manufacture of cellulose acetate was indeed critical to Britain's campaign in the air, then what was the reason for the substantial delay in manufacture? Banbury wished the government to explain:

> Why should a Swiss gentleman – I do not doubt a very excellent man – be picked out to be given what I shall show was practically a monopoly in one of the most important ingredients necessary for making aeroplanes and be allowed to make a big profit even in these times which is not nominally subject to any Excess Profits Tax?[26]

Dreyfus and his investors promised in November 1915 that supplies would be forthcoming within a month, but no manufacture had taken place prior to the registration of the new company on 18 March 1916 which was recorded as having a nominal capital of £4,000 split into 160,000 sixpenny shares. Half of these sixpenny shares were held by Dr Dreyfus, an eighth by Vickers Limited, and the remainder by the Prudential Trust of Canada. The Canadian government had been actively encouraging industrial research and financial investment in armament manufacture not only in response to the immediate demands raised by the present conflict, but also to ensure that the industrial resources of the country were able to compete in international markets once the war was over.[27]

The structure of the nominal capital did not in itself cause undue concern, but in November 1916 questions were raised when British Cellulose issued £120,000 debentures without prior permission from the Treasury.[28] By October 1917, the firm applied to the Treasury to form a new company, this time with a share capital comprised of 2,000,000 £1 shares and a debenture issued at 7 per cent of the same amount, which this naturally started to raise suspicion. Between March 1916 and October 1917, the company had grown from a nominal capital of £4,000 in 6d. shares and 120,000 debentures to a nominal capital of £4,000,000 split between £2,000,000 in £1 shares and £2,000,000 in debentures. This increase in valuation had occurred without a single delivery of any domestically manufactured cellulose acetate from the factory at Spondon which was already exempt from excess profit duties. This was an extraordinary situation in which the government appeared complicit in a business venture that looked extremely profitable for the investors without any direct benefit to the country or the war effort.

Worse was yet to come however when in March 1918 a private company was registered under the name of the British Cellulose and Chemical Manufacturing Parent Company. This new entity recorded a nominal capital of £3,500,000 in £1 shares, of which only £450,000 were paid for in cash. So, the key question on everybody's lips was what had happened to the remaining £3,050,000 and it was here that the scandal really started to break. To dispose of the remainder of the capital in this new company the existing shareholders were to receive 14½ £1 shares for every old 6d. they had previously held. Effectively the original in the £4,000 investment of 1915 was now worth £2,320,000 without a penny ever having been spent on machinery or manufacturing. Banbury explained to the House:

> What took place was this, that gullible people, like myself, had taken these shares, and our money would go – what for? To provide new work, new plant, or new materiel? Not at all, but to put the money into the pockets of these gentlemen who for £4,000 received £2,320,000, always supposing they could sell those shares at par. I say that a more discreditable transaction has never been brought to the knowledge of this House. I do not know this of my own authority, but I am informed that a child company has been issued in America, and one of the statements in the prospectus there has been that the shares are very valuable on account of the monopoly given by the British Government here in England.[29]

The Spectator considered the scandal as a 'sad example of the muddle, waste, and inefficiency caused by lack of organization in the offices concerned' but the negligence extended far beyond the Ministry of Munitions and the War Office.[30]

The MP for Hexham, Mr Richard Holt, had no 'doubt that the men who made those promises knew they were false when they made them' and that the performance of the company 'was so far short of the promise that no person could possibly believe that the men who made those promises supposed at the time that they could fulfil them'.[31] But who were these individuals and why, despite the fact that their business activities had been under government surveillance for some time, had they been gifted such an extraordinarily lucrative monopoly?

For context, the original 6d. shares had become worth £14.10s, and despite the repeatedly staunch defence of the British Cellulose Company's activities in Parliament by the Conservative member for Hammersmith, Sir William Bull, there was no doubt in many minds that something was fundamentally amiss. Some of the key individuals were acquainted through the supply of armaments to the Russian military in 1915. The Canadian Minister of Munitions, General Hughes, had been asked to give reassurances that a contract for two-million shells between the Russians and the Canadian Car and Foundry Company would be delivered on time, whilst Vickers were under scrutiny for failing to supply a quantity of ammunition and guns. Vickers were already involved in an ongoing dispute with the Russian government regarding the Cruiser 'Rurik'. They had been commissioned to construct the vessel and, following numerous modifications, delivered it some two years late in June 1909 – a delay for which the Russian government had withheld final payment.[32] His Russian Imperial Highness, the Grand Duke Sergé, believed that the failure to deliver on contract promises had put the Russian military in a perilous position.[33]

In early 1915, the business dealings of Vickers had come to the attention of the Secretary of State for Foreign Affairs, Sir Edward Grey, via the British ambassador to the United States, Sir Cecil Spring Rice. On 5 May 1915, Spring Rice had written to Grey from Washington, noting he had received reports that Sir Trevor Dawson of Vickers was in regular contact with the disgraced Canadian businessman, Colonel Allison, and he was concerned that information regarding armaments contracts may well be passed onto the enemy:

> I am informed that Trevor Dawson is seeing a great deal of Allison, who again is said to be seeing a lady who is in German pay. As a consequence,

particulars as to contracts may well be in German hands. Is Dawson under the orders of H.M. Government, and if so, is he instructed to do business with Allison, whose reputation here is bad?[34]

The suspicion that information was being passed to the enemy through loose lips was not as fanciful as it might first appear. An agent of Messrs. Vickers, Captain de la Force, had previously ruined a contract for the supply of rifles with a Brazilian manufacturer following similar tactless behaviour. Consequently, Grey drafted a memo to Lord Kitchener recounting the episode and stating that de la Force had:

> Wrecked very promising negotiations by his indiscretions and then refused to leave Rio because, apparently, Sir Trevor Dawson's instructions to him to do so conflicted with instructions sent to him by his other employers at New York – these other employers being, I am given to understand, no other than 'Colonel' Allison's 'Syndicate'.[35]

Grey explained that Allison and his associates had done the British government harm on many occasions despite previous attempts to curb his influences. He also recognized that Messrs. Vickers had, 'by their employment of a person of bad reputation connected with Allison', ruined chances of obtaining arms of the greatest importance to the war effort.[36] There was genuine concern before the United States entered the conflict that German agents operating in New York intended purchasing American factories so that contracts with the Allied powers could then be cancelled. Dawson was himself involved in negotiations for the acquisition of the Bethlehem Steel Company to ensure manufacture was secured and should have been well aware of the need to maintain security.[37]

Knowledge of behaviour of these key individuals in relation to Russian military contracts should have raised alarms with the relevant authorities regarding their involvement in the manufacture of cellulose acetate, but this appears not to have been the case. However, the Sub-Committee on National Expenditure were also suspicious that not only were the delivery promises exaggerated but also that the reports of capital sums expended by British Cellulose on plant and equipment had been similarly inflated. The report considered evidence submitted by the company that claimed the expenditure for construction of a plant capable of producing six tonnes of cellulose acetate per week had cost £350,000 and that additional equipment for the manufacture of up to forty tonnes per week would cost in the region of £1,000,000. The established chemical companies, United Alkali Company and Courtaulds Limited, whose offers to make the same product had been previously rejected by the Ministry of Munitions, had also been asked to give estimated capital costs of their proposed schemes. United Alkali believed that they could construct a complete installation capable of manufacturing at least four to five tonnes per week for approximately £60,000, whilst Courtaulds estimated that a plant producing forty tonnes per week, exclusive of the acquisition of buildings and land, could be put into operation for as little as £150,000.[38] Something, somewhere, in the quantities surveyed by British Cellulose appeared to be rather inaccurate indeed.

In his speech to the House of Commons on 1 August 1918, Mr Holt became increasingly critical of the British Cellulose contract and was determined to draw the attention of those present to the composition of the company's management and shareholders:

> Who are the people who started it? The persons were Sir Trevor Dawson, a director of Vickers, Limited, assisted by Colonel Grant Morden, who is described as being on the staff of the Canadian Minister of Militia. Who was the Canadian Minister of Militia at that time? He was a gentleman called Colonel Sir Samuel Hughes, a person of the worst reputation in Canada, and who happens to be one of the shareholders in the £14 10s. for 6d. transaction.[39]

Holt was particularly critical of the conduct of Sir Trevor Dawson in misleading the government about the capacity for British Cellulose to supply, and, quite apart from the financial nature of the concern, he further considered holding false expectations of such a crucial ingredient of war materiel irreprehensible. Holt concluded that 'persons who do that sort of thing ought to be looked upon with a very great deal of suspicion' and that 'serious steps should be taken by the Government to prevent persons implicated' in the contract from having any further influence over acquisitions.[40]

Holt's assertions would appear to have been justified. Dr Dreyfus had originally promised in November 1915 he would be able to deliver supplies of cellulose acetate within one month and a total of 100 tonnes by August 1916. Nevertheless, a year later deliveries had failed to materialize despite

Colonel Grant Morden confidently stating that the new firm was in a position to manufacture at as little as one week's notice. Despite the ongoing delay Sir Trevor Dawson was called to defend the company's performance, and he argued on 15 February 1916 that the firm was the only concern in England capable of producing the required quantities of cellulose acetate, but no supplies of the materiel were actually manufactured in the UK until April 1917.

Responsibility for Aeronautical Supplies was taken over by the Ministry of Munitions in February 1917, at which time supplies of cellulose acetate were still being obtained entirely from abroad. Some were indeed received from the Dreyfus plant in Basel, but the majority continued to be supplied from the Usines du Rhône as this was still considered to be the superior product.[41] By this date some of the principal British dope manufacturers, such as the British Emaillite Company and Cellon, were desperate to obtain as much of the French product as possible and were endeavouring to privately introduce cellulose acetate manufactured to the du Rhône specification to England.

In fact, both of these British manufacturers had grown significantly since the outbreak of the war in order to meet the increased demand for aeroplane dope. In November 1915, the British Emaillite Company's new factory at Stonebridge Park, London, was working to full capacity, manufacturing dopes compliant with government specifications and proudly advertising that 'in all grades of Emaillite the proportion of Tetrachlorethane has been reduced to the lowest possible limit'.[42] The Cellon Company had to take on additional premises in Richmond in 1917, when their Stratford factory could no longer meet the growing industry demand for their products. However, these manufacturers would become effectively redundant without an adequate supply of cellulose acetate, and it is little wonder that they were prepared to take the responsibility for securing sufficient supply into their own hands.[43]

The slow progress at the British Cellulose factory at Spondon was further exacerbated in July 1917. A temporary shortage of coal had reduced the supply of imports from the French Usines du Rhône factory and consequently the stock of aircraft dope held in the UK became particularly precarious. Dr Dreyfus argued that the reason for the delay at Spondon was due to a lack of understanding on behalf of the Ministry of Munitions regarding the complexity of the operation and the need for additional government financial support. A reluctant government reopened new negotiations with British Cellulose in early 1918 concerning a guarantee of quantities on all future orders.

The claim of insufficient government support was slightly misleading as Sir Auckland Geddes, Minister of National Service, had already made provision for the immediate availability of 2,000 builders to undertake necessary extensions and alterations at Spondon in a memorandum to the War Office in October 1917.[44] Nevertheless, by June 1918 the company announced that a lack of financial resources meant that they were unable to continue manufacturing at Derby unless ongoing contracts and a revision of existing price structures could be quickly placed by the Ministry:

> An agreement was reached at the end of the month under which the original concession regarding the refund of excess profits for five years was revoked with all rights and obligations, and any claims to increases of price under the existing contracts were withdrawn. On the other hand, the Ministry undertook to make loans at interest to the Company to cover a proportion of their approved war capital expenditure, and placed contracts with them of the value of some £3,000,000 on the basis of cost plus a fixed sum for profit and a bonus for economical production.[45]

This new agreement ensured that, despite poor performance, the Ministry of Munitions was entirely dependent upon British Cellulose for Britain's supply of cellulose acetate. In March 1918, the Ministry also prohibited the import of cellulose acetate even from those companies with which they had existing orders, and all other offers to manufacture the product in the UK were categorically refused.

The previous inability of the company to meet even their own performance targets makes this decision even more difficult to understand, but the persistent reports from the aircraft industry regarding the sub-standard quality of the finished product make it utterly incomprehensible. At the time the Ministry decided to grant the monopoly to British Cellulose, officials at the Royal Aircraft Factory, the Technical Branch and the Inspection Department were consistently reporting that the quality of the Spondon product remained sub-standard. If the shortage of cellulose acetate had not been so acute it is likely that mass rejections would have occurred due to persistent variability of the finished materiel, which required careful quality control that caused additional expense whilst all the time actually slowing down the manufacture of standard dope.[46]

After extensive investigation the Select Committee on National Expenditure came to a series of conclusions and recommendations following examination of the evidence. The Committee believed that the government relationship with British Cellulose had remained 'eminently unsatisfactory' until the end of June 1918 before the original agreement concerning the guarantee to refund all capital expenditure had been cancelled. Up until this date there had been no apparent limit to the expenditure which had been incurred by the company for the execution of government orders and no obvious supervision over factory extensions, economy of manufacture, or the quality of the finished product. However, the Committee conceded that 'assistance to a quite unusual degree had been granted by the government to the company, and must continue to be so granted, in order that supplies may be obtained which are essential for the conduct of the war.'[47] The precise reasons for this preferential treatment would later cause further public outrage.

Despite some improvement in relations following the cancellation of the agreement to refund future capital expenditure, British Cellulose still possessed the complete monopoly over manufacture which remained unfavourable to the Ministry of Munitions. In reality, contracts whereby payments are based upon cost are always unsatisfactory, particularly when there was neither supervision over the process nor any financial comparison available from alternative suppliers to ensure value for money.[48] The Committee concluded that the fixed rate of profit was 'based upon a cost which includes materiels at a quite artificial price and is the same whether those materiels are obtained elsewhere or are made by the company themselves'.[49] This was particularly concerning as the raw materiels accounted for between 50 to 75 per cent of the estimated final cost of the finished article. The Committee provided the following summary of findings:

> In view of these considerations, the Committee are strongly of the opinion that the ownership of the factory should immediately be taken over by the Government, and the works completed as far as is necessary, and managed by them. A Technical Committee should be appointed to consider the best use of the works, and to advise upon the necessary steps for the completion

of the factory and its efficient management. The compensation payable should be determined on the same lines as in the case of other properties taken over for war purposes.[50]

The Committee believed that the branch of the Ministry best qualified to take over management at Spondon was the Explosives Department as they had experience of the chemicals under manufacture and qualified personnel familiar with the daily running of such factories. The Committee further concluded:

> At the same time, it should be considered whether an alternative arrangement should not now be made for the manufacture of cellulose acetate in association with the Usines du Rhône. The quantity could not be large in view of the existing works but should be sufficient to enable a comparison to be made between the costs of manufacture. An investigation should be made in order that any portion of the British Cellulose Works, which if not too advanced should be immediately discontinued, and any plant which might prove serviceable to the other manufacturers be diverted to them.[51]

The Sub-Committee were eager to encourage alternative methods of manufacturing cellulose acetate by means of substituting the most expensive ingredients, such as acetic anhydride, to both reduce costs and speed up production. It was also believed that considerable economies could be achieved by replacing methyl acetate with ethyl formate to eliminate any need for imported chemicals. The Royal Aircraft Factory had already been asked to undertake experiments of this kind in the production of a pigmented dope to determine viability.

Ultimately, the situation had exposed the potential flaws in the British procurement system. The determination of the Supply Branches in obtaining critical war materiel without consulting the associated Finance Branches of the Ministry of Munitions had resulted in a situation whereby costs continued to spiral out of control whilst delivery of the finished product remained unsatisfactory or, indeed, non-existent. In addition, capital expenditure was undertaken on the development of production facilities in isolation of the Munitions Works Board, which had little or no input into the structural details and associated costs. The Committee proposed a revision of the procurement system to ensure that departments interested solely in securing output would first have to consult the relevant financial authorities to determine both economy and necessity of the production programme:

> A private monopoly in a key industry cannot be instituted at Government expense or with Government assistance without arousing criticism and, if only for this reason, the Supply Branch would have been better advised to have secured the full authorisation of the Finance Department at every step in their negotiations.[52]

Nevertheless, the report continued to cause outrage long after it was published, which concluded in a public enquiry and revelations involving some of the most senior politicians in the UK.

7

'No departmental favouritism'

The dope scandal (1918–19)

Before the inevitable public enquiry into the affairs of the British Cellulose Company began in earnest during autumn 1918, concerted efforts were made in the House of Commons to defend the reputation of the enterprise, and Sir William Bull remained the principal proponent of the Spondon-based concern.[1] He reminded the House of Commons of 5 August 1918 that following the publication of the Sub-Committees report on 23 July the Company wrote directly to the Ministry of Munitions asking for a full investigation into the charges contained therein.[2] Unsurprisingly, the parliamentary secretary for the Ministry of Munitions was only too happy to accommodate such a request and effectively absolve the Department of any wrongdoing.

As part of this compromise, a letter was sent to the press requesting that they suspend judgement into the allegations made against the Company and the conduct of the Ministry of Munitions pending the forthcoming public enquiry. The majority of British newspapers agreed to await the outcome of the official investigation but the Liberal *Daily Chronicle*, previously supportive of the radical wing of the party under Lloyd George, broke ranks and published an article on 5 August concerning the affairs of the British Cellulose Company in defiance of the previous request to abstain judgement. Bull was furious and, suspecting foul play, pointed the finger for the misdemeanour firmly in the direction of the chairman of the Sub-Committee on National Expenditure, Sir Godfrey Collins. Bull believed that Collins had encouraged the publication of specific extracts from the report by 'sending a typewritten letter, signed by his own hand, to various newspapers, underlining in blue pencil certain passages dealing with the affairs of the British Cellulose Company'.³ Collins naturally refuted the allegation and stated that it was common practice for the salient points of larger reports to be marked prior to circulation to ensure accuracy when reported in the press and reminded the House that 'in so doing I was not doing anything unusual nor was I attempting to cast blame or otherwise on the persons mentioned in the paragraphs'.⁴

Nevertheless, Bull continued to argue that those connected with the company had been treated incredibly unfairly, and they deserved the opportunity to defend themselves in front of an independent tribunal, during which their evidence would be taken upon oath:

> The gentlemen forming this company thought they were doing an extremely patriotic work indeed in getting this acetate of cellulose into this country. It is an extraordinary invention, first invented by an Englishman named Cross about forty years ago, but it was only a laboratory triumph, and it was not until a few years ago that some Swiss chemists named Dreyfus succeeded in turning it into a valuable commodity, which will become more and more valuable as the years go on.⁵

Bull contended that the British government owed a great deal of gratitude to Colonel Grant Morden, who had the foresight to recognize that cellulose acetate would be required in ever increasing quantities by the British aircraft industry as the war progressed and subsequently introduced the Dreyfus method of manufacture to the UK.

In fact, Bull and Colonel Grant Morden were acquainted through the British Commonwealth Union and were both present when the organization was established in December 1916.⁶ This institution not only was protectionist but also aimed to create a strong business-focused group in Parliament, so it is no surprise that Bull should be using his skill as a solicitor in the defence of British Cellulose. Notwithstanding that there was indeed some truth in the fact that Grant Morden had undoubtedly spotted a niche business opportunity – an ability that unquestionably secured his post-war appointment to the Empire Resources Development Committee, which was set up to explore how the state might 'embark upon a policy of engaging for profit, either directly or indirectly, in the establishment and conduct of productive and distributive enterprises'.⁷ The Empire Resources Development Committee were at great pains to point out that they had no desire to discourage private enterprise through their scheme, but Morden's experience with British Cellulose would have undoubtedly been of considerable interest.

The War Office had originally believed that a quarter of a tonne of cellulose acetate per day would be ample to satisfy the requirements for the manufacture of aeroplanes for the Royal Flying Corps. They were also confident that such quantities could easily be secured from foreign suppliers.[8] However, as the aviation services expanded so did the demand for aeroplanes and their constituent component parts until cellulose acetate was required in quantities of between sixty and eighty tonnes per week by August 1918, or approximately ten times the original estimate. There can be little doubt that this original underestimation by the War Office resulted in the continued use of tetrachlorethane as a solvent in aviation dope and the consequent worker deaths and injuries associated with its application.

However, Bull exploited the original government miscalculation to argue that the growth of the company, and its subsequent worth, was not in the least surprising considering the unprecedented increase in demand. He also sought to reassure the honourable members present that all the capital raised had been directly reinvested in the expansion of the Derby works and consequently no profits had been made:

> Their works near Derby are a mile in length and half a mile broad, and they have been put up at a cost of approximately three millions of money. That has been done absolutely at the urgent request of the Government and the particular Department, who have again and again begged that they should turn out more and more of this peculiar composition.[9]

Nevertheless, despite Bull's impassioned and professional defence, it was not enough to sufficiently quell the suspicions of what appeared to many members of the House as a blatant case of war profiteering. In fact, it is likely Colonel Grant Morden had not only identified the potential profit in the manufacture of cellulose during the conflict but had also realized the value in its continued production in the post-war economy. Cellulose was a key component in the manufacture of synthetic silks for the fashion industry and was also vitally important to the increasingly popular motion picture business as a component in unbreakable films. After all, if he could persuade the British government to fund a production facility at the tax-payers expense that had an immediate post-war market beyond aviation, who was he to try and dissuade them?

If the Spondon factory be perfected in the manufacture of artificial silks whilst immune from excess profit duty, then it would ensure lucrative operation once the war contract necessities for aeroplane dope had long expired. This business opportunity had also been identified by the Bank of England, which assisted in the post-war reconversion of the company into British Celanese in the early 1920s precisely for that purpose. Through this investment, Britain secured a foothold in the global emerging acetate rayon industry and initially enjoyed substantial returns.[10] One can only wonder whether someone in the corridors of Whitehall had realized this all along and were quietly weathering the political storm to reap the profits at the cessation of the war.

However, this was certainly not the case in 1918, when Frederick Kellaway, the Parliamentary Secretary to the Ministry of Munitions, announced in the House of Commons on 5 August that he had agreed with the Minister of Munitions that they would immediately set up 'a strong competent body to examine the three recommendations' which the Select Committee has previously made and report the findings at their earliest possible convenience.[11] The apparent urgency reassured those members who wished to qualify the extent of the supposed injustice in the short term, but they would have to wait at least another year and after the jubilation of the armistice before these findings were made public.

One of those most adamant to bring the case before the authorities remained Richard Holt. The Liberal MP for Hexham continued to be amazed that turning a sixpence into £14 10s. could be explained away by the practice of business development and the ease of division for non-existent capital sums. In addition to his parliamentary duties, Holt was also an experienced and successful businessman in the shipping industry and partner in the substantial concern of Alfred Holt & Company of Liverpool.[12] Consequently, his suspicions were founded upon professional expertise rather than hearsay and he believed that taxpayers deserved an explanation as they were not so naive as to imagine that immunity from excess profits duties would ultimately amount to non-financial benefit. To this end, Holt started to do a little bit of investigating of his own.

Whilst consulting the reference library in the House of Commons, Holt discovered a potential connection between British Cellulose and another government department, the Ministry of Information. The key individual linking these two organizations together was Mr C.G. Bryan of the Prudential Trust Company Limited of Canada, who had arranged the original £120,000 investment and also held a senior management position within the British Ministry of Information. Further investigation revealed that another officer of the Ministry was a former director of the Prudential Trust of Canada which had actually managed the British Cellulose account. Holt concluded:

> All this explanation of Colonel Grant Morden is very unsatisfactory. The right honourable Gentleman [Sir William Bull] referred to him as a gentleman who introduced this process into England. We have had other very reputable people in touch with these matters which were not carried on next door to Germany. We ought to have a very full and complete investigation of the whole matter.[13]

There were indeed some strange coincidences, which became increasingly irregular as the case progressed. The entire origin of the Company and its relationship with the government was peculiar, and soon questions were raised about how much German capital was invested in the parent Cellonit Gesellschaft Dreyfus and Company in Basel and why British concerns had not been given the opportunity to arrange for the supply of cellulose acetate.[14] Accusations of government monopoly stifling private enterprise started to resurface reminiscent of those levelled against the Royal Aircraft Factory's design and manufacture of aircraft earlier in the war, but in this case the transactions were far more complicated. Additional suspicion was raised by the fact that Swiss munitions factories were known to be undertaking German armament contracts and that details of that trade were carefully regulated by the German authorities.[15]

It is not too difficult for one to empathize with the scepticism and suspicion. A well-connected Canadian financier, of dubious personal and business reputation, made an introduction at the War Office for two Swiss chemists which resulted in a complete monopoly over the production of an ingredient crucial to the conduct of the air war. In addition, if we then consider Colonel Grant Morden's known association with the disgraced Colonel Wesley Allison and his notorious armaments syndicate, one cannot be too surprised that such misgivings were raised. The leader of the Irish Parliamentary Party, John Dillon, was curious as to why, under these extraordinary circumstance, Sir William Bull would offer a brief in parliament on behalf of a private concern such as the British Cellulose Company. Bull offered the following explanation of his actions:

> The two gentlemen concerned are friends of mine; the papers were attacking them, and I appealed to the House, before deciding the point, to wait until some action can be taken before a more satisfactory tribunal. If this cannot be done, then they must appeal to the Law Courts, unless a satisfactory tribunal is set up which can take evidence on oath. As far as I am concerned I have not a share in this company; I have no interest whatever in it – in fact, I have nothing to do with it.[16]

Actually, Bull was directly connected to government procedure and was the parliamentary secretary to the Secretary of State for the Colonies, Sir Walter Long. Naturally, this makes his impassioned defence of the financial irregularities even more unusual. John Dillion concluded the House of Commons debate of 5 August 1918 with the following warning to the government:

> There is a good deal of scandal going round, and the Government ought to be extremely careful to avoid giving the public the impression that there is anything wrong. I must say, after listening to this Debate and especially to the speech of the honourable Member for Hammersmith [Sir William Bull], that I am convinced that it will be the impression of the public that there is something very unpleasant in this whole transaction, and, if the honourable Member who represents the Ministry of Munitions thinks that he can remove that impression by a Departmental Inquiry, he is labouring under the greatest mistake.[17]

Sir William does not appear to have heeded the above caution.

Only three days later on 8 August 1918, he was once again acting on behalf of his friends and sent a private notice to the Chancellor of the Exchequer, Andrew Bonar Law, requesting to know when the full enquiry under oath would be likely to commence.[18] Urgency was obviously building amongst some of the senior individuals associated with Spondon, but the key question remained why, particularly after the monopoly had been secured and the manufactory was nearing completion. Does this suggest that the government were complicit in the transactions and that the individuals named in the press, now so determined to give evidence under oath, were worried they would be thrown under the bus should the public outcry prove too strong? Whatever the reason, the whole affair continued to become increasingly bizarre.

Colonel Grant Morden was not only a businessman but also the Conservative political candidate for Brentford and Chiswick and was probably eager to portray himself in a positive light in the run up to the 1918 General Election, a seat he subsequently won. As part of raising his public profile he wrote a letter to the pro-conservative weekly magazine, *The Outlook*, in August 1918 on the subject of the Canadian Flying Service. Morden had advocated for an independent Canadian Air Corps throughout the previous year and had even put himself forward as a candidate for Director.[19] *Flight Magazine* were quick to seize upon the opportunity to provide critique on some of the more outlandish claims of the man they now referred to as the Colonel of 'dope fame'.

The Colonel's first assertion was that he had fought closely with Lord Montagu for the establishment of an independent air service, something which had been achieved on 1 April 1918 with the creation of the Royal Air Force and associated Air Ministry. The second, was that the majority of airmen flying in the newly amalgamated air service were Canadian born and that Britain was repeatedly failing to recognize and reward their gallantry. *Flight Magazine* responded accordingly stating that there were two points in which they wished to take issue with the writer of this astonishing letter.

The first was rather a personal matter in which it was acclaimed that they had failed to see how the Colonel had been involved in the creation of a united air service proclaiming that they had 'not seen any prominence given to the name of Colonel Grant Morden, except by the Select Committee on National Expenditure and by the *Daily Chronicle* in connection with the great dope monopoly.'[20] On the second point however, it is worth clarifying that the Canadians played a crucial role in the air war alongside many members of the then defined Crown colonies, but to claim that Canadians formed the bulk of the flying men of the Royal Air Force was simply not true. It was also a mistruth that aircrew from the Crown Colonies received less recognition for gallantry, the military awards conferred on Major Billy Bishop perhaps being the more obvious case in point.[21] The official figure for the total hours flown by all Canadian Training Squadrons during the conflict was 243,566 and although not insubstantial, this number was a proportion, rather than the predominant contribution to the combined war effort.[22] *Flight* concluded that the letter had been written 'in the worst of bad taste' and the glaring inaccuracies may well have represented Colonel Grant Morden's desperation for positive publicity in light of his political ambitions and the negative press received due to his association with British Cellulose.[23]

By October 1918, rumours started to emerge that dope monopoly interests were also intimately linked with the purchase of the *Daily Chronicle*, the very newspaper that had broken ranks and published the initial details of the scandal. The following appraisal of the situation appeared in the 'Airisms From the Four Winds' sections of *Flight Magazine* on 17 October and was undoubtedly circulating amongst the manufactories of the British aircraft industry:

> Curious how rumours get about. At least the assertions that Dope Monopoly interests were intimately concerned in the purchase of the *Daily Chronicle* gave those coupled up an opportunity of denying the soft impeachment. Curious but possibly only coincident, that it was the *Daily Chronicle* which gave such considered criticism to the Special Government Committee's revelations upon the 'Dope' dope. Curious coincident that those criticisms got shut off so suddenly a while ago. Curious coincident that the following inspired, if not official information, should be published at the time of the rumours as to the purchasers of the *Daily Chronicle*.[24]

The dope enquiry was already underway. Chaired by Lord Sumner and supported by Lord Inchape and Lord Colwyn, but the investigation was in its early stages and there was genuine concern that the longer the process took, and the longer it remained out of the public eye, the whole episode would be quietly forgotten. One certain way of ensuring the story remained conveniently buried was to obtain control of the very newspaper that had broken the original story and was most likely to reinvigorate public interest with subsequent reportage.

The *Daily Chronicle* enjoyed a circulation that had doubled during the war years to around 800,000 copies per day. Under the editorship of Robert

Donald, the newspaper successfully maintained an objective opinion offering both praise and criticism of the government's performance as and when the occasion demanded.[25] Whilst Lloyd George effectively remained a prime minister without a party leading the incumbent coalition government, he was anxious to raise his profile through the popular press and had aspirations to see his political allies 'acquire' a Liberal newspaper for the express purposes of his own public relations. Lloyd George believed that the *Daily Chronicle* would be a most suitable publication for this purpose and negotiations between the paper's owners and Lord Leverhulme began in September 1917. Ironically, the route to final acquisition on 3 October 1918 ultimately risked Lloyd George's reputation rather than enhance it.[26]

On 15 October 1918, William Pringle, Liberal MP for Lanarkshire North-West and a barrister by profession, asked the prime minister by means of public notice whether his attention had been called to the recent purchases of London newspapers for the purpose of changing their political allegiance and manipulating editorial content. No doubt Pringle was aware of the rumours surrounding Lloyd George's aspirations for obtaining control of the *Daily Chronicle* and was taking the opportunity to put him on the spot. However, the question was actually taken by the Chancellor of the Exchequer, who acknowledged the recent sales but stated that he had been assured that any traditional political allegiances remained unchanged.[27]

Unsatisfied with attempts by the front bench to swerve a potentially awkward subject, Pringle waited until the afternoon adjournment and took the opportunity to continue his line of questioning during the evening session of Parliament. Pringle was predominantly concerned with a growing tendency of monopolistic control of the press and was frustrated that the government were not prepared to carry out a public enquiry or make an intervention by means of introducing freedom of the press legislation. In truth, nearly all national newspapers of substantial circulation had at this time 'intimate association with the government'.[28] Pringle argued:

> Recently, as everybody is aware, there has been a growth of group interests in newspapers, until now it may be said that with few notable exceptions nearly all the newspapers in this country with large circulations are in the hands of a few groups, and that these groups with a single exception are in intimate association with the Government, if not really subservient to it. The

recent change affects a group of newspapers which certainly were formerly independent. It is somewhat doubtful whether the former independence of this group will be continued under the new system.[29]

Present during this parliamentary session was Sir Henry Dalziel, the Liberal politician for Kirkcaldy Burghs and long-time passionate advocate of Lloyd George. A journalist by trade, Dalziel had acquired ownership of the *Reynold's News, Pall Mall Gazette*, and had recently been appointed by the prime minister as chairman and political director of the *Daily Chronicle*.[30] Dalziel was instrumental in sparking Lloyd George's fascination with the power of the press when in 1909 he had introduced him to the newspaper magnate Alfred Harmsworth, Lord Northcliffe.[31] However, the government didn't simply have control of the press, they were also the regulator of free market paper and access to raw materiel for the purpose of print was entirely at their discretion.

Lloyd George had in fact instigated negotiation for the purchase of the *Daily Chronicle* in early 1917, long before news of the dope scandal actually came to light, but as the paper continued to print articles critical of the government's actions his desire for acquisition intensified. During the initial approaches for purchase it eventually emerged that the real person behind the transaction was none other than the Minister of Information, Lord Beaverbrook. This subsequently resulted in the discussions breaking down, partly due to his personality, partly due to price, but primarily because the incumbent proprietor had no intention of selling the concern to a Tory partisan whatever the price. Following this, Lloyd George arranged a meeting with the managing director on 21 March 1917 and Sir Henry Dalziel assumed control of negotiations.[32] Pringle took up the story in the House of Commons on 15 August 1918:

> The negotiations were kept secret, and no indication was given to anybody that anything had taken place until the 3rd of October, when the late editor of the 'Daily Chronicle' was informed by his proprietor that the property had changed hands, and that my right honourable Friend the Member for Kirkcaldy Burghs was to enter upon his duties as political director of the paper on the following evening. In order to account for the secrecy with which this transaction was carried out – a secrecy which was undoubtedly somewhat strange in view of the late editor's long connection with the paper – the proprietor informed him that he had been bound to secrecy, and that at an interview he had had with the Prime Minister and with my

honourable and gallant Friend the Patronage Secretary to the Treasury, he was pledged to make no disclosure of what was going on, in particular to the editor, because the editor had recently criticised the Government and had published an article in which he said that the Prime Minister 'had a small mind'.[33]

Here, no doubt, was the real reason for the urgency of purchase and transfer of control and ownership. There was also a convenient concern that sensitive intelligence was being leaked to the press and the War Office opened an investigation on 21 June 1918 to determine how the *Daily Chronicle* had obtained secret information about the departure of the home secretary, Sir George Cave, to the Hague earlier that month.[34]

Such breaches were invariably used as justification for the forthcoming acquisition, and it was certainly true that although the newspaper had remained broadly supportive of the government in relation to its prosecution of the war, it was not afraid to utilize its independence in criticism of their practices when it believed it to be necessary. One of the key government failures the editorial team believed the public had a right to know about was the dope scandal, which was then currently under investigation. Pringle lamented that the independent investigation previously conducted by the *Daily Chronicle* had come to such an abrupt end. Not in the least because it was rumoured that Dalziel was associated through financial transactions with none other than Colonel Grant Morden, an accusation the latter subsequently vehemently denied.[35]

Unsurprisingly the whole ordeal was viewed with mounting suspicion by the independent newspapers operating throughout the UK. The *Nottingham Journal and Express* concluded that the entire system of manufactured 'mechanical publicity', operating outside parliamentary control, was not only the creation of Lloyd George but a stab in the back for democracy and warned its readership that 'democracy cannot exist without free expression'.[36]

Nevertheless, following the acquisition of the *Daily Chronicle* and the signing of the armistice of 11 November 1918 that brought the First World War to a military conclusion, reportage concerning the dope scandal became conveniently subdued amongst the bittersweet national mood of victory and associated loss. Yet for some the episode and subsequent delayed investigation was a source of unbearable frustration, as was evident in an anonymous letter published in *The Times* on 14 March 1919 which complained that following the receipt of witness statements there was no reason why the enquiry should remain 'imperfect, incomplete, or secret'.[37] This renewed interest prompted Colonel Wedgewood to publicly ask the prime minister later in the month when the dope enquiry was likely to be completed and the findings reported to the public. The question was answered by Andrew Bonar Law who apologized for the delay and explained that the report was unavoidably overdue because the chairman, Lord Sumner, was in Paris engaged on behalf of the government in preparing the peace settlement, but he was confident the conclusions would be issued shortly.[38] Lord Sumner was a senior British judge, and was sent to France to work on the Versailles Treaty and attended the formal signing on 28 June 1919.[39]

The long-awaited British Cellulose Committee Inquiry Report was finally completed on 31 July 1919 and was addressed to the Chancellor of the Exchequer before the findings were formally published and made public on 14 August. The terms of reference were brief but all encompassing, focused in equal measure on both the activities of the Company itself and the associated government departments. The Inquiry was appointed:

> To enquire into and report upon the formation and financial arrangements of the British Cellulose and Chemical Manufacturing Company, Limited, and Associated Companies, and upon their relations with Departments of the Government.[40]

Lord Sumner's duties on the Continent aside, the Committee expressly wished to highlight that the delay in presenting their conclusions was in fact due to difficulty in obtaining evidence from Dr Camille Dreyfus and the 'unexpectedly elaborate and protracted' report from the eminent accountants Messrs. W.B. Peat, which had been unable to submit the detailed analysis of the Company's accounts until 13 June 1919.[41] The Committee interviewed thirty-two witnesses between 27 November 1918 and February 1919 during a thorough investigation of all the available evidence.

It is worth briefly reiterating that the British Cellulose Company was first registered in England as a private concern on 18 March 1916 with the aim to manufacture cellulose acetate to satisfy the uncompleted portion of a contract between Dr Camille Dreyfus and the War Office signed in July 1915.

The new company was set up for the express purpose of acquiring from Dreyfus British patent rights for the Swiss chemist's method of manufacture. The original business plan was promoted by Lieutenant Colonel Walter Grant Morden, Staff Officer to Sir Sam Hughes, the Canadian Minister of Militia, Sir Arthur Trevor Dawson, director of Vickers Armaments, Ltd., and Mr Edward Robson, a director of the London-based Pinchin, Johnson and Co., Ltd., a major manufacturer of paints and varnishes. It was specifically noted that none of the above individuals had any technical knowledge of the manufacture of cellulose acetate, and the original directors of the Company were listed as follows:

> Shortly after the incorporation of the Company eight directors were nominated in accordance with the provisions of the articles, four for each class of shares, of whom, Sir Trevor Dawson, Col. Grant Morden, Mr. Robson and Mr. Bloch, were nominated by the 'A' shareholders and Captain Clavell, Dr. H. Drefus, Dr. C. Dreyfus and Mr. Rudolph La Roche (described as a banker of Basel) were nominated by the 'B' shareholders. Col. Grant Morden was appointed Chairman.[42]

Captain Alexandre Clavell was one of the principal shareholders in the Cellonite Company (Dreyfus and Co.) of Basel and had been present during a visit to Switzerland by Colonel Grant Morden and Mr Robson in early 1916.

By January 1917, despite a complete lack of production in the UK, the directors considered recapitalization based on the assumed appreciation of the company's existing assets. Interestingly, despite his assertion in Parliament the previous year that he had absolutely nothing to do with the Company, it was revealed that Sir William Bull was actually consulted to advise on the legalities of the ensuing financial transaction.[43] Ultimately, this resulted in the formation of the British Cellulose and Chemical Manufacturing (Parent) Company on 20 March 1918 with a nominal capital of £3,500,000 in £1 shares. The purpose of setting up the parent enterprise was for it to act as a vehicle to finance the existing Company and the analysis of the accounts showed that the new business 'promptly lent to the existing Company the balance of cash remaining in its hands as a result of these operations'.[44] Despite the extensive allegations of financial irregularities, the Committee were unable to find any conclusive proof of financial misconduct.

In terms of the relationship between British Cellulose and the departments of the government there once again appeared to be very little of concern and it was deemed that the original tender was awarded in accordance with the procurement framework. The first contact between the Swiss firm and the War Office occurred in 1914, and subsequently Mr Turner, then in charge of the Aeronautical Contract Branch, began investigations into issuing a tender for 100 tonnes of cellulose acetate of British manufacture.[45] It was also during this period that enquiries were being made into the dangers of tetrachlorethane-based aeroplane dopes and a non-poisonous alternative was being urgently sought.

The Committee believed that, in sharp contrast to previous reports, the Company had successfully satisfied all of the original War Office requests for increased supply and that this was only possible because of the financial concession concerning excess profits duties granted by the government shortly after the incorporation. Early in March 1916, Colonel Grant Morden, on the introduction of Sir Trevor Dawson, met with Sir Charles Harris, the financial secretary to the War Office, during which the formal request for exemption from excess profits duties was made. Harris was an experienced administrator who had been instrumental in the delivery of Richard Haldane's pre-war army reforms when Minister of War.[46] However, the Committee did concede that the next phase of the process had become rather unorthodox indeed:

> Sir Charles Harris at once proceeded to take the opinion of the Treasury authorities unofficially, and received a reply from Sir John Bradbury, in which the latter, whilst deprecating such a concession unless it was absolutely unavoidable, indicated that he considered the least objectionable form in which it could be granted. Some time later, Colonel Morden and Sir A. Trevor Dawson approached the then Chancellor of the Exchequer on the question of a concession as to Excess Profits Duty, the only result being a repetition of the views expressed by Sir John Bradbury in his previous unofficial letter to Sir Charles Harris.[47]

After the Company had been formed and preparations for the construction of the works at Spondon were already underway, the War Office sought the opinions of other government departments and, discovering that the Ministry of Munitions had previously made such grants to contractors, formally applied to the Treasury to sanction the concession. Following further correspondence, responsibility for the decision was placed with the War Office and, after consultation with General Henderson satisfied them on the importance of securing a domestic supply of cellulose acetate, terms were made with the Company on 17 November 1916.

These terms effectively guaranteed that the Company would be refunded for its capital expenditure on plant during the war years up to a maximum equivalent of the excess profits duty, as long as they agreed to quote fair prices and take orders only from the government. Thus, the controversial monopoly was struck by the hand of the War Office and not through the promoters exploiting their extensive list of government contacts.

The Committee refrained from judgement regarding the competitive fairness of the concession but upon examining the evidence believed it to have been both necessary and not unprecedented:

> It is, however, only fair to say that similar concessions, and for similar reasons were being made; that the importance of a British supply of cellulose acetate was obvious and the risk of dependence on a source of supply on the borders of Germany was great; and that, in a considerable measure, Dr. Dreyfus was in a position to command his own terms.[48]

Investigation revealed that in the early phases of operation no profits were made at Spondon and the original concession was cancelled during construction work in which extensions were being made to the Factory to meet additional demands for product on 27 June 1918. Under this new agreement, the Ministry of Munitions made loans to the Company against its expenditure on electrical plant and also granted a fixed percentage loan equivalent to the firm's war capital expenditure on infrastructure up until the end of 1918.[49] This loan was arranged with interest at 1 per cent above that set by the Bank of England, with a minimum interest of 5 per cent per annum, to be repayable within five years of the original agreement.

Under this revised agreement, the Ministry had advanced approximately £900,000 by the end of October 1918. Perhaps one of the most significant omissions in previous reports was the recognition that during the war companies were incorporated in the United States, Italy and France to

Figure 10 Waring and Gillow Furniture Factory, Hammersmith, London, November 1916. Courtesy of Heritage Images/Getty Images.

manufacture cellulose acetate by means of the Dreyfus process and all of which had received financial support from their respective governments.[50] So why then, if the transactions were transparent and lawful, was the dope scandal so momentous in wartime Britain?

The answer may well be found in the fact considerable time was spent during the enquiry in the examination of complaints made by representatives of the British chemical trade who remained infuriated that the government would countenance granting preferential treatment to foreign chemists. Even though concerns had been raised concerning the quality of the finished product and the repeated delays in manufacture and delivery, such ill feeling about the revelation of the monopoly was no doubt exacerbated by the fact that the reputation of British science, and future prospects of the British chemical industry in particular, had enjoyed somewhat of a renaissance whilst engaged in securing the country's supply needs of essential materiel during the conflict. *Science* noted on 29 September 1916:

> The press bears witness, through the appearance of numerous articles and letters, that the people of this country, and even the politicians, have begun to perceive the dangers that will result from a continuance of their former attitude, and to understand that in peace, as in war, civilization is at a tremendous disadvantage in the struggle for existence unless armed by science, and that the future prosperity of the empire is ultimately dependent upon the progress of science, and very specifically of chemistry.[51]

It is easy to see how the author, the eminent University of Glasgow professor of chemistry Gorge Henderson and his colleagues might have been a little put out by the government award of such a seemingly lucrative contract to the Dreyfus brothers at their expense.

Nevertheless, after careful examination of the evidence, and in particular the offers made by Courtlands and United Alkali to manufacture cellulose acetate, the Committee were satisfied that the relationship between the government and British Cellulose was entirely above board:

> We are of the opinion that nothing amounting to favouritism of the Company has been shown by the Aircraft Department. It is undoubtedly, the fact, as is shown above, that from the commencement Dr. Dreyfus, and subsequently the Company, received support and assistance from government officials, and became, in fact, the sole source for which the Service looked for supplies, but we think that the reasons for this are adequate. In this connection it is worthy of comment that, notwithstanding the transfer of the Aeronautical Department from the War Office to the Ministry of Munitions, and the subsequent change of official personnel, the same policy was adopted, namely, to develop to the utmost capacity the resources of the Company's works.[52]

Despite concluding that the formation of the Company and subsequent transactions were legitimate, particularly in light of the necessity to obtain cellulose acetate for the purposes of conducting the air war, Lord Sumner considered the actions of some of promoters to have been less than exemplary and there were two main areas of criticism.

The first related to a meeting of the Company Board on 1 April 1918 during which a Minute was passed that granted to each of the managing directors living and entertainment expenses of £4,500 per annum. The chairman, Colonel Grant Morden, was to receive renumeration for similar purposes amounting to £5,000 per annum with an accompanying veto that no detailed account of his expenses needed be submitted. The second major area of reproach was that the original sixpenny shares had been portrayed as quickly becoming worth £14.10s. even though they were considered to be effectively worthless. Consequently, the Committee concluded that the company directors had 'only themselves to thank' for the treatment they had received in both the House of Commons and the media.[53]

Despite the absolution contained in the final report, scepticism remained as to the findings and the grumblings continued concerning the exclusion of British manufacturers and exclusivity of supply.[54] Furthermore, there remained some doubt regarding the financial arrangements of the shareholders which appeared so blatantly underhand in an environment where 'satisfactory definitions of profiteering' were notoriously difficult to demonstrate.[55] There were also other examples of the Company's supposed underhandedness, such as the illegal sale of second-hand railway wagons without a permit from the Ministry of Munitions. Whether a blatant disrespect for the law or an example of professional oversight, such reportage did little to raise the public confidence in the reputation of the Company.[56] In addition, in the appendices of the final report there were listed thirty-two shareholders of the British Cellulose and Chemical Manufacturing (Parent) Company and their shareholdings as of 2 May 1918. Once again, this only served to raise further suspicion relating to the previous business activities of certain individuals.

The majority of the shares were unsurprisingly held by the Dreyfus brothers and Captain Alexandre Clavell, the previous owners of the Cellonite Company of Basel, and amounted to 74,998. The second and third highest shareholders were the Prudential Trust Company of Canada, with 41,830 shares, and Vickers Limited, with 16,487. Of the major protagonists previously named in the press for their involvement in the 'dope scandal', Colonel Grant Morden held 1,705 shares, whilst Sir Trevor Dawson acquired 2,204. Another name which drew attention was that of General Sir Sam Hughes, the Canadian Minister of Militia and Defence. Despite Hughes being a known associate of Colonel Allison, he had been officially absolved of misconduct during the Canadian government's Shell Committee enquiry of 1916. Nevertheless, he was listed as holding 1,000 British Cellulose shares, which he later transferred to the Prudential Trust Company.

Notwithstanding the irregularities, and in particular the supposedly obvious examples of war profiteering, the findings of the independent enquiry were considered final, and one might have been forgiven for believing that the government might wish to put the whole episode behind them. But remarkably, the British government not only took an ardent interest in the repurposing of the manufactory's post-war operations but also made additional financial investment in the British Cellulose and Chemical Manufacturing (Parent) Company and became the majority shareholder – a revelation that some found difficult to accept.

Conclusions: 'A plane truth'

Post-war industrial applications of cellulose (1919 onwards)

Following the issue of Lord Sumner's findings, the British Cellulose and Chemical Manufacturing (Parent) Company Ltd. quietly began to restructure the business in order to widen their influence beyond aviation and meet the challenging operating conditions of the post-war economy. Interestingly, the government retained its involvement in the company and chose to exchange their rights to reclaim the sums expended on previous capital investment for the award of 1,450,000 preference shares. These shares were advertised to the public on 3 March 1920 as providing a guaranteed fixed dividend of 7½ per cent and one-quarter of the balance of any profits would be distributed to the shareholders each year.[1] The government also appointed two directors to the board, Sir Philip Henriques and Sir John Field Beale, to further protect their investment, and Treasury civil servants specifically stated that they were only concerned with the company policy in so far as it affected their own security.[2]

However, the government's decision to retain financial association did not go unnoticed. On 2 March 1920, Henry Cautley, MP East Grinstead, was curious to ascertain from the Chancellor of the Exchequer the reasons why he had approved of the government taking 1,450,000 of British Cellulose preference shares rather than insist upon the company's property being sold and the government's investments being repaid. He was also keen to ascertain the government's justification for its association in the industry of producing film and under what circumstances the government had become financially interested in the British Cellulose Company.[3]

In response to such challenging questions, Austen Chamberlain reiterated that the relationship had existed between the government and the British Cellulose Company during the war years and that the Ministry of Munitions had agreed to advance 'to the company a proportion of its expenditure on plant and buildings for the purpose'. Towards the end of 1918, the government were determined to secure these advances in the public interest as the total investment amounted to £1,250,000, in addition to a previous loan of £200,000. This sum was secured on the issue of preference shares which provided the company with sufficient capital for the development and exploration of new and emerging business opportunities, whilst the government retained its share of initial investment and potential future profits. Nevertheless, the chancellor reminded the House:

> Experience has shown, however, that in these circumstances it would not be possible for the Company to raise the necessary funds to continue its undertaking, and accordingly, after very careful consideration and as part of a scheme for the reconstruction of the Company, I approved the proposal of the Minister of Munitions to take 1,450,000 at 7½ per cent. accumulative participating preference shares in place of the existing mortgage and debentures. It is a condition of this arrangement that in case of war the government shall have the right to take control of the management of the factory for the purpose of producing munitions, and that the Company unreservedly abandons certain large claims put forward by them in connection with their transactions with the government during the war. The alternative suggested by the Honourable Member, namely, the liquidation of a new industry, which is essential in war and which under peace conditions may, I hope, prove to be of great benefit to this country, would not, in my opinion, have been in the best interests of the nation.[4]

It was likely that Chamberlain was in an impossible situation. In May 1919, a board had been appointed to oversee the liquidation of the Ministry of Munitions under the chairmanship of Frederick Kellaway. It was soon discovered that the disposal of assets that had been funded by the government in wartime raised significant problems, principally because the agreements with contractors were often unique and complex in nature and that the owners of the sites were realistically the only possible purchasers of capital assets that remained in situ.[5] No doubt Chamberlain saw the option of shares as a compromise in the hope of both a future financial return and the avoidance of further complicated negotiations.

Nevertheless, Cautley remained concerned by the fact that the government interest was being used by the company as a means of demonstrating institutional confidence in their operation. Ultimately, this amounted to a seal of approval by the government and was being used as a method of enticing investors to take out additional shares on the grounds that the concern had already made considerable profits during the war and thus were able to pay off their liabilities. Despite the challenge, the government decision to continue business association prevailed and in the early stages of the post-war restructure even appeared to be a shrewd financial investment.

Initially, the divergence of manufacture into artificial silks and cine-film proved successful. The company's principal product, a lustrous thread of continuous length formed from acetic ester of cellulose, won scientific acclaim and was in high demand with textile manufacturers.[6] However, the transition to new markets required a considerable reconfiguration of the existing factory and additional capital investment that had a significant impact on the early distribution of profits. Nevertheless, the directors remained confident that when full output was achieved, manufacturing costs would be significantly reduced, enabling the conduct of a profitable business.[7] Despite the optimism, however, in January 1921 manufacturing at Spondon was significantly reduced and the market price of the company's shares consequently fell rapidly. The decline in prospects was largely due to the stagnation in the artificial silk trade upon which the directors and the government had placed such high hopes.[8]

There was briefly, however, the possibility that the evolving post-war aviation industry may once again come to the company's rescue, and on 12 June 1922 a scheme was proposed to the Chancellor of the Exchequer by Charles Dennistoun Burney, a retired Royal Navy commander and aeronautical engineer. Burney was consulting for Vickers Ltd. and believed that a regular commercial airship service could be maintained from Great Britain to Egypt, India and Australia. Although the scheme was ultimately unsuccessful, it was directly responsible for the government investment in the construction of large airships such R100 and R101, the contracts for which were placed with the newly constituted Airship Guarantee Company, a subsidiary of Vickers.[9]

The surface area of an airship was considerably greater than the wings of the largest aeroplane and required significantly more dope. Unsurprisingly, both Vickers and the government were exploring schemes in which they could utilize assets in which they had already heavily invested such as in the production of cellulose acetate. Nevertheless, civil servants had become understandably wary of such business arrangements involving both public and private funds, and the report specifically mentioned the problems faced by the government when they entered schemes as joint subscribers with the public:

> If the undertaking gets into difficulties the public complain that they were misled by the fact of Government taking an interest in it into investing their own money. This has lately been urged at the meeting of British Cellulose Company notwithstanding that in that case the Government merely forewent their mortgage rights on money advanced for war purposes and accepted preference shares in lieu.[10]

In peacetime, the government were unable to act in the same way as a private capitalist and Parliament rightly controlled public expenditure once again after emergency wartime powers had been rescinded. It was obvious that the government remained cautious of becoming entangled in another scandal like that experienced with British Cellulose, particularly as the Spondon product would be required in large quantities if the airship programme were to prove successful. However, even post-war, the legacy of the dope scandal was still fresh in the minds of those at Westminster who remained adverse to any additional national expenditure on speculative schemes, especially when they had been conceived by an armaments manufacturer such as Vickers.

The prospects of the British Cellulose continued to decline, and all-too-familiar questions were raised in Parliament regarding the judgement of the government and its determination to continue to support what appeared to most onlookers to be an ailing concern. James Kiley, the Liberal Member for Stepney Whitechapel and St George's, enquired of the Chancellor of the Exchequer on 8 May 1922 whether the government were still represented on the board by two appointed directors salaried at £500 per annum. And, if so, whether the chancellor proposed to continue to support such appointments considering the poor performance of the company.[11] The Financial Secretary to the Treasury, Mr Hilton Young, responded in the affirmative, although by this date Sir John Field Beale had been replaced on the board by Sir William Alexander. This encouraged the following response from Kiley:

> In view of the disastrous results to the investors who invested their money in the British Cellulose Company on the grounds that His Majesty's Government were large shareholders and had two directors on the board, steps will be taken to dispense with the services of these two directors and for the Government to cease all connection with this concern?[12]

Young responded that this was not planned because the government believed it to be undesirable to attempt to sell such a large a block of shares and it was still hoped that market changes would eventually lead 'to an enhancement of the value of the government asset'.

The appointment of government directors remained contentious and their continued involvement in the British Cellulose Chemical Manufacturing Company was once again raised in the House of Commons in March 1923. In response, Stanley Baldwin, then Chancellor of the Exchequer, reminded the House that a government director was 'there on purpose to watch the interests of the government and the taxpayer' and was 'paid as their guardian and representative', but the argument was beginning to wear increasingly thin.[13] In spite of this, the government continued its association with the manufacturer even following its change of name to British Celanese in 1923, and Sir Philip Henriques continued to act on behalf of the national interest as a director, a position that could not be removed without the consent of the government whilst they retained not less than 250,000 preference shares.[14] This awkward relationship continued well into the 1930s, but it is worth recognizing that the Spondon factory gave invaluable service during the Second World War. It even enjoyed success in the 1950s with the introduction of cellulose acetate packing foil, now more widely known as cling-film.[15]

The legacy of the British Cellulose Inquiry continued to haunt those who were originally associated with the scandal. Grant Morden's involvement became a primary cause of irritation following his selection as the official candidate for the Coalition Unionist's in the Brentford and Chiswick Division in October 1918. At the time of his selection the Committee of Inquiry into the affairs surrounding the creation of British Cellulose was still ongoing. Consequently, any discussion on the subject remained *sub judice*, which caused some to argue that for this reason alone he should not have been put forward as a government candidate whilst under investigation.

There can be little doubt that both the government and the local Unionist Association would have known that Morden was immune from questioning before the selection was actually made.[16] The political disregard was likely the result of his association with Walter Long, the Secretary of State to the Colonies. Long was instrumental in the resignation of Asquith and the formation of the first coalition government and had accepted a loan from Morden in 1917 in order to relieve personal financial difficulties.[17] Despite the impropriety, Morden won the election in 1918 and held the seat until his retirement from public service following a declaration of bankruptcy on 15 April 1931. He died 25 June 1952 at the age of fifty-one.[18] Sir Trevor Dawson passed away the same year but was largely spared the embarrassment of association with the cellulose scandal. The company was eventually sold to Courtaulds in 1958 and manufacturing continued at the Spondon site until 2012. The Factory was eventually demolished between 2015 and 2017 and the 120-acre site has since been redeveloped without trace.[19]

In the years immediately preceding the outbreak of the First World War, the acclaimed aviation pioneer, F.W. Lanchester, argued that until a new or emerging technology had a definite strategic direction, enabling investigation that could be carried out in the laboratory, scientific progress would not only remain slow, but confined to the hands of a few dedicated pioneers. This was certainly the case in relation to the development of the British aircraft industry prior to its rapid expansion to meet the technological demands of the war. Lanchester mused:

> The moment the problem has been formulated, and the direction in which research is desirable has been pointed out, the conditions are changed, and the number of workers and the volume of work turned out goes up by leaps and bounds. Up to the present time the scientific work that has been done in the direction of elucidating the principles of flight has consisted of individual sporadic efforts, in some cases by workers insufficiently equipped both as to apparatus ands training, and the results are discordant to the extent of being conflicting; complete disagreement frequently exists, not only as to the conclusions be even as to the most elementary facts.[20]

It was the formulation of the problem pertaining to the military application of heavier-than-air flying machines coupled with the initially reluctant acknowledgement of their potential by the Secretary of State for War, Richard Haldane, that enabled government-funded scientific investigation of a meaningful scale. However, Haldane was soon converted from sceptic to believer and became an important advocate for future investment in the progress of British aeronautical science and its application for war purposes. Speaking in the House of Commons on 2 August 1909 he argued that the availability of national funds enabled great strides to be made in the experimentation of the principles of flight, but current investment was only sufficient 'to make machines that will fly, whether dirigibles or aeroplanes' and not machines suitable for war purposes.[21]

The Royal Aircraft Factory originally took up the challenge of producing an aeroplane suitable for military purposes and the B.E.2 design was perfected by the aircraft designers namely Geoffrey de Havilland and Edward Teshmaker Busk. The aeroplane made its first flight on 1 February 1912 and proved the benchmark of aerodynamic principle upon which private manufacturers based their future designs. Nevertheless, despite its initial success, the design was never far from criticism and controversy, an unfortunate situation that continued to dog the aeroplane throughout its service career.

On 23 October 1912, the Conservative MP for Brentford, Mr Joynson-Hicks, questioned how many of these new B.E.2 machines were under construction at the Royal Aircraft Factory and how many firms had been engaged in the manufacture of parts. The Under-Secretary of State for War, Harold Tennant, explained that thirteen machines were currently on order, all of which were being completed by private firms. This was no doubt an attempt to pacify those suspicious of government motives regarding aeroplane construction. However, perhaps what was more important in terms of context was the response from Tennant when asked how many aeroplanes were owned by the British Army:

> Thirty-six effective aeroplanes are in the possession of the British Army, of which twelve are at the Central Flying School. Of these nineteen are of English manufacture. In addition, four machines are under reconstruction at the Royal Aircraft Factory.[22]

From these humble beginnings the British aircraft industry would grow beyond all expectations during the ensuing conflict and the total number of B.E.2 designs manufactured would exceed 3,500. Through a combination of strategic procurement policies, government loans and the mobilization of sub-contractor frameworks, the aircraft industry expanded from fourteen major companies in October 1914 to twenty-six by 1916.[23] By 26 July 1918, the combined workforce of the six government Aircraft Factories located at Aintree, Birmingham, Croydon, Farnborough, Hayes and Sudbury stood at 11,206 alone.[24] Deliveries of aeroplanes increased accordingly as the military demand grew and the average of 246 deliveries in 1915 soon increased to 593 by 1916, and by the signing of the armistice in 1918 British factories were capable producing 800 military aeroplanes per week.[25] In fact, by the last year of the war, when the Royal Air Force possessed some 22,000 aeroplanes, aircraft manufacturing capability had for the first time outstripped the availability of the trained pilots to fly them.[26]

In the official history of the air war, Walter Raleigh acknowledged that without the efforts of the Royal Aircraft Factory, and Mervyn O'Gorman in particular, the rapid growth of British airpower would not have been possible. However, Raleigh also recognized that the relationships between Farnborough and private enterprise threatened to undermine the development of British aviation. A good example of this suspicion was in the development of engines. The Royal Aircraft Factory technicians specified the performance parameters of aviation engines and built a wind tunnel and laboratory specifically for the purpose of testing powerplant designs from the industry. There was, however, one very critical problem. The manufacturers themselves refused to send their designs for performance tests and attract potential scrutiny but the Factory refused to pass any engines fit for inclusion in new aeroplane designs without them first being approved safe for operation. This ultimately resulted in a stalemate about which Raleigh subtly noted the following observations:

> There was a misunderstanding, which after a time became acute, between the Factory, zealous for the public interest, believed that it could best serve their interest by encouraging, and co-ordinating the efforts of the makers. The makers, jealous of supervision and control, did not accept that view.[27]

During these early stages of aviation development, it was certainly true that the majority of progress had been achieved by private enterprise and government support had been rather slow to materialize. Therefore, the private firms feared the restraints of bureaucracy which might lead, in their minds, to a state monopoly of the industry.

Nevertheless, such unprecedented technological progression and increase in production capabilities during the war was ultimately the result of that 'necessity' to which Lanchester had previously alluded. But the primary threat to the British ability to manufacture aeroplanes was not disconnect between the objectives of the government and private industry, nor an inability to disseminate to independent manufacturers the results of scientific analysis conducted at Farnborough, but the shortage of a key component as simple as aircraft dope. In fairness to the British government and the War Office, nobody could have foreseen the huge increase in demand for aircraft at the outbreak of the conflict and even twenty-first-century industries can still be caught out by sudden demand and subsequent supply shortages. Perhaps the most recent example has been the chip crisis that effectively forced many of the automobile giants to curtail manufacture and store millions of almost completed vehicles whilst awaiting the delivery of tiny, seemingly inconsequential, semi-conductors. These shortages caused factories to suspend production and delays in customer deliveries which, although frustrating, admittedly would not have had the potentially devastating consequence of the Allies losing their aerial supremacy during the First World War due to a lack of cellulose acetate.

By 1916, however, there was a very real and increasing threat that all the progress attained in British aeronautical development and manufacturing capability could be undone due to the shortage of aviation dope. This no doubt contributed to the prolonged manufacture of dopes that contained deadly solvents such as tetrachlorethane, and once the fatalities and illnesses within the aeroplane dope shops were openly reported, the government had little choice but to invest in the manufacture of non-poisonous substitutes and ensure a domestically produced supply. It was this increasingly difficult situation that resulted in the government's association with the Dreyfus brothers and their spurious promoters which culminated in what became known as the 'dope scandal'. However, even as the arguments raged regarding the government's relationship with the British Cellulose Company there was still room in the aviation press for some good-humoured satire.

In a letter printed in the correspondence section of *Flight Magazine* in September 1917, Douglas Thorburn regretted that he had been unable to attend any of the numerous recent sports gatherings held by British aircraft manufacturers due to a 'prolonged stay in France'. Thorburn picked nostalgic fun at the pre-war circuit races around pre-set courses and suggested some more contemporary alternatives:

> I read of the same old flat races – or round races, according to the shape of the course – the same old competitions with eggs and spoons, and the same old sack races. I am not going to suggest that prizes should be awarded to the employee who has had the sack the most often or to the damsel of the dope department who knows most about spoons, but surely it is possible to introduce items a little more closely associated with the aircraft industry. A competition to decide who could dope a tail elevator or rudder in the shortest time could be made quite exciting and would also have a beneficial effect on those taking part.[28]

The mentions of 'spoons' was a witticism at the expense of *Flight*'s founder and editor, Stanley Spooner, but the references to the process of applying aeroplane dope are clear evidence of the extent to which such a seemingly inconsequential product had entered the public psyche.

Even following the Armistice, the Aircraft Disposal Department, which had been tasked with the sale of excess wartime aviation materiels, were soon advertising large quantities of dope for sale on the open market. In November 1919 these included 18,292 gallons of cellulose acetate dope, 7,252 gallons of nitro cellulose dope, 1,843 gallons of mixed dope and 6,000 gallons of S.33 dope solvent. These were stored at depots throughout the country, including the Royal Aircraft Factory at Farnborough, and if nothing else, serve as testament to how far future supply had been secured during the closing stages of the war.[29] There was even sufficient excess dope available for the supply of a significant quantity to the United States in 1918 to assist them in the delivery of their aircraft programme.[30]

Nevertheless, despite the exoneration of both the Ministry of Munitions and those promoters originally associated with the British Cellulose Company, the bitter legacy of the 'dope scandal', and the controversies surrounding early manufacture of aeroplanes at the Royal Aircraft Factory, remained fresh in the minds of those working within the British aircraft industry well into the 1920s. The former British Aeroplane Varnish Company, rebranded as Titanine Limited in 1922 after their flagship product, were at pains to ensure consumers were aware that they were responsible for producing the first products 'along the lines of elimination of the deleterious ingredients', and 'produced the original non-poisonous dope with such satisfactory results that the British Government later prohibited the use of tetrachlorethane'.[31]

However, the authorities had been originally suspicious of Titanine because it used a more flammable nitro-cellulose base rather than the acetyl cellulose foundation that was the preference of government scientists, and as a consequence the company was obliged to prove the qualities of their composition. Ultimately, the fundamental qualities of durability, adhesion and flexibility, combined with the ability to resist fire, were successfully demonstrated and Titanine became the favoured product of aeroplane manufacturers such as A.V. Roe for covering their machines once the use of government specified dopes had been relaxed.[32] In terms of the Royal Aircraft Factory, which had been renamed the Royal Aircraft Establishment in 1918 to avoid being confused with the newly formed Royal Air Force, there were still rumblings regarding supposed government monopolies in early manufacture. In a 1923 report of the Gothenburg Airshow, the decision of the Swedes to only manufacture aeroplanes in government factories was likened by British aeronautical commentators to 'the state of affairs that obtained in this country in the evil days when all British military machines were produced at the Royal Aircraft Factory by the best brains in the country'.[33]

In January 1934, *The Times* reported the successful order for forty-five tonnes of British-manufactured 'Cellon' aeroplane dope for export to the Turkish government. The article noted that this was particularly satisfying because the market had been almost exclusively dominated by France, a fact that caused some surprise considering the government's extensive wartime investment in the British Cellulose Company.[34] Even following technological progression which ensured aircraft airframes were manufactured predominantly of aluminium, there remained a need for a plentiful supply of aeroplane dope to treat fabric-covered control surfaces. In fact, the airframes of many of the principal British training aircraft such as the De Havilland Tiger Moth, Avro Anson and Airspeed Oxford retained their fabric coverings.[35] By the late 1930s, when Britain found itself once again in the shadow of global conflict, familiar questions regarding the security of aeroplane dope supply were once again being raised in the House of Commons.

On the 24 November 1937, the Under-Secretary of State for Air, Lieutenant-Colonel Anthony Muirhead, gave the following reassurance to the House when asked how many companies were supplying aeroplane dope to the government as Air Ministry contractors and 'under what conditions new manufacturers who may wish to supply this materiel' were allowed to tender:

> Seven firms are approved for the supply of aeroplane dope. As regards the second part of the question new manufacturers are required to submit the materiel offered to laboratory and service tests, each of six months' duration, with a view to ascertaining that the required standards as regards adhesion to fabric, tautening properties, durability, etc., are complied with.[36]

Those members of the House that were old enough to remember the legacy of the First World War were no doubt determined to avoid a repeat of the circumstances that had previously caused such embarrassment to the government. Although previously little remembered in the twenty-first century, the 'dope scandal' is an integral ingredient in the story of the development of the British military airpower and the subsequent progress of commercial aviation. The next great strides in the history of the aeroplane are likely to be found in securing alternative power sources and experiments have recently taken place with cellulosic biofuels made from wood pulp to power commercial aircraft.[37] However, these investigations have revealed that although technically possible, the use of carbon offset remains negligible, and further work will inevitably be required to secure the future development of the British aircraft industry. However, it would seem fitting indeed to think that cellulose could in fact prove to be a potential solution to the future of aviation and the past scandal regarding its manufacture may well be worth remembering.

Notes

Introduction

1. H. Driver, *The Birth of British Military Aviation: Britain 1903–1914* (Suffolk: Boydell & Brewer, 1997).
2. W. Raleigh, *The War in the Air: Being the Story of the Part Played in the Great Air War by the Royal Air Force* (Oxford: Clarendon Press, 1922); H.M.S.O., *The Official History of the Ministry of Munitions: Volume VIII, Control of Industrial Capacity and Equipment* (London: H.M.S.O., 1922); H.M.S.O., *The Official History of the Ministry of Munitions: Volume IX, Part II, Design and Inspection* (London: H.M.S.O., 1922); H.M.S.O., *The Official History of the Ministry of Munitions: Volume XII, The Supply of Munitions* (London: H.M.S.O., 1921); H.M.S.O., *The Official History of the Ministry of Munitions: Volume XII, Part I, Aircraft* (London: H.M.S.O., 1921); A.J. Jackson, *AVRO Aircraft since 1908* (London: Putman & Company, 1965).
3. L.E. Opdycke, 'O Romeo, Romeo, Wherefore Art Thou Romeo? – or … Aviation Reporting and the Aviation Press', *Aerospace Historian*, Vol. 35, no. 2 (1988): 120–2.
4. J. Black, *Rethinking Military History* (London: Routledge, 2004), 202–3.
5. A. Fage, J.L. Nayler, E.F. Relf and G. Temple, 'Leonard Bairstow: 1880–1963', *Biographical Memoirs of Fellows of the Royal Society*, Vol. 11 (November 1965): 22–40, 23.
6. A. Jungdahl, 'Public Influence on the Proliferation of Military Aviation 1907–1912', *Air Power History*, Vol. 60, no. 1 (Spring 2013): 28–39, 34–5.
7. 'The Government and Aerial Navigation', *The Times*, 6 May 1909, 14.
8. 'The Cross-Channel Flight', *The Times*, 26 July 1909, 9.
9. Ibid., 35.
10. 'The Gordon Bennett Cup', *The Times*, 27 August 1909, 8.
11. G.C. Loening, 'Lessons of the 1911 International Cup Race', *Scientific American*, Vol. 105, no. 8 (19 August 1911): 170–7.
12. L. d'Orcy, 'How the War Has Modified the Aeroplane', *Scientific American*, Vol. 113, no. 10 (4 September 1915): 196–7, 196.

13 'Dropping Bombs on Balloons and Targets', *Scientific American*, Vol. 107, no. 13 (28 September 1912): 254.
14 Hansard Parliamentary Debates: HC Deb, Vol. 4 (27 November 1912): cc.1242–1245.
15 'The Reported Visits of Airships', *The Times*, 26 February 1913, 8.
16 B. Holman, 'The Phantom Airship Panic of 1913: Imagining Aerial Warfare in Britain before the Great War', *Journal of British Studies*, Vol. 55, no. 1 (January 2016): 99–121, 120–1.
17 D. Henderson, *Military Aeroplane Competition 1912: Report of the Judges Committee* (London: H.M.S.O., 1912), 3.
18 G. de Havilland, '*Sky Fever*' (Shrewsbury: Airlife Ltd., 1979), 77.
19 T. Treadwell, *British & Allied Aircraft Manufacturers of the First World War* (Stroud: Amberley Publishing Ltd., 2011), 179–80.
20 A.J. Jackson, *AVRO Aircraft since 1908* (London: Putman & Company, 1965), 59–61.
21 T. Jenkins, *The Airborne Forces Experimental Establishment* (Solihull: Helion & Company, 2015), 57.
22 Hansard Parliamentary Debates: HL Deb, Vol. 22 (1 August 1916): cc.1008–1009.
23 G. de Havilland, '*Sky Fever*' (Shrewsbury: Airlife Ltd., 1979), 89–90.
24 Hansard Parliamentary Debates: HC Deb, Vol. 56 (30 July 1913): c.541.
25 'The Cross-Channel Flight Accomplished', *The Times*, 26 July 1909, 8.
26 Hansard Parliamentary Debates: HC Deb, Vol. 56 (30 July 1913): c.668.
27 H. Driver, *The Birth of British Military Aviation: Britain 1903–1914* (Suffolk: Boydell & Brewer, 1997), 92–5.
28 *Canada at War: Speeches Delivered by the Right Honourable Sir Robert Laird Borden* (December 1914), 25.
29 H.M.S.O., *British Cellulose Committee Inquiry Report* (London: H.M.S.O., 1919), 7.
30 K. Robert, 'Constructions of "Home", "front", and Women's Employment in the First World War', *History and Theory*, Vol. 52, no. 3 (2013): 319–43.
31 D. French, *The Strategy of the Lloyd George Coalition, 1916–1918* (Oxford: Clarendon Press, 1999), 84.
32 D. Ahlstrom, 'The Hidden Reason Why the First World War Matters Today: The Development and Spread of Modern Management', *The Brown Journal of World Affairs*, Vol. 21, no. 1 (2014): 201–18, 214.
33 V. Simmonds, & G. Alan, *Britain and World War I* (London: Routledge, 2012), 74.

34 K. Grieves, 'Lloyd George and the Management of the British War Economy', R. Chickering & S. Förster (ed), Great War, *Total War: Combat and Mobilization on the Western Front, 1914-1918* (Cambridge: Cambridge University Press, 2000), 380-1.
35 J. Sweetman, 'Crucial Months for Survival: The Royal Air Force, 1918-19', *Journal of Contemporary History*, Vol. 19, no. 3 (1984): 529-47, 530.
36 V. Simmonds, & G. Alan, *Britain and World War I* (London: Routledge, 2012), 11.

Chapter 1

1 R. Higham, 'Quantity vs. Quality: The Impact of Changing Demand on the British Aircraft Industry, 1900 – 1960', *Business History Review*, Vol. 42, no. 4 (1968): 443-6, 445.
2 C.H. Claudy, 'England's Aircraft Industry', *Scientific American*, Vol. 120, no. 13 (29 March 1919): 314.
3 M. Paris, 'Air Power and Imperial Defence', *Journal of Contemporary History*, Vol. 24, no. 2 (1989): 209-25, 214, 215.
4 A. Gollin, 'The Mystery of Lord Haldane and Early British Military Aviation', *A Quarterly Journal Concerned with British Studies*, Vol. 11, no. 1 (1979): 46-65, 48.
5 'Count Zeppelin's Air Ship', *The Morning Post*, 31 October 1900, 5.
6 'The Conquest of the Air: Its National Importance', *The Times*, 13 July 1908, 10.
7 'Balloons in War', *Pall Mall Gazette*, 23 May 1900, 3.
8 'Cody Kites for the British Army', *Scientific American*, Vol. 97, no. 1 (6 July 1907): 8.
9 H.M.S.O., *Army Appropriation Account 1912-1913* (London: H.M.S.O., 1914), 61.
10 The predecessor to the Royal Flying Corps, which was formed on 13 April 1913.
11 Hansard Parliamentary Debates: HC Deb, Vol. 32 (4 December 1911): cc1178-81.
12 Ibid.
13 '£75 The Cost of a Pilot's Certificate', *The Penny Illustrated Paper*, 16 November 1916, 619.
14 'Women's Aerial League', *The Times*, 30 December 1909, 8.
15 E. Bruce, *Aircraft in War* (London: Hodder & Stoughton, 1914), 144-5.
16 'The War Office and Aeroplanes', *The Times*, 11 March 1909, 8.

17 W. Wright, 'Flying as a Sport and Its Possibilities', *Scientific American*, Vol. 98, no. 9 (29 February 1908): 139.
18 'The Wright Brothers in France', *The Times*, 23 July 1908, 17.
19 O. Wright & W. Wright, 'Mechanical Flight', *Science*, Vol. 23, no. 588 (6 April 1906): 557–8.
20 Santos-Dumont's record was awarded by the Fédération Aéronautique Internationale for a flight of 220 metres in 21.5 seconds.
21 'Military Aeronautics: Debate in the French Senate', *The Times*, 1 April 1910, 5.
22 A. Jungdahl, 'Public Influence on the Proliferation of Military Aviation 1907–1912', *Air Power History*, Vol. 60, no. 1 (2013): 28–39, 34.
23 'The Future of Aviation in England', *The Times*, 3 February 1912, 6.
24 War Office, *Memorandum on Naval and Military Aviation* (London: H.M.S.O., 1912), 2–4.
25 C. Grahame-White & H. Harper, *The Aeroplane in War* (London: T. Werner Laurie, 1912), 72–3.
26 T.N.A, F.O. 371, Volume: 2092: Russian Aeroplane Built by Sikorsky (13 March to 19 July 1914).
27 'The Royal Aircraft Factory: Its Present Position', *The Times*, 24 April 1912, 6.
28 War Office, *Memorandum on Naval and Military Aviation*, 11.
29 M. O'Gormon, 'Aeroplane Efficiency', *Journal of the Royal Society of Arts*, Vol. 60, no. 3081 (8 December 1911): 100.
30 'The International Aero Exhibition at Olympia', *Journal of the Royal Society of Arts*, Vol. 61, no. 3144 (21 February 1913): 384–5, 384.
31 D. Henderson, *Military Aeroplane Competition 1912: Report of the Judges Committee* (London: H.M.S.O., 1912), 3.
32 Ibid.
33 'Funeral of Mr. Cody', *The Times*, 12 August 1913, 5.
34 'The Aerial League of the British Empire' was founded in 1909 for the promotion of British Aeronautics and to combat their perceived government apathy to aviation research.
35 J. Strutt, *Treasury Committee to Consider Desirability of Establishing National Physical Laboratory* (London: H.M.S.O., 1898), 1.
36 H.M.S.O., *Report of the Advisory Committee for Aeronautics: For the Year 1910–11* (London: H.M.S.O., 1910), 10–11.
37 Ibid., 20–6.
38 J. Seely, *Memorandum of the Secretary of State Relating to the Army Estimates for 1913–1914* (London: H.M.S.O., 1913), 11.

39 'Aeronautics: Advisory Committee Report', *The Times*, 13 November 1912, 26.
40 H.M.S.O., *Report of the Advisory Committee for Aeronautics: For the Year 1911–12* (London: H.M.S.O., 1912), 4.
41 H.M.S.O., *History of the Ministry of Munitions: Volume VIII, Control of Industrial Capacity and Equipment* (London: H.M.S.O., 1922), 38.
42 'The German Airmen', *New York Times Current History of the European War*, 1 March 1915, 933.
43 H.M.S.O., *Report of the Advisory Committee for Aeronautics: For the Year 1909–10* (London: H.M.S.O., 1910), 8.
44 H.M.S.O., *Report of the Advisory Committee for Aeronautics: For the Year 1912–13* (London: H.M.S.O., 1913), 17–18.
45 H.M.S.O., *Report of the Advisory Committee for Aeronautics: For the Year 1913–14* (London: H.M.S.O., 1914), 21.
46 R.T. Glazebrook, *Report of the Departmental Committee on the Accidents to Monoplanes* (London: H.M.S.O., 1912), 9.
47 I.W.M., Emp 62/4, *National Physical Laboratory Report for the Year 1914–15* (Teddington: W.F. Parrot, 1915), 24.
48 'Aeronautics and the Air Service', *The Times*, 8 January 1914, 4.
49 Hansard Parliamentary Debates: HC Deb, Vol. 58 (17 February 1914): c753.
50 Hansard Parliamentary Debates: HC Deb, Vol. 58 (18 February 1914): cc928–929.
51 Hansard Parliamentary Debates: HC Deb, Vol. 61 (20 April 1914): c577.
52 H.M.S.O., *Report of the Advisory Committee for Aeronautics: For the Year 1913–14* (London: H.M.S.O., 1914), 21.
53 Ibid.
54 Hansard Parliamentary Debates: HC Deb, Vol. 61 (29 April 1914): cc1684–1751.
55 Ibid.

Chapter 2

1 H.M.S.O., *Memorandum on Military and Naval Aviation* (London: H.M.S.O., 1913), 1–2.
2 D. Henderson, *Military Aeroplane Competition 1912: Report of the Judges Committee* (London: H.M.S.O., 1912), 2–5.
3 P. Fearon, 'The Formative Years of the British Aircraft Industry, 1913–1924', *The Business History Review*, Vol. 43, no. 4 (Winter 1969), 476–95, 482–3.

4   H.M.S.O., *Memorandum on Military and Naval Aviation*, 6–7.
5   J.A. Fairlie, 'Advisory Committees in British Administration', *The American Political Science Review*, Vol. 20, no. 4, (November 1926): 812.
6   'The Royal Aircraft Factory: Its Present Position', *The Times*, 24 April 1912, 6.
7   C. Grahame-White, *Aviation* (London: Collins, 1912) 209–10.
8   'The King and Methods of Warfare: Flying at Farnborough', *The Times*, 18 May 1912, 8.
9   F.W. Lanchester, *Aircraft in Warfare: The Dawn of the Fourth Arm* (London: Constable & Company, 1916) 172.
10 'Aviation as an Investment', *The Times*, 13 September 1912, 13.
11 'Aeronautics: Advisory Committee Report', *The Times*, 13 November 1912, 26.
12 'Aeronautical Society: Aeroplane Stability Devices', *The Times*, 29 January 1913, 24.
13 'Engineers at the R.A.F.', *Flight Magazine*, Vol. V, no. 11 (15 March 1913): 298.
14 Ibid.
15 'The Royal Aircraft Factory', *The Times*, 8 January 1914, 4.
16 H.M.S.O., *Memorandum on Military and Naval Aviation*, 2.
17 'The Supply of Aircraft', *The Times*, 13 January 1914, 10.
18 Ibid.
19 W. A. Robson, *Aircraft in War and Peace* (London: Macmillan, 1916), 121–2.
20 H.M.S.O., *The Official History of the Ministry of Munitions: Volume IX, Part II, Design and Inspection* (London: H.M.S.O., 1921), 18–19.
21 'The Royal Aircraft Factory and the Industry', *Flight Magazine*, Vol. VI, no. 5 (31 January 1914): 105.
22 C. MacLeod, 'Reluctant Entrepreneurs: Patents and State Patronage in New Technosciences, circa 1870–1930', *Isis*, Vol. 103, no. 2 (June 2012): 328–39, 336.
23 B. Williams, 'The War Aeroplane Here and Abroad', *Scientific American*, Vol. 115, no. 19 (4 November 1916): 412.
24 'Wright Aircraft Patents', *The Times*, 7 October 1916, 5.
25 C. Macleod, 'Reluctant Entrepreneurs: Patents and State Patronage in New Technosciences, circa 1870–1930', 337.
26 'The Royal Aircraft Factory and the Industry', *Flight Magazine*, Vol. VI, no. 5 (31 January 1914): 113.
27 'The Royal Aircraft Factory and the Industry: Letters', *Flight Magazine*, Vol. VI, no. 5 (31 January 1914): 125.
28 Ibid.
29 'British Progress in the Air', *The Times*, 26 February 1914, 7.

30 M. O'Gormon, 'The RAF and the Private Constructor', Flight Magazine, Vol. VI, no. 22 (17 July 1914): 747–8.
31 Idid.
32 H.M.S.O., Army Estimates of Effective and Non-Effective Services for the Year 1914–15 (London: H.M.S.O., 1914), 68.
33 Hansard Parliamentary Debates: HC Deb, Vol. 60 (24 March 1914): cc240–2.
34 The F.E.2a entered squadron service in 1915 in the fighter/reconnaissance role but was soon superseded by more powerful variants of the design.
35 Ibid.
36 'Nailed to the Counter', Flight Magazine, no. 20, Vol. 6 (15 May 1914): 506.
37 'Army Aeroplanes – Reports on Recent Accidents', The Times, 31 July 1914, 4.
38 Hansard Parliamentary Debates: HC Deb, Vol. 60 (24 March 1914): cc242–3.
39 Ibid.
40 Hansard Parliamentary Debates: HC Deb, Vol. 60 (24 March 1914): cc282–4.
41 H. Bannerman-Phillips, 'The New British "Mark R.E." Biplane', Scientific American, Vol. 111, no. 3 (18 July 1914): 42.
42 D. Egerton, England and the Aeroplane: Militarism, Modernity and Machines (London: Penguin, 2013), 11–12.
43 H.M.S.O., The Official History of the Ministry of Munitions: Volume XII, Part I, Aircraft (London: H.M.S.O., 1921) 17–18.
44 Ibid., 1.
45 M.R. Irwin, 'A Note on Public Sector Integration: The Decline of British Naval Aviation, 1914–1945', Review of Industrial Organization, Vol. 14, no. 1 (February 1999), 85–90, 86–7.
46 'Aircraft in War', Scientific American, Vol. 111, no. 11 (5 September 1915): 170–2, 170.
47 'An Airman's Duel', The Times, 30 September 1914, 8.
48 University of Coventry: Frederick Lanchester Archive: Typed Copy of a Note by Frederick Lanchester on the Question of Attack on Aircraft by Aircraft for the Sub-Committee, Aeroplanes (4 October 1915).
49 Hansard Parliamentary Debates: HC Deb, Vol. 70 (23 February 1915): cc167–168.
50 Hansard Parliamentary Debates: HC Deb, Vol. 73 (19 July 1915): cc1173–4.
51 The Department of Military Aeronautics was created in 1913, when the control of military aviation was separated from the Master-General of the Ordnance.
52 Hansard Parliamentary Debates: HC Deb, Vol. 73 (19 July 1915): cc1173–4.

53 University of Coventry: Frederick Lanchester Archive, Typed Report (T.673-8) of the Advisory Committee for Aeronautics: Sub-Committee on the Capabilities of an Aeroplane in Relation to Its Size (April 1916), 6.
54 T.N.A., CAB 24/1/32, War Policy: Report and Supplementary Memoranda of a Cabinet Committee, by A. Henderson (12 October 1915).

Chapter 3

1 H.M.S.O., *Minutes of Evidence and Appendices of The Departmental Committee on Celluloid* (London: H.M.S.O., 1913), 124.
2 J. Kinloch, 'An Investigation of the Best Methods of Destroying Lice and Other Vermin', *The British Medical Journal*, Vol. 1, no. 2892 (3 June 1916): 789–93, 792.
3 H.M.S.O., *The Official History of the Ministry of Munitions: Volume XII, The Supply of Munitions* (London: H.M.S.O., 1921), 137.
4 A. Hamilton, 'Dope Poisoning in the Manufacture of Aeroplane Wings', *Monthly Review of the U.S. Bureau of Labor Statistics*, Vol. 5, no. 4 (October 1917): 18–19.
5 H.M.S.O., *The Official History of the Ministry of Munitions: Volume XII, The Supply of Munitions*, 136.
6 'Fabrics for Aeroplanes Wings', *The Times*, 10 December 1913, 24.
7 National Physical Laboratory: Last Year's Work, *The Times*, 21 May 1913, 26.
8 A. Hamilton, 'Dope Poisoning in the Making of Airplanes', *Monthly Review of the U.S. Bureau of Labor Statistics*, Vol. 6, no. 2 (February 1918): 37–64, 37.
9 Ibid., 38–9.
10 'Mysterious Disease of the Liver', *The Times*, 21 December 1914, 3.
11 W.H. Willcox, *An Outbreak of Toxic Jaundice due to Tetrachlorethane Poisoning: A New Type Amongst Aeroplane Workers* (London: The Lancet Office, 1915), 3–4.
12 Ibid., 4.
13 Ibid., 7.
14 Hansard Parliamentary Debates: HC Deb, Vol. 69 (11 February 1915): c703.
15 W. Schereschewsky, 'Maintenance of Health in Industries: Its Relation to the Adequate Production of War Materiels', *Public Health Reports*, Vol. 32, no. 22 (1 June 1917): 835–9, 837.
16 Hansard Parliamentary Debates: HC Deb, Vol. 69 (11 February 1915): c703.
17 Ibid., 12.

18 'Home Office Workmen's Compensation Act 1906, 15 July 1916', *The London Gazette*, 16 July 1915, 6961–2.
19 'Health in the Munition Factory', *The Times*, 27 March 1916, 5.
20 Ministry of Munitions, *Health of Munitions Workers Committee: Final Report: Industrial Health and Efficiency* (London: H.M.S.O., 1918).
21 W.H. Thompson, *The Industrial Injuries Act: A New Era for the Injured Worker* (London: Twentieth Century Press, 1948), 21.
22 Hansard Parliamentary Debates: HC Deb, Vol. 74 (16 September 1915): cc149–50.
23 Hansard Parliamentary Debates: HC Deb, Vol. 76 (8 December 1915): cc1402–403.
24 Ibid.
25 R.H. Brade, 'Courtrai Flax Notice: Issued on Behalf of the Army Council', *The London Gazette*, 9 January 1917, 379.
26 'Defence of the Realm Act: Prohibition of the Purchase and Sale of Russian Flax', *The London Gazette*, 28 January 1916, 1131.
27 'Defence of the Realm Act: Prohibition of the Purchase and Sale of Russian Flax', *The London Gazette*, 21 March, 3068.
28 R.H. Brade, 'Army Council Order: Cotton, Flax and Hemp Industries', *The London Gazette*, 27 April 1917, 3956.
29 Joint Order by the Admiralty and Army Council, 'Flax, Hemp and Jute Goods: Priority for Government Orders, 31 March 1917', *The London Gazette*, 20 April 1917, 3755.
30 War Office, 'The Flax Seed (Ireland) Order by R.H. Wade, 12 July 1917', *The London Gazette*, 17 July 1917, 7311.
31 H.M.S.O., *The Official History of the Ministry of Munitions: Volume XII, The Supply of Munitions* (London: H.M.S.O., 1921), 127.
32 Ibid.
33 'Flax-Growing in Ireland', *The Times*, 7 January 1918, 3.
34 J.H. Grisdale & R.J. Hutchinson, *Grow Flax for Fibre* (Ottawa: Dominion Experimental Farms, 1918).
35 'Notice of General License for Purchase of Blast Furnace Dust for Use as a Fertilizer under the Order of the Minister of Munitions', *The London Gazette*, 8 February 1918, 1834.
36 'Side Winds', *Flight Magazine*, Vol. 9, no. 24 (14 June 1917): 604.

Chapter 4

1. I.W.M., EMP 71/1, *Committee on Production: Findings (March 1915–May 1917)* (London: H.J. Wilson, 1917), 103.
2. 'Health in the Munitions Factory', *The Times*, 27 March 1916, 5.
3. Hansard Parliamentary Debates: HC Deb, Vol. 82 (11 May 1916): c899.
4. 'Cellon Extensions', *Flight Magazine*, Vol. 5, no. 29 (19 July 1913): 805.
5. Hansard Parliamentary Debates: HC Deb, Vol. 82 (11 May 1916).
6. 'Dope Poisoning', *Review of the U.S. Bureau of Labor Statistics*, Vol. 3, no. 5 (November 1916): 105–8, 108.
7. 'A Non-Poisonous Dope', *Flight Magazine*, Vol. 7, no. 13 (26 March 1915): 220.
8. 'A New British Dope Free of Tetrachlorethane and all Heavy Spirits', *Flight Magazine* (2 April 1915): 235.
9. Ibid., 235.
10. 'A New Non-Poisonous Dope', *Flight Magazine* (16 April 1915): 271.
11. 'Dopes – Poisonous and Otherwise', *Flight Magazine*, Vol. 8, no. 14 (6 April 1916): 280.
12. Hansard Parliamentary Debates, HC Deb: Vol. 83 (21 June 1916): cc141–2.
13. Ibid.
14. 'Dope Poisoning Troubles', *Flight Magazine*, Vol. 8, no. 13 (30 March 1916): 275.
15. 'The Supply of Dope', *Flight Magazine*, Vol. 8, no. 26 (29 June 1916): 550.
16. 'The Air Inquiry: Functions of the Factory', *The Times*, 13 July 1916, 5.
17. I.W.M., Document: 7142, Private Papers of Miss G.M. West, 1916–1917.
18. 'Dope Poisoning', *Flight Magazine*, Vol. 8, no. 14 (6 April 1916): 228.
19. 'Dope Poisoning', *Flight Magazine* (30 March 1916): 257.
20. Ibid.
21. Hansard Parliamentary Debates: HC Deb: Vol. 80 (7 March 1916): cc1366–7.
22. Hansard Parliamentary Debates: HC Deb: Vol. 80 (9 March 1916): cc1704.
23. 'Dope Poisoning', *Flight Magazine*, Vol. 8, no. 13 (30 March 1916): 257.
24. 'Dope Poisoning Troubles', *Flight Magazine* (6 April 1916): 302.
25. Hansard Parliamentary Debates: HC Deb: Vol. 83 (22 June 1916): cc313–314.
26. Ibid.
27. Ibid.
28. Hansard Parliamentary Debates: HC Deb: Vol. 85 (7 August 1916): cc662–3.
29. Hansard Parliamentary Debates: HC Deb: Vol. 85 (8 August 1916): cc854–55.
30. 'Dopes', *Flight Magazine*, Vol. 8, no. 18 (4 May 1916): 370.

31 I.W.M., MUN VII/19, *Ministry of Reconstruction, Report of the Engineering Trades (New Industries) Committee* (London: H.M.S.O., 1918), 25.
32 S. Welch, 'Cellulose Acetate', *British Medical Journal*, Vol. 2, no. 3327 (4 October 1924): 644.
33 I.W.M., EMP 45/4, *Factories & Workshops Department, Annual Report of the Chief Inspector of Factories and Workshops for the Year Ending 1917* (London: H.M.S.O., 1918), 18–20.
34 I.W.M., EMP 45/19, *A.M. Anderson, Women Workers and the Health of the Nation* (London: John Bale, Sons & Danielsson, 1918), 16.

Chapter 5

1 R.T. Wakelam, 'The Roaring Lions of the Air: Air Substitution and the Royal Air Force's Struggle for Independence after the First World War', *Air Power History*, Vol. 43, no. 3 (1996): 50–63, 50.
2 'The Air Committee Fiasco', *The Times*, 13 April 1916, 9.
3 H. Wynn, 'The Royal Air Force: Its Origin and History, 1918–1970', *Aerospace Historian*, Vol. 23, no. 3 (1976): 154–67, 154–6.
4 M. Cooper, 'Blueprint for Confusion: The Administrative Background to the Formation of the Royal Air Force, 1912–19', *Journal of Contemporary History*, Vol. 22, no. 3 (July 1987): 437–53, 438–40.
5 'The Air Election', *The Times*, 14 January 1916, 5.
6 Pemberton-Billing founded his own aeroplane company in 1913 constructing flying boats in Southampton; the business was sold to Hubert Scott-Paine in 1916 and renamed the Supermarine Aviation Works Ltd.
7 Hansard Parliamentary Debates: HC Deb, Vol. 80 (14 March 1916): cc1933.
8 Hansard Parliamentary Debates: HC Deb 16, Vol. 80 (14 March 1916): cc2249.
9 Hansard Parliamentary Debates: HC Deb, Vol. 82 (11 May 1916): cc900–2.
10 Ibid.
11 Hansard Parliamentary Debates: HC Deb, Vol. 82 (11 May 1916), cc899–900.
12 Hansard Parliamentary Debates: HC Deb, Vol. 82 (8 May 1916): c272.
13 Hansard Parliamentary Debates: HC Deb, Vol. 80 (14 March 1916): c1882.
14 T.N.A., CAB 24/2/29, Report of the Committee on the Royal Aircraft Factory by R. Burbidge (12 May 1916), 1.
15 Ibid.
16 Ibid., 4.

17 'Aircraft Factory Methods: The View of the Air Board', *The Times*, 27 July 1916, 9.
18 T.N.A., CAB 24/2/29, Report of the Committee on the Royal Aircraft Factory by R. Burbidge (12 May 1916), 5.
19 T.N.A., CAB 42/16/9, The Royal Aircraft Factory: Report by the President of the Air Board to the War Committee, by Lord Curzon (19 July 1916), 2.
20 Ibid., 3.
21 G. de Havilland, *'Sky Fever'* (Shrewsbury: Airlife Ltd., 1979), 72–3.
22 Hansard Parliamentary Debates: HL Deb, Vol. 22 (1 August 1916): cc1026.
23 Hansard Parliamentary Debates: HC Deb, Vol. 81 (22 March 1916): cc246.
24 Hansard Parliamentary Debates: HC Deb, Vol. 81 (28 March 1916): c619.
25 H.M.S.O., *Interim Report of the Committee on the Administration and Command of the Royal Flying Corps* (London: H.M.S.O., 1916), 3.
26 'R.F.C. Inquiry', *Flight Magazine*, Vol. 8, no. 26 (29 June 1916): 550.
27 *'Reform in the Air Services'*, *The Times*, 16 May 1916, 9.
28 Ibid.
29 Ibid.
30 Hansard Parliamentary Debates: HC Deb, Vol. 82 (17 May 1916): cc1572–618.
31 Ibid.
32 'The Air Enquiry: Lord Montagu's Evidence', *The Times*, 27 May 1916, 4.
33 'Presentation of the Aero Club Medals to the Wright Brothers', *The Scientific American*, Vol. 100, no. 25 (19 June 1909): 459.
34 'The Air Enquiry: Lord Montagu's Evidence', *The Times*, 27 May 1916, 4.
35 'Notes', *The Times Engineering Supplement*, 9 October 1907, 4.
36 G. Wallace, *Flying Witness: Harry Harper and the Golden Age of Aviation* (London: Putman, 1958), 55–6.
37 R. Higham, 'The Peripheral Weapon in Wartime', *The Air Power Historian*, Vol. 8, no. 2 (April 1961): 67–78, 68–9.
38 'The Air Enquiry: Lord Montagu's Evidence', *The Times*, 27 May 1916, 4.
39 H., Harper, *Ace Air Reporter* (London: John Gifford Ltd., 1943), 111.
40 'The Air Enquiry: Lord Montagu's Evidence', *The Times*, 27 May 1916, 4.
41 Fokker was a Dutch aircraft manufacturer based in Germany. The original designs for the *Die Fliegertruppe* were based on the French pre-war Morane-Saulnier G racing monoplane.
42 M. Cooper, 'The Development of Air Policy and Doctrine on the Western Front, 1914–1918', *Aerospace Historian*, Vol. 28, no. 1 (1981): 38–51, 42.
43 'The Air Enquiry: Sir Alfred Mond's Criticisms', *The Times*, 2 June 1916, 6.
44 C. Grahame-White & H. Harper, *Aircraft in the Great War: A Record & Study* (Chicago: A.C. McClurg & Co., 1915), 328–9.

45 'Divided Air Service: Lord Montagu on Army and Navy Jealousy', *The Times*, 2 June 1916, 6.
46 'The Air Inquiry: Observers and Their Prospects', *The Times*, 5 July 1916, 5.
47 Ibid.
48 'Aircraft Factory: Allegations and a Reply', *The Times*, 12 July 1916, 5.
49 Ibid.
50 Ibid.
51 Hansard Parliamentary Debates: HC Deb, Vol. 85 (16 August 1916): cc1850–51.
52 R.T. Glazebrook, *Report of the Departmental Committee on the Accidents to Monoplanes* (London: H.M.S.O., 1912).
53 Lord Rayleigh & F.J. Selby, 'Richard Tetley Glazebrook (1854–1935)', *Obituary Notices of Fellows of the Royal Society*, Vol. 2, no. 5 (December 1936): 28–56, 39.
54 'Aircraft Factory: Allegations and a Reply', *The Times*, 12 July 1916, 5.
55 'The Air Inquiry: Functions of the Factory', *The Times*, 13 July 1916, 5.
56 Ibid.
57 H.M.S.O., *Interim Report of the Committee on the Administration and Command of the Royal Flying Corps* (London: H.M.S.O., 1916), 8.
58 Ibid.
59 'The Royal Aircraft Factory Committee Report', *Flight Magazine*, Vol. VIII, no. 31 (3 August 1916): 637–40.
60 T.N.A., CAB 40/20/11, Supply of Aeroplanes, by Edwin Montagu (20 September 1916) 3.
61 Ibid.
62 Hansard Parliamentary Debates: HC Deb, Vol. 85 (10 August 1916): cc1216.
63 'The Air Board: Lord Montagu on Its Defective Position,' *The Times*, 23 October 1916, 5.
64 Lord Montagu, 'The Air Crisis: The Board and the Services', *The Times*, 6 November 1916, 3.
65 T.N.A., CAB 24/3/31, Duties and Functions of the Air Board, and Its Relationship with the Admiralty, War Office, and Ministry of Munitions, by H.P. Harvey (1 February 1917).
66 'The Committee and the R.A.F.', *Flight Magazine*, Vol. 8, no. 82 (28 December 1916): 1135.
67 T.N.A., CAB 24/6/60, State of the Air Service with the British Expeditionary Force, by Field-Marshal Haig (15 February 1917).
68 G. Sheffield, *The Chief: Douglas Haig and the British Army* (London: Aurum Press, 2012), 151–2.

69 T.N.A., CAB 24/6/60, War Office Response to Letter from Field Marshal, Commander-in-Chief, British Armies in France, by B.E. Cubbit (24 February 1917).
70 Ibid.
71 T.N.A., CAB 24/6/91, Air Board Response to Letter from Field Marshal, Commander-in-Chief, British Armies in France, by H.P. Harvey (1 March 1917).
72 Hansard Parliamentary Debates: HC Deb, Vol. 92 (26 April 1917): cc2626–7.
73 T.N.A, CAB 24/7/6, Air Board Report to the Cabinet, by H.P. Harvey (3 March 1917).
74 Ibid.
75 T.N.A., CAB 24/10/76, Letter to the Secretary of the War Cabinet in Response to Correspondence from Field-Marshal Haig, by H.P. Harvey (17 April 1917).
76 E. Grove, 'Air Force, Fleet Air Arm – or Armoured Corps? The Royal Naval Air Service at War', in T. Benbow (ed), *British Naval Aviation: The First 100 Years* (Surrey: Ashgate Publishing Limited, 2011), 45–6.

Chapter 6

1 A. Gollin, S.W. Whitehall, D. Lloyd George, & J.L. Garvin, 'Freedom or Control in the First World War: (The Great Crisis of May 1915)', *Historical Reflections*, Vol. 2, no. 2 (Winter 1976): 135–55, 140–2.
2 R. J. Q. Adams, 'Delivering the Goods: Reappraising the Ministry of Munitions: 1915–1916', *Albion: A Quarterly Journal Concerned with British Studies*, Vol. 7, no. 3 (Autumn, 1975): 232–44, 235–6.
3 H.M.S.O., *Ministry of Munitions Bill* (London: H.M.S.O., 1915).
4 'A Step in Government Control', *The Times*, 11 March 1915, 9.
5 K. Neilson, 'R. H. Brand, the Empire and Munitions from Canada', *The English Historical Review*, Vol. 126, no. 523 (December 2011): 1430–55, 1435–6.
6 H.M.S.O., *History of the Ministry of Munitions: Part IV, Vol. II, Munitions Organisation in Canada* (London: H.M.S.O., 1920), 77.
7 'Fuse Contract Enquiry in Canada', *The Times*, 31 May 1916, 7.
8 'The British Empire', *Political Science Quarterly*, Vol. 31, no. 3 (September 1916): 42–50, 48.
9 H.M.S.O., *History of the Ministry of Munitions: Part IV, Vol. II, Munitions Organisation in Canada*, 77.

10 K. Nielson, 'Russian Foreign Purchasing in the Great War: A Test Case', *The Slavonic and East European Review*, Vol. 60, no. 4 (1982): 574–5.
11 T.N.A. F.O. 371, Volume 2447: Provision of Munitions Russia, Col. Allison, Russian Orders from U.S. And Canada (January–February 1915).
12 T.N.A. F.O. 371, Volume 2448 Russian Orders in America; Colonel Alison (15–22 January 1915).
13 'Commission on Canadian Fuse Contract', *The Times*, 16 May 1916, 7.
14 'The Great Dope Monopoly', *Flight Magazine*, no. 31, Vol. X (1 August 1918): 847–8.
15 'New Industry for Derby', *The Derbyshire Advertiser*, 4 August 1916, 4.
16 H.M.S.O., *The Official History of the Ministry of Munitions: Volume VIII, Control of Industrial Capacity and Equipment, Part I, Review of State Manufacture* (London: H.M.S.O., 1921), 53.
17 H.M.S.O., *History of the Ministry of Munitions: The Supply of Munitions: Volume XII* (London: H.M.S.O., 1921), 136.
18 Ibid.
19 'The Great Dope Monopoly', *Flight Magazine*, Vol. X, no. 38 (1 August 1918): 847–8.
20 Ibid.
21 H.M.S.O., *Reports of the Select Committee on National Expenditure* (London: H.M.S.O., 1918), 2.
22 Hansard Parliamentary Debates: HC Deb, Vol. 109 (1 August 1918): cc662–772.
23 Ibid.
24 Ibid.
25 H.M.S.O., *Reports of the Select Committee on National Expenditure*, 50.
26 Ibid.
27 'Industrial Research in Canada' *Science*, Vol. 44, no. 1145 (8 December 1916): 810–1.
28 A debenture is long-term debt companies used by companies to raise capital.
29 Hansard Parliamentary Debates: HC Deb, Vol. 109 (1 August 1918): cc662–772.
30 'The Select Committee on National Expenditure', *The Spectator*, 3 August 1918, 115.
31 Hansard Parliamentary Debates: HC Deb, Vol. 109 (1 August 1918): cc662–772.
32 T.N.A., F.O. 371, Volume: 2444: Fine Imposed on Messrs. Vickers By Russian Government (15 March 1915).

33. T.N.A., F.O.371, Volume 2447: Decypher of Telegram from Sir G. Buchanan (9 March 1915).
34. T.N.A., F.O.371, Volume 2447: Decypher of Telegram from Sir C. Spring-Rice, Washington (5 May 1915).
35. T.N.A., F.O.371, Volume 2447: Draft Memo to Lord Kitchener from Sir Edward Grey (May 1915).
36. Ibid.
37. 'American Munition Supplies: The Alleged German Plot to Buy Control of Their Sources', *The New York Times Current History of the European War*, Vol. 2, no. 4 (July 1915): 673–8, 677.
38. H.M.S.O., Reports of the Select Committee on National Expenditure.
39. Hansard Parliamentary Debates: HC Deb, Vol. 109 (1 August 1918): cc662–772.
40. Ibid.
41. H.M.S.O., Reports of the Select Committee on National Expenditure.
42. 'General Aviation Accessories', *Flight Magazine Supplement: Aviation Clothing and Accessories* (19 November 1915): 3–4.
43. 'Cellon Progress', *Flight Magazine*, Vol. IX, no. 19, (10 May 1917): 466.
44. T.N.A., CAB 24/4/44, Problem of the Maintenance of the Armed Forces, by Sir Auckland Geddes (November 1917), 6.
45. H.M.S.O., Reports of the Select Committee on National Expenditure.
46. 'Contracts for Cellulose Acetate', *Flight Magazine*, no. 38, Vol. (1 August 1918): 864–7.
47. H.M.S.O., Reports of the Select Committee on National Expenditure.
48. 'Criticism of Munitions Contract', *The Times*, 27 July 1918, 3.
49. H.M.S.O., Reports of the Select Committee on National Expenditure.
50. Ibid.
51. Ibid.
52. Ibid.

Chapter 7

1. Sir William Bull was a Conservative politician and solicitor. He was closely associated with Sir Trevor Dawson through the Imperial Society of Knights Bachelor and Colonel Grant Morden through committees.
2. Hansard Parliamentary Debates: HC Deb, Vol. 109 (5 August 1918): cc1035–54.

3   Ibid.
4   Ibid.
5   Ibid.
6   J.A. Turner, 'The British Commonwealth Union and the General Election of 1918', *The English Historical Review*, Vol. 93, no. 368 (July 1978): 528–59, 532–3.
7   T.N.A., CAB 25/4/49, The Empire Resources Development Committee (5 June 1919).
8   H.M.S.O., *The Official History of the Ministry of Munitions: Volume XII, The Supply of Munitions* (London: H.M.S.O., 1921), 137–8.
9   Hansard Parliamentary Debates: HC Deb, Vol. 109 (5 August 1918): cc1035–54.
10 V. Cerretano, 'The Treasury, Britain's Postwar Reconstruction, and the Industrial Intervention of the Bank of England 1921–1929', *The Economic History Review*, Vol. 62, no. 1 (August 2009): 80–100, 92–3.
11 Hansard Parliamentary Debates: HC Deb, Vol. 109 (5 August 1918): cc1035–1054.
12 'Sir Richard Durning Holt Obituary', *Journal of the Royal Society of Arts*, Vol. 89, no. 4584 (4 April 1941): 312.
13 Hansard Parliamentary Debates: HC Deb, Vol. 109 (5 August 1918): cc1035–54.
14 'The Cellulose Acetate Monopoly', *Flight Magazine*, Vol. 10, no. 32 (8 August 1918): 893–6.
15 T.N.A., CAB 24/57/96, Summary of Blockade Information (5–11 July 1918), 4–5.
16 'The Cellulose Acetate Monopoly', *Flight Magazine*, 895.
17 Ibid.
18 Hansard Parliamentary Debates: Vol. 109 (8 August 1918): cc1545–6.
19 J. Pariseau, 'Circuits and Bumps: The Story of the RCAF's Aborted Takeoffs, 1909–1938', *Aerospace Historian*, Vol. 32, no. 3 (September 1985): 173–83, 177.
20 'A Canadian Flying Service', *Flight Magazine*, Vol. 10, no. 33 (15 August 1918): 904.
21 Canadian Major 'Billy' Bishop, born in Owen Sound, Ontario, was one of the highest scoring aces of the First World War credited with seventy-one aerial victories.
22 F.H. Ellis, *Canada's Flying Heritage* (Toronto: University of Toronto Press, 1981), 128.
23 'A Canadian Flying Service', *Flight Magazine*, Vol. 10, no. 33 (15 August 1918): 904.

24 'Airisms from the Four Winds' *Flight Magazine*, Vol. 10, no. 42 (17 October 1918): 1170.
25 K. O. Morgan, 'Lloyd George's Premiership: A Study in Prime Ministerial Government' *The Historical Journal*, Vol. 13, no. 1 (March 1970): 130–57, 139–40.
26 'Lloyd George's Acquisition of the Daily Chronicle in 1918', *Journal of British Studies*, Vol. 22, no. 1 (1982): 127–44, 131–3.
27 Hansard Parliamentary Debates: HC Deb, Vol. 110 (15 October 1918): c25.
28 'Newspapers & Monopolies', *The Times*, 16 October 1918, 12.
29 Hansard Parliamentary Debates: HC Deb, Vol. 110 (15 October 1918): cc78–94.
30 J.M. McEwen, 'The National Press during the First World War: Ownership and Circulation', *Journal of Contemporary History*, Vol. 17, no. 3 (July 1982): 459–86, 473–4.
31 J.M. McEwen, 'Northcliffe and Lloyd George at War, 1914–1918' *The Historical Journal*, Vol. 24, no. 3 (September 1981): 651–72, 651–2.
32 J.M. McEwen, 'Lloyd George's Acquisition of the Daily Chronicle in 1918', *Journal of British Studies*, Vol. 22, no. 1 (1982): 127–44, 135–6.
33 Hansard Parliamentary Debates: HC Deb, Vol. 110 (15 October 1918): cc78–94.
34 T.N.A., CAB 24/54/96, War Cabinet: Departure of Sir George Cave to the Hague (21 June 1918).
35 Hansard Parliamentary Debates: HC Deb, Vol. 110 (15 October 1918): cc78–94.
36 'Public Poison', *The Nottingham Journal and Expresss*, 6 August 1918, 2.
37 'The Cellulose Scandal: Still a Case for Inquiry', *The Times*, 14 March 1919, 6.
38 Hansard Parliamentary Debates: Vol. 113 (19 March 1919): cc2084–2085.
39 T.N.A., F.O. 1011/118-0006, *Paris Peace Conference: Guest List for Signing of The Treaty* (24 June 1919).
40 H.M.S.O., *British Cellulose Committee Inquiry Report* (London: H.M.S.O., 1919), 3.
41 Ibid.
42 Ibid., 4.
43 Hansard Parliamentary Debates: HC Deb, Vol. 109 (5 August 1918): cc1035–4.
44 H.M.S.O., *British Cellulose Committee Inquiry Report* (London: H.M.S.O., 1919), 6.
45 Ibid., 8.
46 A.J. Antony Morris, 'Haldane's Army Reforms 1906–8: The Deception of the Radicals', *History*, Vol. 56, no. 186 (February 1971): 17–34, 19.

47 H.M.S.O., *British Cellulose Committee Inquiry Report* (London: H.M.S.O., 1919), 10.
48 Ibid.
49 Ibid., 11.
50 B.C. Hesse, 'The Contribution of the Chemist to the Industrial Development of the United States', *Science*, Vol. 41, no. 1062 (7 May 1915): 665–75, 667.
51 G.G. Henderson, 'The Present Position and Future Prospects of the Chemical Industry in Great Britain', *Science*, Vol. 44, no. 1135 (29 September 1916): 435–48, 435.
52 H.M.S.O., British Cellulose Committee Inquiry Report (London: H.M.S.O., 1919), 12.
53 'No Departmental Favouritism' *The Times*, 15 August 1919, 8.
54 'The Cellulose Inquiry', *Flight Magazine*, Vol. 11, no. 34 (21 August 1919): 1119.
55 'A Case for Inquiry', *The Times*, 8 August 1918, 7.
56 'British Cellulose Company Fined', *The Times*, 8 January 1919, 3.

Conclusion

1 'British Cellulose: Forthcoming Investment', *The Times*, 25 February 1920, 21.
2 'British Cellulose: The Government's Position', *The Times*, 2 March 1920, 6.
3 Hansard Parliamentary Debates: HC Deb, Vol. 126 (2 March 1920): cc247–50.
4 Ibid.
5 H.M.S.O., *The Official History of the Ministry of Munitions: General Organisation of Munitions Supply, Volume II, Part I, Supplement, Liquidation of the Ministry of Munitions* (London: H.M.S.O., 1920), 41–2.
6 C.F. Cross, 'Recent Research in Cellulose Industry', *Journal of the Royal Society of Arts*, Vol. 68, no. 3541 (1 October 1920): 725–6.
7 'Company Meetings: British Cellulose & Chemical Manufacturing Company Ltd.', *The Times*, 10 December 1920, 19.
8 'British Cellulose Position: Official View of the Situation', *The Times*, 15 January 1921, 13.
9 T.N.A., CAB 24/137/23, Airships: Commander Burney's Scheme. Memorandum for the Chancellor of the Exchequer (12 June 1922).
10 Ibid.
11 Hansard Parliamentary Debates: HC Deb, Vol. 153 (8 May 1922): cc1822–3.
12 Ibid.

13 Hansard Parliamentary Debates: HC Deb, Vol. 161 (13 March 1923): cc1281–2.
14 Hansard Parliamentary Debates: HC Deb, Vol. 206 (26 May 1927): cc2175.
15 'Products and Appliances', *The Journal of the Royal Institute of Public Health and Hygiene*, Vol. 9, no. 12(December 1946): 405–7, 407.
16 'Brentford & Chiswick: Colonel Grant Morden and Cellulose', *The Times*, 6 December 1918, 10.
17 R. Murphy, 'Walter Long, the Unionist Ministers, and the Formation of Lloyd George's Government in December 1916', *The Historical Journal*, Vol. 29, no. 3. (September 1986): 737–8.
18 Lieutenant-Colonel Grant Morden, *The Times*, 27 June 1932, 19.
19 'When the Chemical Plant Echoed to the Sound of more than 20,000 Workers', *Derby Telegraph*, 28 April 2020, 22.
20 F.W. Lanchester, 'Mechanical Flight', *The Times Engineering Supplement*, 7 April 1909, 18.
21 Hansard Parliamentary Debates: HC Deb, Vol. 8 (2 August 1909): cc1564–8.
22 Hansard Parliamentary Debates: HC Deb, Vol. 42 (23 October 1912): cc2166–7.
23 J.H. Morrow Jr., 'Industrial Mobilization in World War I: The Prussian Army and the Aircraft Industry', *The Journal of Economic History*, Vol. 37, no. 1 (March 1977): 36–51, 43.
24 I.W.M., MUN.V/49, *Ministry of Munitions (Intelligence & Statistics Section): Report on Labour in Government Establishments in July 1918 (1918)*, 9.
25 C.H. Claudy, 'England's Aircraft Industry', *Scientific American*, Vol. 120, no. 13 (29 March 1919): 314.
26 P. Kennedy, 'Britain in the First World War', in A.R., Millet, & W., Murray (eds), *Military Effectiveness: Volume 1, The First World War* (Cambridge: Cambridge University Press, 2010), 34–5.
27 W. Raleigh, *The War in the Air: Being the Story of the Part Played in the Great Air War by the Royal Air Force* (Oxford: Clarendon Press, 1922), 162.
28 D. Thorburn, 'Aircraft Stunts for Aircraft Sports', *Flight Magazine*, Vol. 9, no. 38 (20 September 1917): 972.
29 'Aircraft Disposal Department', *The Times*, 20 November 1919, 16.
30 H.M.S.O., *The Official History of the Ministry of Munitions: General Organisation of Munitions Supply, Volume II, Part VIII, Inter-Allied Organisation* (London: H.M.S.O., 1920), 74.

31 'Titanine Ltd.', *Flight Magazine*, Vol. XIV, no. 59 (14 December 1922): 31.
32 Ibid.
33 'The Gothenburg Aero Show', *Flight Magazine*, Vol. 15, no. 30 (26 July 1923): 422.
34 'Aeroplane Dope for Turkey', *The Times*, 26 January 1934, 14.
35 A.J. Jackson, *AVRO Aircraft since 1908*, 319–20.
36 Hansard Parliamentary Debates: HC Deb, Vol. 329 (24 November 1937): cc1248–1249.
37 R. Bridger, *The Plane Truth: Aviation's Real Impact on People and the Environment* (London: Pluto Press, 2013), 41–2.

Bibliography

Primary sources

The National Archives, Kew

Cabinet office records

CAB 24/1/32, War Policy: Report and Supplementary Memoranda of a Cabinet Committee, by A. Henderson (12 October 1915).
CAB 24/2/29, Report of the Committee on the Royal Aircraft Factory by R. Burbidge (12 May 1916).
CAB 24/3/31, Duties and Functions of the Air Board, and Its Relationship with the Admiralty, War. Office, and Ministry of Munitions, by H.P. Harvey (1 February 1917).
CAB 24/4/44, Problem of the Maintenance of the Armed Forces, by Sir Auckland Geddes (November 1917).
CAB 24/6/60, State of the Air Service with the British Expeditionary Force, by Field-Marshal Haig (15 February 1917).
CAB 24/6/60, War Office Response to Letter from Field Marshal, Commander-in-Chief, British Armies in France, by B.E. Cubbit (24 February 1917).
CAB 24/6/91, Air Board Response to Letter from Field Marshal, Commander-in-Chief, British Armies in France, by H.P. Harvey (1 March 1917).
CAB 24/7/6, Air Board Report to the Cabinet, by H.P. Harvey (3 March 1917).
CAB 24/10/76, Letter to the Secretary of the War Cabinet in Response to Correspondence from Field-Marshal Haig, by H.P. Harvey (17 April 1917).
CAB 24/54/96, War Cabinet: Departure of Sir George Cave to the Hague (21 June 1918).
CAB 24/57/96, Summary of Blockade Information (5–11 July 1918).
CAB 24/137/23, Airships: Commander Burney's Scheme. Memorandum for the Chancellor of the Exchequer (12 June 1922).
CAB 25/4/49, The Empire Resources Development Committee (5 June 1919).
CAB 40/20/11, Supply of Aeroplanes, by Edwin Montagu (20 September 1916).
CAB 42/16/9, The Royal Aircraft Factory: Report by the President of the Air Board to the War Committee, by Lord Curzon (19 July 1916).
F.O. 371, Volume 2447: Provision of Munitions Russia, Col. Allison, Russian Orders from U.S. And Canada (January–February 1915).

F.O. 371, Volume: 2444: Fine Imposed on Messrs. Vickers By Russian Government (15 March 1915).

F.O. 371, Volume 2447: Decypher of Telegram from Sir G. Buchanan (9 March 1915).

F.O. 371, Volume 2447: Decypher of Telegram from Sir C. Spring-Rice, Washington (5 May 1915).

F.O. 371, Volume 2447: Draft Memo to Lord Kitchener from Sir Edward Grey (May 1915).

F.O. 371, Volume 2448 Russian Orders in America; Colonel Alison (15–22 January 1915).

F.O. 371, Volume: 2092: Russian Aeroplane Built by Sikorsky (13 March to 19 July 1914).

F.O. 1011/118-0006, Paris Peace Conference: Guest List for Signing of The Treaty (24 June 1919).

Imperial war museums:

Document: 7142, Private Papers of Miss G.M. West, 1916–17.

EMP 45/4, *Factories & Workshops Department, Annual Report of the Chief Inspector of Factories and Workshops for the Year Ending 1917* (London: H.M.S.O., 1918).

EMP 45/19, *A.M. Anderson, Women Workers and the Health of the Nation* (London: John Bale, Sons & Danielsson, 1918).

EMP 62/4, National Physical Laboratory Report for the Year 1914–15 (Teddington: W.F. Parrot, 1915).

EMP 71/1, Committee on Production: Findings *(March 1915–May 1917)*, (London: H.J. Wilson, 1917).

I.W.M., MUN.V/49, *Ministry of Munitions (Intelligence & Statistics Section): Report on Labour in Government Establishments in July 1918* (1918).

MUN VII/19, *Ministry of Reconstruction, Report of the Engineering Trades (New Industries) Committee* (London: H.M.S.O., 1918).

University of Coventry archive:

University of Coventry: Frederick Lanchester Archive: Typed Copy of a Note by Frederick Lanchester on the Question of Attack on Aircraft by Aircraft for the Sub-Committee, Aeroplanes (4 October 1915).

University of Coventry: Frederick Lanchester Archive, Typed Report (T.673-8) of the Advisory Committee for Aeronautics: Sub-Committee on the Capabilities of an Aeroplane in Relation to Its Size (April 1916).

H.M.S.O. official histories:

History of the Ministry of Munitions: Part IV, Vol. II, Munitions Organisation in Canada (London: H.M.S.O., 1920).

The Official History of the Ministry of Munitions: Volume VIII, Control of Industrial Capacity and Equipment (London: H.M.S.O., 1922).

The Official History of the Ministry of Munitions: Volume IX, Part II, Design and Inspection (London: H.M.S.O., 1922).

The Official History of the Ministry of Munitions: Volume XII, The Supply of Munitions (London: H.M.S.O., 1921).

The Official History of the Ministry of Munitions: Volume XII, Part I, Aircraft (London: H.M.S.O., 1921).

The Official History of the Ministry of Munitions: General Organisation of Munitions Supply, Volume II, Part I, Supplement, Liquidation of the Ministry of Munitions (London: H.M.S.O., 1920).

The Official History of the Ministry of Munitions: General Organisation of Munitions Supply, Volume II, Part VIII, Inter-Allied Organisation (London: H.M.S.O., 1920).

H.M.S.O. published parliamentary reports and papers:

Treasury Committee to Consider Desirability of Establishing National Physical Laboratory (London: H.M.S.O., 1898).

Report of the Advisory Committee for Aeronautics: For the Year 1909–10 (London: H.M.S.O., 1910).

Report of the Advisory Committee for Aeronautics: For the Year 1910–11 (London: H.M.S.O., 1910).

Report of the Advisory Committee for Aeronautics: For the Year 1911–12 (London: H.M.S.O., 1912).

Report of the Departmental Committee on the Accidents to Monoplanes (London: H.M.S.O., 1912).

Military Aeroplane Competition 1912: Report of the Judges Committee (London: H.M.S.O., 1912).

Memorandum on Naval and Military Aviation (London: H.M.S.O., 1912).

Memorandum on Military and Naval Aviation (London: H.M.S.O., 1913).

Memorandum of the Secretary of State Relating to the Army Estimates for 1913–1914 (London: H.M.S.O., 1913).

Minutes of Evidence and Appendices of the Departmental Committee on Celluloid (London: H.M.S.O., 1913).

Report of the Advisory Committee for Aeronautics: For the Year 1912-13 (London: H.M.S.O., 1913).
Army Appropriation Account 1912-1913 (London: H.M.S.O., 1914).
Army Estimates of Effective and Non-Effective Services for the Year 1914-15 (London: H.M.S.O., 1914).
Report of the Advisory Committee for Aeronautics: For the Year 1913-14 (London: H.M.S.O., 1914).
Ministry of Munitions Bill (London: H.M.S.O., 1915).
Interim Report of the Committee on the Administration and Command of the Royal Flying Corps (London: H.M.S.O., 1916).
Health of Munitions Workers Committee: Final Report: Industrial Health and Efficiency (London: H.M.S.O., 1918).
Reports of the Select Committee on National Expenditure (London: H.M.S.O., 1918).
British Cellulose Committee Inquiry Report (London: H.M.S.O., 1919).

Hansard parliamentary debates:

Hansard Parliamentary Debates: HC Deb, Vol. 8 (2 August 1909): cc1564–1568.
Hansard Parliamentary Debates: HC Deb, Vol. 32 (4 December 1911): cc1178–1181.
Hansard Parliamentary Debates: HC Deb, Vol. 42 (23 October 1912): cc2166–2167.
Hansard Parliamentary Debates: HC Deb, Vol. 4 (27 November 1912): cc1242–1245.
Hansard Parliamentary Debates: HC Deb, Vol. 56 (30 July 1913): c541.
Hansard Parliamentary Debates: HC Deb, Vol. 56 (30 July 1913): c668.
Hansard Parliamentary Debates: HC Deb, Vol. 58 (17 February 1914): c753.
Hansard Parliamentary Debates: HC Deb, Vol. 58 (18 February 1914): cc928–929.
Hansard Parliamentary Debates: HC Deb, Vol. 60 (24 March 1914): cc240–242.
Hansard Parliamentary Debates: HC Deb, Vol. 60 (24 March 1914): cc242–243.
Hansard Parliamentary Debates: HC Deb, Vol. 61 (20 April 1914): c577.
Hansard Parliamentary Debates: HC Deb, Vol. 61 (29 April 1914): cc1684–1751.
Hansard Parliamentary Debates: HC Deb, Vol. 69 (11 February 1915): c703.
Hansard Parliamentary Debates: HC Deb, Vol. 70 (23 February 1915): cc167–168.
Hansard Parliamentary Debates: HC Deb, Vol. 73 (19 July 1915): cc1173–1174.
Hansard Parliamentary Debates: HC Deb, Vol. 74 (16 September 1915): cc149–150.
Hansard Parliamentary Debates: HC Deb, Vol. 76 (8 December 1915): cc1402–1403.
Hansard Parliamentary Debates: HC Deb: Vol. 80 (7 March 1916): cc1366–1367.
Hansard Parliamentary Debates: HC Deb: Vol. 80 (9 March 1916): cc1704.
Hansard Parliamentary Debates: HC Deb, Vol. 82 (11 May 1916): cc900–902.
Hansard Parliamentary Debates: HC Deb, Vol. 80 (14 March 1916): c1882.

Hansard Parliamentary Debates: HC Deb, Vol. 80 (14 March 1916): cc1933.
Hansard Parliamentary Debates: HC Deb 16, Vol. 80 (14 March 1916): cc2249.
Hansard Parliamentary Debates: HC Deb, Vol. 81 (22 March 1916): cc246.
Hansard Parliamentary Debates: HC Deb, Vol. 81 (28 March 1916): c.619.
Hansard Parliamentary Debates: HC Deb, Vol. 82 (8 May 1916): c272.
Hansard Parliamentary Debates: HC Deb, Vol. 82 (11 May 1916): c899.
Hansard Parliamentary Debates: HC Deb, Vol. 82 (17 May 1916): cc1572–1618.
Hansard Parliamentary Debates, HC Deb: Vol. 83 (21 June 1916): cc141–142.
Hansard Parliamentary Debates: HC Deb: Vol. 83 (22 June 1916): cc313–314.
Hansard Parliamentary Debates: HL Deb, Vol. 22 (1 August 1916): cc1008–1009.
Hansard Parliamentary Debates: HL Debs, Vol. 22 (1 August 1916): cc1026.
Hansard Parliamentary Debates: HC Debates: Vol. 85 (7 August 1916): cc662–663.
Hansard Parliamentary Debates: HC Deb: Vol. 85 (8 August 1916): cc854–855.
Hansard Parliamentary Debates: HC Deb, Vol. 85 (10 August 1916): cc1216.
Hansard Parliamentary Debates: HC Deb, Vol. 85 (16 August 1916): cc1850–1851.
Hansard Parliamentary Debates: HC Deb, Vol. 92 (26 April 1917): cc2626–2627.
Hansard Parliamentary Debates: HC Deb, Vol. 109 (1 August 1918): cc662–772.
Hansard Parliamentary Debates: HC Deb, Vol. 109 (5 August 1918): cc1035–1054.
Hansard Parliamentary Debates: Vol. 109 (8 August 1918): cc1545–1546.
Hansard Parliamentary Debates: HC Deb, Vol. 110 (15 October 1918): c25.
Hansard Parliamentary Debates: HC Deb, Vol. 110 (15 October 1918): cc78–94.
Hansard Parliamentary Debates: Vol. 113 (19 March 1919): cc2084–2085.
Hansard Parliamentary Debates: HC Deb, Vol. 126 (2 March 1920): cc247–250.
Hansard Parliamentary Debates: HC Deb, Vol. 153 (8 May 1922): cc1822–1823.
Hansard Parliamentary Debates: HC Deb, Vol. 161 (13 March 1923): cc1281–1282.
Hansard Parliamentary Debates: HC Deb, Vol. 206 (26 May 1927): cc2175.
Hansard Parliamentary Debates: HC Deb, Vol. 329 (24 November 1937): cc1248–1249.

Books and articles:

Bannerman-Phillips, H., 'The New British "Mark R.E." Biplane', *Scientific American*, Vol. 111, no. 3 (18 July 1914): 42.

Bruce, E., *Aircraft in War* (London: Hodder & Stoughton, 1914).

Claudy, C.H., 'England's Aircraft Industry', *Scientific American*, Vol. 120, no. 13 (29 March 1919).

Cross, C.F., 'Recent Research in Cellulose Industry', *Journal of the Royal Society of Arts*, Vol. 68, no. 3541 (1 October 1920): 725–6.

d'Orcy, L. 'How the War Has Modified the Aeroplane', *Scientific American*, Vol. 113, no. 10 (4 September 1915): 196–7.

Fairlie, J.A., 'Advisory Committees in British Administration', *The American Political Science Review*, Vol.20, no. 4, (November 1926): 812.

Grahame-White, C., *Aviation* (London: Collins, 1912).

Grahame-White, C., & Harper, H., *The Aeroplane in War* (London: T. Werner Laurie, 1912).

Grahame-White, C., & Harper, H., *Aircraft in the Great War: A Record & Study* (Chicago: A.C. McClurg & Co., 1915).

Grisdale, J.H., & Hutchinson, R.J., *Grow Flax for Fibre* (Ottawa: Dominion Experimental Farms, 1918).

Hamilton, A., 'Dope Poisoning in the Manufacture of Aeroplane Wings', *Monthly Review of the U.S. Bureau of Labor Statistics*, Vol. 5, no. 4 (October 1917): 18–19.

Hamilton, A., 'Dope Poisoning in the Making of Airplanes', *Monthly Review of the U.S. Bureau of Labor Statistics*, Vol. 6, no. 2 (February 1918): 37–64.

Havilland, G., '*Sky Fever*' (Shrewsbury: Airlife Ltd., 1979).

Henderson, G.G., 'The Present Position and Future Prospects of the Chemical Industry in Great Britain', *Science*, Vol. 44, no. 1135 (29 September 1916): 435–48.

Hesse, B.C., 'The Contribution of the Chemist to the Industrial Development of the United States', *Science*, Vol. 41, no. 1062 (7 May 1915): 665–75, 667.

Kinloch, J. 'An Investigation of the Best Methods of Destroying Lice and Other Vermin', *The British Medical Journal*, Vol. 1, no. 2892 (3 June 1916): 789–93.

Lanchester, F.W., 'Mechanical Flight', *The Times Engineering Supplement*, 7 April 1909, 18.

Lanchester, F.W., *Aircraft in Warfare: The Dawn of the Fourth Arm* (London: Constable & Company, 1916).

Loening, G.C., 'Lessons of the 1911 International Cup Race', *Scientific American*, Vol. 105, no. 8 (19 August 1911): 170–7.

O'Gormon, M., 'Aeroplane Efficiency', *Journal of the Royal Society of Arts*, Vol. 60, no. 3081 (8 December 1911): 100–2.

O'Gormon, M., '*The RAF and the Private Constructor*', Flight Magazine, Vol. VI, no. 22 (17 July 1914): 747–8.

Raleigh, W., *The War in the Air: Being the Story of the Part Played in the Great Air War by the Royal Air Force* (Oxford: Clarendon Press, 1922).

Robson, W.A., *Aircraft in War and Peace* (London: MacMillan, 1916).

Schereschewsky, W., 'Maintenance of Health in Industries: Its Relation to the Adequate Production of War Materiels', *Public Health Reports*, Vol. 32, no. 22 (1 June 1917): 835–9.

Thompson, W.H., *The Industrial Injuries Act: A New Era for the Injured Worker* (London: Twentieth Century Press, 1948).

Thorburn, D., 'Aircraft Stunts for Aircraft Sports', *Flight Magazine*, Vol. 9, no. 38 (20 September 1917): 972.

Welch, S., 'Cellulose Acetate', *British Medical Journal*, Vol. 2, no. 3327 (4 October 1924): 644.

Willcox, W.H., An Outbreak of Toxic Jaundice Due to Tetrachlorethane Poisoning: A New Type amongst Aeroplane Workers (London: The Lancet Office, 1915), 3–7.

Williams, B., 'The War Aeroplane Here and Abroad', *Scientific American*, Vol. 115, no. 19 (4 November 1916): 412.

Wright, O., & Wright, W., 'Mechanical Flight', *Science*, Vol. 23, no. 588 (6 April 1906): 557–8.

Wright, W., 'Flying as a Sport and its Possibilities', *Scientific American*, Vol. 98, no. 9 (29 February 1908): 139.

Unattributed books and articles:

'Cody Kites for the British Army', *Scientific American*, Vol. 97, no. 1 (6 July 1907): 8.

'Presentation of the Aero Club Medals to the Wright Brothers', *The Scientific American*, Vol. 100, no. 25 (19 June 1909): 459.

'Dropping Bombs on Balloons and Targets', *Scientific American*, Vol. 107, no. 13 (28 September 1912).

'The International Aero Exhibition at Olympia', *Journal of the Royal Society of Arts*, Vol. 61, no. 3144 (21 February 1913): 384–5.

'Engineers at the R.A.F.', *Flight Magazine*, Vol. V, no. 4 (15 March 1913): 298.

'Cellon Extensions', *Flight Magazine*, Vol. 5, no. 29 (19 July 1913): 805.

'The Royal Aircraft Factory and the Industry', *Flight Magazine*, Vol. VI, no. 5 (31 January 1914): 105.

'The Royal Aircraft Factory and the Industry: Letters', *Flight Magazine*, Vol. VI, no. 5 (31 January 1914): 125.

'Nailed to the Counter', *Flight Magazine*, Vol. 6, no. 20 (15 May 1914): 506.

Canada at War: Speeches Delivered by the Right Honourable Sir Robert Laird Borden (December 1914).

'A Non-Poisonous Dope', *Flight Magazine*, Vol. 7, no. 13 (26 March 1915): 220.

'A New British Dope Free of Tetrachlorethane and All Heavy Spirits', *Flight Magazine*, (2 April 1915): 235.

'A New Non-Poisonous Dope', *Flight Magazine* (16 April 1915): 271.

'American Munition Supplies: The Alleged German Plot to Buy Control of Their Sources', *The New York Times Current History of the European War*, Vol. 2, no. 4 (July 1915): 673–8.

'Aircraft in War', *Scientific American*, Vol. 111, no. 11 (5 September 1915): 170–2.

'General Aviation Accessories', *Flight Magazine Supplement: Aviation Clothing and Accessories* (19 November 1915): 3–4.

'Dope Poisoning', *Flight Magazine*, Vol. 8, no. 13 (30 March 1916): 257.

'Dope Poisoning', *Flight Magazine*, Vol. 8, no. 14 (6 April 1916): 228.

'Dope Poisoning Troubles', *Flight Magazine* (6 April 1916): 302.

'Dopes – Poisonous and Otherwise', *Flight Magazine*, Vol. 8, no. 14 (6 April 1916): 280.

'Dopes', *Flight Magazine*, Vol. 8, no. 18 (4 May 1916): 370.

'The Supply of Dope', *Flight Magazine*, Vol. 8, no. 26 (29 June 1916): 550.

'R.F.C. Inquiry', *Flight Magazine*, Vol. 8, no. 26 (29 June 1916): 550.

'The Royal Aircraft Factory Committee Report', *Flight Magazine*, Vol. VIII, no. 31 (3 August 1916): 637–40.

'The British Empire', *Political Science Quarterly*, Vol. 31, no. 3 (September 1916): 42–50.

'Dope Poisoning', *Review of the U.S. Bureau of Labor Statistics*, Vol. 3, no. 5 (November 1916): 105–8.

'Industrial Research in Canada', *Science*, Vol. 44, no. 1145 (8 December 1916): 810–11.

'The Committee and the R.A.F', *Flight Magazine*, Vol. 8, no. 82 (28 December 1916): 1135.

'Cellon Progress', *Flight Magazine*, no. 19, Vol. IX (10 May 1917): 466.

'Side Winds', *Flight Magazine*, no. 24, Vol. 9 (14 June 1917): 604.

'The Great Dope Monopoly', *Flight Magazine*, no. 38, Vol. (1 August 1918): 847–8.

'Contracts for Cellulose Acetate', *Flight Magazine*, no. 31, Vol. X (1 August 1918): 864–7.

'The Cellulose Acetate Monopoly', *Flight Magazine*, Vol. 10, no. 32 (8 August 1918): 893–6.

'Airisms from the Four Winds' *Flight Magazine*, Vol. 10, no. 42 (17 October 1918): 1170.

'The Cellulose Inquiry', *Flight Magazine*, Vol. 11, no. 34 (21 August 1919): 1119.

'Titanine Ltd.', *Flight Magazine*, Vol. XIV, no. 59 (14 December 1922): 31.

'The Gothenburg Aero Show', *Flight Magazine*, Vol. 15, no. 30 (26 July 1923): 422.

'Sir Richard Durning Holt Obituary', *Journal of the Royal Society of Arts*, Vol. 89, no. 4584 (4 April 1941): 312.

'Products and Appliances', *The Journal of the Royal Institute of Public Health and Hygiene*, Vol. 9, no. 12 (December 1946): 405–7.

Newspaper articles

'Balloons in War', *Pall Mall Gazette*, 23 May 1900, 3.
'Count Zeppelin's Air Ship', *The Morning Post*, 31 October 1900.
'Notes', *The Times Engineering Supplement*, 9 October 1907, 4.
'The Conquest of the Air: Its National Importance', *The Times*, 13 July 1908, 10.
'The War Office and Aeroplanes', *The Times*, 11 March 1909, 8.
'The Government and Aerial Navigation', *The Times*, 6 May 1909.
'The Wright Brothers in France', *The Times*, 23 July 1908, 17.
'The Cross-Channel Flight', *The Times*, 26 July 1909.
'The Cross-Channel Flight Accomplished', *The Times*, 26 July 1909.
'The Gordon Bennett Cup', *The Times*, 27 August 1909.
'Women's Aerial League', *The Times*, 30 December 1909, 8.
'Military Aeronautics: Debate in the French Senate', *The Times*, 1 April 1910, 5.
'The Future of Aviation in England', *The Times*, 3 February 1912, 6.
'The Royal Aircraft Factory: Its Present Position', *The Times*, 24 April 1912, 6.
'The King and Methods of Warfare: Flying at Farnborough', *The Times*, 18 May 1912, 8.
'Aviation as an Investment', *The Times*, 13 September 1912, 13.
'Aeronautics: Advisory Committee Report', *The Times*, 13 November 1912, 26.
'Aeronautical Society: Aeroplane Stability Devices', *The Times*, 29 January 1913, 24.
'The Reported Visits of Airships', *The Times*, 26 February 1913.
National Physical Laboratory: Last Year's Work, *The Times*, 21 May 1913, 26.
'Funeral of Mr. Cody', *The Times*, 12 August 1913, 5.
'Fabrics for Aeroplanes Wings', *The Times*, 10 December 1913, 24.
'Aeronautics and the Air Service', *The Times*, 8 January 1914, 4.
'The Royal Aircraft Factory', *The Times*, 8 January 1914, 4.
'The Supply of Aircraft', *The Times*, 13 January 1914, 10.
'British Progress in the Air', *The Times*, 26 February 1914, 7.
'Army Aeroplanes – Reports on Recent Accidents', *The Times*, 31 July 1914, 4.
'An Airman's Duel', *The Times*, 30 September 1914, 8.
'Mysterious Disease of the Liver', *The Times*, 21 December 1914, 3.
'The German Airmen', *New York Times Current History of the European War*, 1 March 1915, 933.
'A Step in Government Control', *The Times*, 11 March 1915, 9.
'Defence of the Realm Act: Prohibition of the Purchase and Sale of Russian Flax', *The London Gazette*, 28 January 1916, 1131.
'The Air Election', *The Times*, 14 January 1916, 5.
'Health in the Munition Factory', *The Times*, 27 March 1916, 5.
'The Air Committee Fiasco', *The Times*, 13 April 1916, 9.

'Energy Without Organization', *The Times*, 10 May 1916, 9.
'Commission on Canadian Fuse Contract', *The Times*, 16 May 1916, 7.
'Reform in the Air Services', *The Times*, 16 May 1916, 9.
'The Air Enquiry: Lord Montagu's Evidence', *The Times*, 27 May 1916, 4.
'Fuse Contract Enquiry in Canada', *The Times*, 31 May 1916, 7.
'Divided Air Service: Lord Montagu on Army and Navy Jealousy', *The Times*, 2 June 1916, 6.
'The Air Enquiry: Sir Alfred Mond's Criticisms', *The Times*, 2 June 1916, 6.
'The Air Inquiry: Observers and Their Prospects', *The Times*, 5 July 1916, 5.
'Aircraft Factory: Allegations and a Reply', *The Times*, 12 July 1916, 5.
'The Air Inquiry: Functions of the Factory', *The Times*, 13 July 1916, 5.
'Home Office Workmen's Compensation Act 1906, 15 July 1916', *The London Gazette*, 16 July 1915, 6961–2.
'Aircraft Factory Methods: The View of the Air Board', *The Times*, 27 July 1916, 9.
'New Industry for Derby', *The Derbyshire Advertiser*, 4 August 1916, 4.
'Wright Aircraft Patents', *The Times*, 7 October 1916, 5.
'The Air Board: Lord Montagu on Its Defective Position,' *The Times*, 23 October 1916, 5.
Lord Montagu, 'The Air Crisis: The Board and the Services', *The Times*, 6 November 1916, 3.
'£75 The Cost of a Pilot's Certificate', *The Penny Illustrated Paper*, 16 November 1916, 619.
'Courtrai Flax Notice: Issued on Behalf of the Army Council', *The London Gazette*, 9 January 1917, 379.
'Defence of the Realm Act: Prohibition of the Purchase and Sale of Russian Flax', *The London Gazette*, 21 March 1917, 3068.
'Joint Order by the Admiralty and Army Council, Flax, Hemp and Jute Goods: Priority for Government Orders, 31 March 1917', *The London Gazette*, 20 April 1917, 3755.
'Army Council Order: Cotton, Flax and Hemp Industries', *The London Gazette*, 27 April 1917, 3956.
'The Flax Seed (Ireland) Order by R.H. Wade, 12 July 1917,' *The London Gazette*, 17 July 1917, 7311.
'A Canadian Flying Service', *Flight Magazine*, Vol. 10, no. 33 (15 August 1918): 904.
'Flax-Growing in Ireland', *The Times*, 7 January 1918, 3.
'Notice of General License for Purchase of Blast Furnace Dust for Use as a Fertilizer under the Order of the Minister of Munitions', *The London Gazette*, 8 February 1918, 1834.

'Criticism of Munitions Contract', *The Times*, 27 July 1918, 3.
'The Select Committee on National Expenditure', *The Spectator*, 3 August 1918, 115.
'Public Poison', *The Nottingham Journal and Express*, 6 August 1918, 2.
'A Case for Inquiry', *The Times*, 8 August 1918, 7.
'Newspapers & Monopolies', *The Times*, 16 October 1918, 12.
'Brentford & Chiswick: Colonel Grant Morden and Cellulose', *The Times*, 6 December 1918, 10.
'British Cellulose Company Fined', *The Times*, 8 January 1919, 3.
'The Cellulose Scandal: Still a Case for Inquiry', *The Times*, 14 March 1919, 6.
'No Departmental Favouritism' *The Times*, 15 August 1919, 8.
'Aircraft Disposal Department', *The Times*, 20 November 1919, 16.
'British Cellulose: Forthcoming Investment', *The Times*, 25 February 1920, 21.
'British Cellulose: The Government's Position', *The Times*, 2 March 1920, 6.
'Company Meetings: British Cellulose & Chemical Manufacturing Company Ltd.', *The Times*, 10 December 1920, 19.
'British Cellulose Position: Official View of the Situation', *The Times*, 15 January 1921, 13.
Lieutenant-Colonel Grant Morden, *The Times*, 27 June 1932, 19.
'Aeroplane Dope for Turkey', *The Times*, 26 January 1934, 14.
'When the Chemical Plant Echoed to the Sound of More Than 20,000 Workers', *Derby Telegraph*, 28 April 2020, 22.

Secondary sources

Books and articles:

Adams, R.Q.M., 'Delivering the Goods: Reappraising the Ministry of Munitions: 1915–1916', *Albion: A Quarterly Journal Concerned with British Studies*, Vol. 7, no. 3 (Autumn, 1975): 232–44.

Ahlstrom, D., 'The Hidden Reason Why the First World War Matters Today: The Development and Spread of Modern Management', *The Brown Journal of World Affairs*, Vol. 21, no. 1 (2014): 201–18.

Black, J., *Rethinking Military History* (London: Routledge, 2004).

Bridger, R., *The Plane Truth: Aviation's Real Impact on People and the Environment* (London: Pluto Press, 2013).

Cerretano, V., 'The Treasury, Britain's Postwar Reconstruction, and the Industrial Intervention of the Bank of England 1921–1929', *The Economic History Review*, Vol. 62, no. 1 (August 2009): 80–100.

Cooper, M., 'The Development of Air Policy and Doctrine on the Western Front, 1914–1918', *Aerospace Historian*, Vol. 28, no. 1 (1981): 38–51.

Cooper, M., 'Blueprint for Confusion: The Administrative Background to the Formation of the Royal Air Force, 1912–19', *Journal of Contemporary History*, Vol. 22, no. 3 (July 1987): 437–53.

Driver, D., *The Birth of British Military Aviation: Britain 1903–1914* (Suffolk: Boydell & Brewer, 1997).

Egerton, D., *England and the Aeroplane: Militarism, Modernity and Machines* (London: Penguin, 2013).

Ellis, F.H., *Canada's Flying Heritage* (Toronto: University of Toronto Press, 1981).

Fage, A., Nayler, J.L., Relf, E.F., & Temple, G., 'Leonard Bairstow: 1880–1963', *Biographical Memoirs of Fellows of the Royal Society*, Vol. 11 (November 1965): 22–40.

Fearon, P., 'The Formative Years of the British Aircraft Industry, 1913–1924', *The Business History Review*, Vol. 43, no. 4 (Winter 1969): 476–95.

French, D., *The Strategy of the Lloyd George Coalition, 1916–1918* (Oxford: Clarendon Press, 1999).

Gollin, A., Whitehall, S.W., Lloyd George, D., & Garvin, J.L., 'Freedom or Control in the First World War: (The Great Crisis of May 1915)', *Historical Reflections*, Vol. 2, no. 2 (Winter 1976): 135–55.

Gollin, A., 'The Mystery of Lord Haldane and Early British Military Aviation', *A Quarterly Journal Concerned with British Studies*, Vol. 11, no. 1 (1979): 46–65.

Grieves, K., 'Lloyd George and the Management of the British War Economy', in R. Chickering & S. Förster (ed), *Great War, Total War: Combat and Mobilization on the Western Front, 1914–1918* (Cambridge: Cambridge University Press, 2000).

Grove, E., 'Air Force, Fleet Air Arm – or Armoured Corps? The Royal Naval Air Service at War', in T. Benbow (ed), *British Naval Aviation: The First 100 Years* (Surrey: Ashgate Publishing Limited, 2011).

Harper, H., *Ace Air Reporter* (London: John Gifford Ltd., 1943).

Higham, R., 'The Peripheral Weapon in Wartime', *The Air Power Historian*, Vol. 8, no. 2 (April 1961): 67–78.

Higham, R., 'Quantity vs. Quality: The Impact of Changing Demand on the British Aircraft Industry, 1900–1960', *Business History Review*, Vol. 42, no. 4 (1968): 443–6.

Holman, B., 'The Phantom Airship Panic of 1913: Imagining Aerial Warfare in Britain before the Great War', *Journal of British Studies*, Vol. 55, no. 1 (January 2016): 99–121.

Hunsaker, J.C., 'A Half Century of Aeronautical Development', *Proceedings of the American Philosophical Society*, Vol. 98, no. 2 (15 April 1954): 121–30.

Irwin, M.R., 'A Note on Public Sector Integration: The Decline of British Naval Aviation, 1914–1945', *Review of Industrial Organization*, Vol. 14, no. 1 (February 1999): 85–90.

Jackson, A.J., *AVRO Aircraft since 1908* (London: Putman & Company, 1965).

Jenkins, T., *The Airborne Forces Experimental Establishment* (Solihull: Helion & Company, 2015).

Jungdahl, A., 'Public Influence on the Proliferation of Military Aviation 1907–1912', *Air Power History*, Vol. 60, no. 1 (Spring 2013): 28–39.

Kennedy, P., 'Britain in the First World War', in A.R., Millet, & W., Murray (eds), Military Effectiveness: Volume 1, The First World War (Cambridge: Cambridge University Press, 2010).

MacLeod, C., 'Reluctant Entrepreneurs: Patents and State Patronage in New Technosciences, circa 1870–1930', *Isis*, Vol. 103, no. 2 (June 2012): 328–39.

McEwen, J.M., 'Northcliffe and Lloyd George at War, 1914–1918' *The Historical Journal*, Vol. 24, no. 3 (September 1981): 651–72.

McEwen, J.M., 'Lloyd George's Acquisition of the Daily Chronicle in 1918', *Journal of British Studies*, Vol. 22, no. 1 (1982): 127–44.

McEwen, J.M., 'The National Press during the First World War: Ownership and Circulation', *Journal of Contemporary History*, Vol. 17, no. 3 (July 1982): 459–86, 473–4.

Morgan, K.O., 'Lloyd George's Premiership: A Study in Prime Ministerial Government' *The Historical Journal*, Vol. 13, no. 1 (March 1970): 130–57.

Morris, Antony, A.J., 'Haldane's Army Reforms 1906–8: The Deception of the Radicals', *History*, Vol. 56, no. 186 (February 1971): 17–34.

Morrow, J.H. (Jr)., 'Industrial Mobilization in World War I: The Prussian Army and the Aircraft Industry', *The Journal of Economic History*, Vol. 37, no. 1 (March 1977): 36–51.

Murphy, R., 'Walter Long, the Unionist Ministers, and the Formation of Lloyd George's Government in December 1916', *The Historical Journal*, Vol. 29, no. 3. (September 1986): 735–45.

Nielson, K., 'Russian Foreign Purchasing in the Great War: A Test Case', *The Slavonic and East European Review*, Vol. 60, no. 4 (1982): 574–5.

Neilson, K., 'R. H. Brand, the Empire and Munitions from Canada', *The English Historical Review*, Vol. 126, no. 523 (December 2011): 1430–55.

Opdycke, L.E., 'O Romeo, Romeo, Wherefore Art Thou Romeo? — or ... Aviation Reporting and the Aviation Press', *Aerospace Historian*, Vol. 35, no. 2 (1988): 120–2.

Paris, P., 'Air Power and Imperial Defence', *Journal of Contemporary History*, Vol. 24, no. 2 (1989): 209–25.

Pariseau, J., 'Circuits and Bumps: The Story of the RCAF's Aborted Takeoffs, 1909–1938', *Aerospace Historian*, Vol. 32, no. 3 (September 1985): 173–83.

Rayleigh, Lord & Selby, F.J., 'Richard Tetley Glazebrook (1854–1935)', *Obituary Notices of Fellows of the Royal Society*, Vol. 2, no. 5 (December 1936): 28–56.

Robert, K., 'Constructions of "Home", "Front", and Women's Employment in the First World War', *History and Theory*, Vol. 52, no. 3 (2013): 319–43.

Sheffield, G., *The Chief: Douglas Haig and the British Army* (London: Aurum Press, 2012), 151–2.

Simmonds, V., & Alan, G., *Britain and World War I* (London: Routledge, 2012).

Sweetman, J., Crucial Months for Survival: The Royal Air Force, 1918–19, *Journal of Contemporary History*, Vol. 19, no. 3 (1984): 529–47.

Treadwell, T., *British & Allied Aircraft Manufacturers of the First World War* (Stroud: Amberley Publishing Ltd., 2011).

Turner, J.A., 'The British Commonwealth Union and the General Election of 1918', *The English Historical Review*, Vol. 93, no. 368 (July 1978): 528–59.

Wallace, G., *Flying Witness: Harry Harper and the Golden Age of Aviation* (London: Putman, 1958).

Wakelam, R.T., 'The Roaring Lions of the Air: Air Substitution and the Royal Air Force's Struggle for Independence after the First World War', *Air Power History*, Vol. 43, no. 3 (1996): 50–63.

Wynn, H., 'The Royal Air Force: Its Origin and History, 1918–1970', *Aerospace Historian*, Vol. 23, no. 3 (1976): 154–67.

Index

Advisory Committee for Aeronautics 29, 31, 33, 36, 42, 57, 106
Aeronautical Inspection Department 55, 79, 132
Air Board 13, 31, 83, 88, 94, 95, 96, 103, 110–116
Air Committee 40, 87, 99
Air Ministry 13, 31, 88, 111–112, 143, 168
Airco D.H.2 53
Aircraft Manufacturing Company (Airco) 53
Airship Guarantee Company 159
Alexander Motor Prize Competition 27
Allison, John Wesley
    Member of General Hughes' Staff 118, 120–122, 128–129, 141, 154
American Ammunition Company 119, 121
Anderson, Adelaide Mary
    Principal Lady Inspector of Factories 86
Army Balloon Factory 17
Asquith, Herbert
    British Prime Minister 42, 88, 90, 111–112, 117, 162
AVRO 504 8

B.E.2 3, 7–10, 25–26, 29–30, 34, 40, 44, 47, 52–54, 100, 104, 106–108, 163–164
Baden Powell, Baden
    Aeronautical Society of Great Britain 46–47
Bailhache, Clement
    Chief Lord Justice 79, 96–99, 108
Bairstow, Leonard
    Aeronautical Engineer 2
Baldwin, Stanley
    Chancellor of the Exchequer 161
Banbury, Frederick
    MP for City of London 125–127
Barnwell, Frank
    British Aircraft Designer 102

Baron, Annie
    Aeroplane Worker 81
Bennett-Goldney, Francis
    MP for Canterbury 77, 79
Bleriot, Louis
    French Aircraft Designer 2, 4–5, 9, 21–22, 26, 46, 54
Bonar Law, Andrew
    Chancellor of the Exchequer 126, 142, 148
Borden, Robert
    Canadian Prime Minister 10, 118–120
Bowerman, Charles
    MP for Deptford 74–77
Brace, William
    Under-Secretary of State for the Home Department 68, 74–75, 82
Brand, Robert
    1st Baron Brand of Eydon 118
Brewer, Griffith
    Wright Brothers UK Patent Agent 47
Bristol Scout 102
British Aeroplane Varnish Company
    Aeroplane Dope Manufacturers 75–76, 81, 167
British Cellulose & Chemical
    Manufacturing Company 11, 85–86, 122–134, 137–139, 141–142, 144, 148–150, 153–155, 157–158, 160–161, 166–167
British Commonwealth Union 138
Bryan, George
    Aeronautical Engineer 2
Bull, William
    MP for Hammersmith 128, 137–139, 141–142, 149
Burbidge, Richard
    Chair of the Committee on the Royal Aircraft Factory 91, 94–95, 110
Busk, Edward Teshmaker
    Aeronautical Engineer 3, 163

Index

Cautley, Henry
    MP for East Grinstead 158–159
Cellon Ltd., Messrs.
    Aeroplane Dope Manufacturers 72, 74, 123, 131, 167
Cellonit Gesellschaft Dreyfus & Company
    Celluloid Manufacturers 141
Celluloid 59–60
Cellulose Acetate 10–12, 59–60, 83, 85, 122–127, 129–132, 134, 138–139, 141, 148–153, 160–161, 165–166
Chamberlain, Austen
    Chancellor of the Exchequer 158
Chanute, Octave
    Aviation Pioneer 20
Churchill, Winston
    First Lord of the Admiralty 6
Clark, Ellen Jane
    Aeroplane Worker 81
Cody, Samuel Franklin
    Aviation Pioneer 7, 17–18, 27–28, 40
Collins, Godfrey
    Chairman of the Sub-Committee on National Expenditure 137–138
Colonel Grant Morden 125, 130–131, 138–139, 141, 143–144, 147, 149–150, 154, 161–162
Committee of Imperial Defence 3, 7, 40, 87
Courtaulds Limited 130, 162
Crayford Aeroplane Works 64–65
Curzon, George
    Lord Curzon 88, 94–95, 103, 111–112

D.94 Royal Aircraft Factory Dope Compound 77–79
Daily Chronicle 137, 143–147
Dalziel, Henry
    MP for Kirkcaldy Burghs 146–147
Dawson, Trevor
    Managing Director of Vickers Ltd. 125–126, 128–131, 149–150, 154, 162
de Havilland, Geoffrey
    Aircraft Designer 3, 7–9, 13, 53, 94–95, 163
Defence of the Realm Act 69, 118
Dennistoun Burney, Charles
    Aeronautical Engineer 159

Department of Metallurgy and Metallurgical Chemistry 32
Donald, Robert
    Editor Daily Chronicle 145
Dope Scandal 11, 146–147, 152, 154, 160, 165, 167–168
Duncan, Charles
    MP for Barrow-in-Furness 106

Edwards Valve Company of Chicago 119

Farman, Henri
    French Aircraft Designer 2, 21, 41, 46, 48
Farnborough See Royal Aircraft Factory
Flax 68–72
Forster, Henry
    Financial Secretary to the War Office 106
Fowler, Henry
    Superintendent Royal Aircraft Factory 31, 94

Geddes, Aukland
    Minister for National Service 132
Glazebrook, Richard Tetley
    Director National Physical Laboratory 106
Gordon Bennett Trophy 5
Gothenburg Airshow 167
Grahame-White, Claude
    British Aviation Pioneer 5, 23, 100
Green, Frederick
    British Aeronautical Engineer 7
Green's Motor Patents Syndicate 28
Grey, Charles
    Founder of Aeroplane Magazine 44–45
Grey, Edward
    Secretary of State for Foreign Affairs 128–129

Haig, Douglas
    Commander-in-Chief British Armies in France 113–114
Haldane, Richard
    Secretary of State for War 17, 19, 150, 163
Hamilton, Alice
    American Physician & Research Scientist 61

Hamilton, John
   1st Viscount Sumner 144, 148, 153, 157
Harmsworth, Alfred
   Lord Northcliffe 146
Harmsworth, Cecil
   Secretary of State for the Home Department 65–66
Harper, Harry
   Britain's First Air Correspondent 100
Harris, Charles
   Financial Secretary to the War Office 150
Health of Munitions Workers Committee 65, 67
Heckstall-Smith, Smitheyt
   Assistant Superintendent Royal Aircraft Factory 91–92
Heffter, Arthur
   German Chemist and Pharmacologist 62
Henderson, Arthur
   Minister Without Portfolio 57
Henderson, David
   Director-General Military Aeronautics 56, 91, 94, 100, 102–104, 151
Henderson, George
   Prof. of Chemistry, University of Glasgow 153
Hewlett and Blondeau
   Aeroplane Manufacturers 48
Holt, Richard
   MP for Hexham 128, 130, 140–141
Hughes, Samuel
   Canadian Minister of Militia & Defence 119–121, 125, 128, 130, 149, 154

James Rowlands
   Liberal MP for Dartmouth 65–66, 68, 81–83
Joint War Air Committee 12, 99
Joynson-Hicks, William
   MP Brentford 18–19, 35–36, 50–52, 97, 163

Kellaway, Frederick
   Parliamentary Secretary to the Ministry of Munitions 140, 158
Kiley, James
   MP for Stepney Whitechapel 160–161

Lanchester, Frederick
   British Aeronautical Engineer 42, 55, 57, 162, 165
Laurier, Wilfred 118
Legge, Thomas Morrison
   Home Office Medical Inspector of Factories 64–65
Lloyd George, David
   British Prime Minister 112, 137, 145–146
   Minister of Munitions 12, 67, 118
Long, Walter
   Parliamentary Secretary to the Secretary of State for the Colonies 120–121, 142, 162
Luxmore Drew, Clifford Luxmore
   H.M. Coroner 64
Lynch, Arthur
   MP Clare West 56, 90, 102

Markham, Arthur
   MP Mansfield Division 90, 131, 167
Messrs. Siebe Gorman and Company
   Aeroplane Dope Manufacturers 82
Messrs. Usines de Rhône
   French Chemical Company 60, 122, 131, 134
Metcalf, Annie
   Aeroplane Worker 82
Ministry of Munitions 12, 31, 70–72, 111–112, 114, 117–118, 123–124, 127, 130–134, 137, 140, 142, 150–151, 153–154, 158, 166
Moddy, Gilbert
   French Polisher 63
Mond, Alfred
   Liberal MP for Swansea 101–102
Montagu, John Walter Edward Douglas-Scott
   Lord Montagu of Beaulieu 8, 88, 97–101, 103, 105, 108, 110–111, 143
Morden, Walter Grant
   Canadian Financier and Politician 125, 130–131, 138–139, 141, 143–144, 147, 149–150, 154, 161
Muirhead, Anthony
   Under Secretary of State for Air 168

Index

National Physical Laboratory 2, 8, 27, 29, 31, 39, 77–78, 82, 91, 106–107
Novadope
   Aeroplane Dope 76
Nullis Secundus
   British Army Airship 100

O'Gorman, Mervyn
   Superintendent Royal Aircraft Factory 7, 25, 29–31, 42–43, 49–50, 57, 79, 80, 91–92, 94–95, 101, 105, 108, 164
O'Grady, James
   MP for Leeds East 111

Parsons, Charles
   British Engineer 91, 104
Pearson, Weetman
   Lord Cowdray 112
Pemberton, Noel Pemberton
   The First Air Member 89–90, 95–96, 98–99, 103–104, 109
Perley, George
   Candian High Commissioner 120
Pringle, William
   MP for Lanarkshire North-West 145–147
Prudential Trust Company Limited of Canada 126, 141, 154–155

Rayleigh (Lord) *see* Strutt, John
Robson, Edward
   Director of Pinchin, Johnson & Co., Ltd. 149
Roe, Alliot Verdon
   British Aircraft Designer 8, 13, 167
Rowlands, James
   Liberal MP for Dartmouth 65–66, 68, 81–83
Royal Air Force 12, 13, 18, 143, 164, 167
Royal Aircraft Establishment 18, 167
Royal Aircraft Factory 4, 7–9, 18, 24–25, 29, 33–36, 39–40, 43–46, 48–58, 60, 76–80, 88–95, 100–104, 107–110, 113, 115, 132, 134, 141, 163–167
Royal Flying Corps 7–13, 23–24, 28, 30, 32, 36–37, 39–40, 48, 49, 51–57, 78, 87, 90, 96–103, 107–108, 113–114, 122, 139
Royal Naval Air Service 8, 12, 55, 57, 87, 89–90, 98–99, 107

Samuel, Herbert
   Home Secretary 82
Sandys, George
   MP for Wells 53
Santos-Dumont, Alberto
   Brazlian Aviation Pioneer 21, 46
Sage and Company, Messrs. F.
   Aeroplane Sub-Contactors 74
Seeley, John Edward Bernard
   Secretary of State for War 42
Seely, John Edward Bernard
   Secretary of State for Air 9, 18–19, 28, 35, 53
Selwood, Charles
   Aeroplane Worker 68
Shell Committee 118–119, 121, 155
Shell Crisis 117
Short Bothers Seaplane Works 67
Sikorsky, Igor
   Aircraft Designer & Manufacturer 23
Smith, Herbert
   Chief Designer at Sopwith Aviation Company 107
Smith, Sydney
   Superintendent Royal Aircraft Factory 31
Sopwith Aviation Company 13, 41, 107
Sopwith Pup 107
Sopwith 1½ Strutter 107
Sopwith Tabloid 52
Sopwith, Thomas
   Aviation Pioneer 52
Spilsbury, Bernard
   Pathologist at St. Mary's Hospital 63–64
Spondon *See* British Cellulose
Spooner, Stanley
   Founder of Flight Magazine 50, 166
Spring Rice, Cecil
   British Ambassador to the United States 120, 128
Sproxton, Foster
   Chief Chemist at the British Xylonite Company 60
Stanley, Edward
   Lord Derby 88
Steele, James
   Aeroplane Worker 80

Strutt, John William
    Chair of the Advisory Committee for Aeronautics 31
Sumner (Lord) *see* Hamilton, John

Templer, Colonel James Lethbridge Brooke
    Balloon Pioneer 17
Tennant, Harold
    Under-Secretary of State for War 56, 77–78, 89, 163
Tetrachlorethane 11, 60, 62–68, 74–86, 108, 131, 139, 150, 165, 167
The Aeronautical Society of Great Britain 46
The Amalgamated Society of Engineers 43
The Army Aeroplane Competition 7, 26–28
The Aster Engineering Company 28
The International Arms and Fuse Company 118–119
Titanine
    British Aeroplane Dope 75–76, 81–82, 167
Trenchard, Hugh
    General Officer Commanding Royal Flying Corps 113–114

Tyson-Wilson, William
    Trade Unionist and Labour Politician 56

United Alkali Company 123, 130, 153
United French Polisher's London Society 73

Vickers F.B.5 'Gunbus' 101

War Office 6–7, 17, 20, 25–26, 30–31, 33, 35–36, 40, 47, 49, 54, 56, 65, 69, 72, 73, 75, 77–78, 81–83, 87, 90–97, 99, 102, 106, 110, 112, 114, 119, 121–127, 132, 139, 141, 147–153, 165
Wedgewood, Josiah Clement
    MP Newcastle-under-Lyme 148
White, William
    Canadian Finance Minister 119
Wilcox, William Henry
    Home Office Pathologist 63
Wolseley Tool and Motor Car Company 28
Wright, Orville
    Aviation Pioneer 47
Wright, Wilbur
    Aviation Pioneer 20, 53

www.ingramcontent.com/pod-product-compliance
Lightning Source LLC
Chambersburg PA
CBHW052113300426
44116CB00010B/1654